MW00558832

Southern Tufts

Southern Tufts

The Regional Origins and National Craze for Chenille Fashion

ASHLEY CALLAHAN   THE UNIVERSITY OF GEORGIA PRESS   ATHENS AND LONDON

Published by the University of Georgia Press

Athens, Georgia 30602

www.ugapress.org

© 2015 by Ashley Callahan

All rights reserved

Designed by Erin Kirk New

Set in Scala

Printed by Everbest through Four Colour Print Group, Louisville, KY.

The paper in this book meets the guidelines for
permanence and durability of the Committee on
Production Guidelines for Book Longevity of the
Council on Library Resources.

Most University of Georgia Press titles are
available from popular e-book vendors.

Printed in China

19 18 17 16 15 c 5 4 3 2 1

Library of Congress Cataloging-in-Publication Data

Callahan, Ashley.
    Southern tufts : the regional origins and national craze for
chenille fashion / Ashley Callahan.
        pages   cm
    Includes bibliographical references and index.
    ISBN 978-0-8203-4516-1 (hardcover : alkaline paper) 1. Chenille—
Southern States—History. 2. Coverlets—Southern States—History.
3. Chenille—United States—History. 4. Clothing and dress—United
States—History. 5. Fashion—United States—History. I. Title.
    NK9015.C35   2015
    746'.04617—dc23   2014046932

British Library Cataloging-in-Publication Data available

i: Chenille robe, U.S. patent design by France Schaeffee,
filed August 22, 1940, granted October 8, 1940, des. 123,021.

ii: Model wearing a chenille robe, ca. 1950. Bandy Heritage Center for
Northwest Georgia, Carpet and Rug Institute Photograph Collection.

v: From Tristram & Fuller ad, *Wilton (Conn.) Bulletin*, June 20, 1940.

vi: From private collection, November 1944.

xvi: Map by Flying W Graphics

xxiii: Chenille robe, U.S. patent design by Charles Shapiro,
filed August 22, 1940, granted October 1940, des. 123,022.

This project was made possible
in part by the generosity of the
Brown-Whitworth Foundation;
the Center for Craft, Creativity & Design,
Inc.; the Harry and Helen Saul
Foundation; Norville Industries;
and Shaw Industries.

Contents

Foreword   MADELYN SHAW

- - - GEORGIA'S TUFTED TEXTILES—both the hand-crafted and machine-made versions—lie at the crossroads of two other components of American textile and fashion history: southern cotton mills and northern apparel trades.

Historians have studied many aspects of the textile industries across the southern states from the late nineteenth into the mid-twentieth centuries, from the organization of capital and labor to the roles played by race and gender, to the interplay between agrarian and industrial ways of life. But the products of these industries have rarely been given much emphasis. The endless yards of sheetings and shirtings—or denims and tickings—that emerged from those mills were not the stuff of fashion or innovation. They were staples, not novelties. They were necessities, not luxuries. These unglamorous materials became the work clothes and utilitarian household textiles of the nation and beyond. They also became the basis for tufted bedspreads and clothing.

Similarly, the emergence of the American fashion industries has also been studied in some detail, both by historians of the organization and production methods of the garment industry and by design historians looking at individual makers and manufacturing firms. But scholarship has rarely gone beyond the fashion centers of New York and California and the production centers of the mid-Atlantic and New England states, and the concentration of design or style leadership in these places has been accepted without question.

OPPOSITE: Women using sergers to make chenille robes (detail), Sparks, Inc., Dalton, Georgia, early 1950s, collection of Alice Sparks Young

- - - ix

Women, four of whom are
wearing chenille robes,
ca. 1945, found photograph,
private collection

This book shows us a new facet of American fashion: how a few women
in the rural South used readily available materials to create a product that
responded to a specific market niche and then adapted and expanded that
one narrow product into an industry, one that attracted bigger capital investment, new technologies, new owners and workers, and new relationships
between producers and consumers.

By the 1890s, when the cottage industry in tufted bedspreads was beginning, southern cotton mills had already begun the growth that would
steadily erode New England's cotton textile manufacturing base after 1900.
Southern mills had several advantages, proximity to the raw material and
a labor surplus among them. Perhaps the most important for the tufted
textile industry were the paternalistic structure of the mill villages, a family
employment pattern that encouraged low wages, and a public emphasis on
nonimmigrant white labor. The relationships between the owners and
various levels of workers in the tufted textiles businesses explored throughout this volume reflect these aspects of the broader southern textiles industries. And, of course, because most of the products of southern spinning
and weaving mills in the early years were staples—plain cotton yarns and
plain-weave cloth, bleached and unbleached—tufters had easy access to the
raw materials they required.[1]

American fashion, as we have come to understand the term today, was
nonexistent in the first decade of the twentieth century, when the first tufted
bedspreads were being produced as a cottage industry in the Georgia highlands. The influence of the 1876 centennial of American independence

had fostered a Colonial Revival style in many of the country's decorative arts, including household textiles such as rugs and coverlets, but there was no question of any such fad in fashionable apparel. Style leadership in the garment trade came from Europe—more specifically Paris, where a few important houses created custom clothing for the well-to-do women of many nations, which percolated downward to women of all social classes via fashion journals and women's magazines. Even American dress pattern companies followed the French mode; their monthly or quarterly magazines, such as the Butterick Company's *The Delineator*, helped disseminate French fashion across the United States, whether the patterns were used by home sewers or by small dressmakers with local businesses.[2]

By 1913 some American designers and industrialists were questioning this adherence to the French mode. In November 1913 the *Ladies' Home Journal* published work by New York–based fashion designer Ethel Traphagen, with decorative elements inspired by American Indian art. Traphagen was becoming known in American fashion: she had been awarded first prize in a 1912–13 *New York Times* competition to encourage American "style creators."[3] The New York–based silk manufacturer H. R. Mallinson and Company flexed its style muscles in early 1914 with the introduction of a group of printed silks called Mexixe, inspired by motifs from Mexican folk art and southwestern Indian art, studied by the firm's design staff at the Metropolitan Museum of Art, the Brooklyn Museum, and the American Museum of Natural History. Also in 1914, Chicago corset manufacturer Henry W. Gossard, who had himself begun in business as an importer of European-made corsetry, sponsored a trophy for the best American dress design, to be given by the Fashion Art League of America (an association of dressmakers whose semiannual conventions were held in Chicago). Winners received widespread notice in the press, perhaps particularly since they were often from towns other than the fashion centers of New York and Chicago and so made good local and regional copy. In 1916, partially in response to the design isolation from Europe imposed by the Great War, the "Designed in America" campaign was introduced. Spearheaded by Morris De Camp Crawford, an editor at *Women's Wear*, a small group of New York–based writers, educators, and manufacturers organized and supported this campaign, which brought designers into museums to broaden their design education and unleash their own creative instincts, unfettered by the dictates of Paris couturiers and Lyons silk manufacturers. Between

1916 and 1922, American textile and apparel designers competed for prizes in a variety of "Made in America" contests (one-of-a-kind and production textiles, and custom and ready-to-wear clothing, for example) reported on in *Women's Wear* and the rest of the fashion press.

In essence, these designers were still creating fashion from the top down, on the model inherited from Europe, based on the needs and desires of a social elite that had the leisure and wealth to devote to acquiring and displaying a custom wardrobe. But they also opened the door for the creation of American style on a different model, one that emerged from the needs of the country's millions of ordinary women, who did not have a lady's maid, who did much of their own housework and laundry, and for whom the newly emerging ready-to-wear industry would ensure, "She can come from a small town, but she doesn't look it. No one's a country cousin, a jay, a hick anymore."[4]

Women's ready-made clothing took on a new respectability as an industry when silhouettes simplified in the late 1910s and early 1920s. Fashion's straighter lines, less-defined waistlines, looser fit, and rejection of fussy drapery made standardized sizing simpler than had been possible with the unforgiving styles of many decades past that had layered tightly fitting bodices over corseted bodies. Although it was possible in the nineteenth century to buy many essential parts of a woman's wardrobe as ready-to-wear, in practice few women of any means at all did so, preferring the more personalized fit of custom clothing. But by the 1920s ready-to-wear was booming and the custom trade was diminishing, seen more and more as only for the elite. While ready-made clothing might not necessarily fit as well as custom-made, and may have been made from cheaper or less durable materials than a woman might have purchased on her own to take to her dressmaker, it had the theoretical advantage of coming from a fashion center and being of the current mode. The exclusivity and individuality of custom clothing was traded for the time-saving convenience of ready-to-wear. And in that trade emerged the notion of throwaway fashion, inexpensive additions to a basic wardrobe that filled a short-term need, or perhaps just a frivolous desire, and would not require several trips to the dressmaker and hours of fittings to acquire. The chenille beach capes or sundresses purchased from Dixie Highway spreadlines (tufted textile roadside retailers) on the drive from Detroit to Florida for a midwinter vacation represent this. These garments were easy fitting or unfitted, well suited to what was—at least originally—an unsophisticated production process.

Chenille dress,
cotton, 53 inches
long, ca. 1935,
private collection,
photograph by
Michael McKelvey

Harold's Chenille and Gift Shop, South Folkston, Georgia, Harold Ayers, proprietor, ca. 1945, postcard published by Tichnor Brothers, Boston, collection of Bradley Putnam

Although tufted garments emerged from the tufted bedspread, a form that had its roots in Colonial Revival style, the garments themselves do not reflect what might be termed "regional Americana." The tufting designs and garment styles were not quintessentially southern highland. We find no imitations of Appalachian woven coverlets, for example, in tufted spreads or robes. In contrast, the American Indian–inspired Pendleton Woolen Mills blanket and bathrobe, or the Stetson hat and cowboy shirt, which were also popularized in the 1910s and 1920s, clearly evoked the Old West, albeit in a romanticized, even nostalgic manner that reflected Wild West shows and Tom Mix cowboy movies more than any dimly remembered late nineteenth-century reality. Tufted garments represent something very different and quite new in American fashion: a style developed independently of Paris or New York, piggybacking on a regional specialty in terms of technique but applying that technique to adaptations of the current mode, a bottom-up rather than top-down fashion item. Georgia's tufters created a regional fashion icon from scratch. As such, tufted garments may be akin to Levi's jeans—but Levi's took much longer to transition from workingman's clothing to fashion statement than the chenille robe took to move from tufted bedspread to household staple.

Style is only part of the story, however. The tufted garment industry was successful as much because its product was developed in response to a particular set of circumstances that, somewhat serendipitously, allowed it to flourish. Henry Ford's Model-T and the democratization of automobile travel and tourist camp or motor court holidays allowed middle-class Americans to explore their country. The advent of the idea of a vacation in the sun and the increasingly busy route to the beaches of Florida (and its enormous real estate boom of the 1920s) directed many of those automobiles through Georgia. And the easy dissemination of popular culture through the movies and through print media (such as women's magazines, dress pattern publications, and the women's pages of newspapers) ensured a shared national vocabulary of fashion. Pendleton Woolen Mills, for example, printed its first catalog, with color images of its Indian-inspired product line, in the mid-1910s, at about the time that color images were becoming more common in popular magazine features and advertisements.

The tufted robes and beach capes and playsuits and sundresses made by entrepreneurial women and the manufacturers that followed their lead were one part of the sea change in how American women bought their clothes and perceived fashion brought about by the ready-to-wear industry. Casual clothing that met a real need, and was not only functional but had roots in America's regional heritage, became a hallmark of American fashion design in the 1930s and remains so today. *Southern Tufts: The Regional Origins and National Craze for Chenille Fashion* is an absorbing and entertaining examination of this notable first in American fashion.

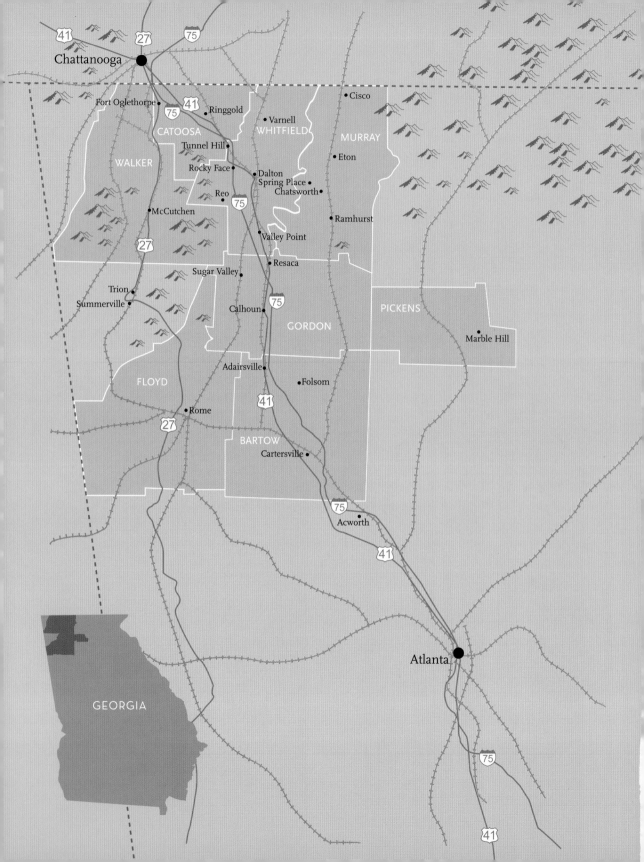

Preface

‒ ‒ ‒ THE ENCHANTING SPECTACLE of rows and rows of brightly colored bedspreads, gently flapping in the breeze along the side of an old highway in the foothills of the Blue Ridge Mountains, was a defining image of northwestern Georgia for generations. Now faded from memory are the coats, capes, robes, and other articles of clothing that hung near the spreads. In their combination of traditional needlework and modern styles, Georgia's tufted garments (made from the 1920s through well past midcentury) are an innovative regional expression of American fashion.

The tufted bedspread industry, which developed in the 1910s and remained strong into the 1950s, has been a popular topic for newspaper and magazine articles since the 1930s, and these writings all offer roughly the same story: the revival of a traditional needlework technique by a young woman in Dalton, Georgia, in Whitfield County, led to the development of a major industry.

The only book to focus exclusively on Dalton's tufted textile industry is Thomas M. Deaton's *Bedspreads to Broadloom: The Story of the Tufted Carpet Industry* (1993), which addresses both chenille and carpet and includes brief mentions of garments. Deaton records stories that capture the colorful personalities of many individuals involved in the industry and provides clear explanations about the industry's technological evolution. Deaton conducted more than eighty interviews beginning in 1979 that document key oral histories related to the tufted textile industry, and he donated his research files, with interview transcripts, to the Bandy Heritage Center for

Hand-Tufted Bedspreads, U.S. 41, Georgia, ca. 1940, postcard published by W. M. Cline Company, Chattanooga, collection of Bradley Putnam

Northwest Georgia at Dalton College. Though the center was still in the process of preparing archival collections for researchers when I was preparing this book, the director, Dr. John D. Fowler, kindly made them available to me, for which I am grateful. Additional scholars have included aspects of tufted textile history in formal publications on other topics, such as Douglas Flamming in *Creating the Modern South: Millhands and Managers in Dalton, Georgia, 1884–1984* (1992), Jane S. Becker in *Selling Tradition: Appalachia and the Construction of an American Folk, 1930–1940* (1998), Randall L. Patton with David B. Parker in *Carpet Capital: The Rise of a New South Industry* (1999), and Philis Alvic in *Weavers of the Southern Highlands* (2003).

In the 1980s and 1990s, local historian Cheryl Wykoff conducted extensive interviews related to the tufted textile industry. Some of her research is presented in a series of locally published booklets, *Tufted Bedspreads* (1984), *Tufted Bedspread Sampler* (1989), and *Peacock Alley* (1992), but much more is contained in an overstuffed three-ring binder now in the collection of the Whitfield-Murray Historical Society's Crown Gardens & Archives in Dalton. Wykoff's work is cited throughout this book, and I admire her enthusiastic efforts to preserve so many personal accounts and her foresight in making her unpublished materials available to future scholars. The Whitfield-Murray Historical Society has some incredible archival materials, and I appreciate executive director Jennifer Detweiler's willingness to assist me with my efforts to glean as much as possible from that collection.

Southern Tufts: The Regional Origins and National Craze for Chenille Fashion is the first book to bring focused attention to the garments produced by the tufted textile industry. There are many reasons this area has been overlooked. First, garment production was never as large as bedspread production and generated fewer fortunes. Second, a discussion of the creation of bedspreads and tufted throw rugs—flat, domestic textiles—leads more naturally to a discussion of the production of carpet, and the story of carpet came to define Dalton. Also, numerous leaders of garment manufacturing companies either moved away or passed away before scholars began conducting interviews, so many of their stories are now lost. Garments, though, interact with the world differently than bedspreads—which are confined to a single function in a single room—and an investigation of the design, manufacture, and meaning of tufted garments expands the discussion of tufted textiles and contributes to our knowledge and understanding of this important American clothing.

In addition to documenting the history of the tufted fashion industry, this book provides new context for its birth and development, placing it within the Southern Appalachian Craft Revival, to illustrate how it was part of a larger blossoming of regional craft, and the Colonial Revival, to demonstrate its role as part of a national interest in early Americana. Also, while previous scholars have had to rely largely on oral history, which poses the challenges of uncertain dates and reconciling conflicting memories, evolving digital technology facilitates charting the industry's progress through historical advertisements and assigning a more precise timeline. Increasingly sophisticated online search engines and expanding databases also helped me identify many early newspaper and magazine articles that have not been part of previous tufted textile scholarship. I did not ignore old technology and spent hours scrolling through microfilm of Dalton's newspapers. Once those are digitized, I am certain that additional information will become readily accessible about many chenille garment businesses.

Like Deaton and Wykoff, I conducted oral history interviews. I visited some individuals who have spoken many times about the industry's history, but when asked specifically about garments, they revealed new facts. I also interviewed individuals whose family stories had not been documented, and I am pleased to be able to provide a record of their experiences here.

Everyone I met, in person and on the phone and online, was generous in sharing information, and I am honored by their kindness to me and willingness to help with this project.

Southern Tufts begins with a history of Northwest Georgia's tufted textiles, addressing why and where the technique was popular and how Dalton's location allowed the industry to blossom. The text then traces the development of tufted garments through individual forms—kimonos and aprons; dresses, coats, and capes; and robes—following a roughly chronological approach. The most extensive chapter is on robes, which thrived for the longest period of time—about the mid-1930s through the late 1950s—and experienced the most widespread manufacture and consumption. The book concludes with a chapter on the revival of tufted fashion toward the end of the twentieth century.

Several chapters include sections in ecru that focus on individuals who made tufted garments or companies that made them. Some of these makers are documented here for the first time, and others, though discussed by previous scholars, never have had their work with fashion highlighted. Neither these focus sections nor the extended appendix with brief biographies of

Girls and women in a prayer circle, some wearing chenille robes, ca. 1958, found photograph, private collection

companies and individuals associated with the manufacture of tufted garments includes every person or business involved. The stories of individuals, though, convey the conditions and innovations typically involved with small businesses in this industry, and the stories of larger companies hint at the impressive scale of production that existed. Surprisingly little information surfaced from the largest manufacturers, but I captured what I could and I will continue to hope that more material has survived and will eventually be appreciated and archived.

I explain terminology in detail as it arises in the text, but a few key terms should be introduced briefly here. All of the garments and accessories discussed in *Southern Tufts* are considered *tufted textiles*. They were created through an embroidery process in which a series of plain stitches are sewn into a sheet of fabric (usually cotton), then are clipped on the top of the fabric and fluffed to make tufts—resulting in short pieces of yarn (usually cotton) that look like regular stitches on the bottom of the fabric and fuzzy pompoms on top. The earliest spreads were white-on-white, like the early nineteenth-century embroidered spreads that inspired them, and later ones featured color. Tufted garments likely were introduced after color became common among northwest Georgia's tufted bedspread creations. When the tufting is done by hand, it is called *candlewick*, a traditional embroidery term. When it is done by machine, the resulting textile is called *chenille*, after the French for "caterpillar." (Complicating these definitions is the fact that *chenille* is the term most commonly associated with all of northwestern Georgia's tufted textiles now, regardless of whether they are made by hand or machine.) A popular method of decoration for chenille was *overlay*, which has two layers of tufting. First the fabric is tufted with a basic chenille pattern, usually straight rows, then a design motif, such as flowers or a bow, is tufted over the first layer of chenille—overlaid on the existing tufting. Period advertisements often use the words *robe*, *housecoat*, and *dressing gown* interchangeably, and generally I have used *robe* in the text because it is the term with the broadest definition.

The topic of tufted fashion can be evaluated from a variety of standpoints, including economic studies, gender studies, cultural studies, roadside history, social history, and race and ethnicity studies. As a decorative arts historian, I have approached it from the perspective of decorative arts, design, and material culture. My goal for *Southern Tufts* is to document as much about chenille fashion as I can because this is a rapidly disappearing history.

Woman wearing a chenille robe on the rooftop of a thirteen-story building, Los Angeles, ca. 1940, found photograph, private collection

I want to provide enough information for experts in other specialized areas of study to be able to develop more research and include tufted garments in their projects. I also want to present the information in a way that reflects the often informal and entertaining nature of the topic. In addition to professional photographs of tufted garments and formal advertising images, *Southern Tufts* includes brightly colored postcards of roadside chenille stands to convey their garish glory and black-and-white found photographs to suggest how pervasive chenille garments were in the American landscape. Chenille is fascinating, and this scholarship is serious, but *Southern Tufts* is meant to be fun, a celebration of an exciting Georgia creation.

Woman wearing a chenille robe, ca. 1942, found photograph, private collection

Southern Tufts

Chapter One

The History of Candlewick Bedspreads in Northwest Georgia

— — — LOCATED IN THE SCENIC FOOTHILLS of the Blue Ridge Mountains in southern Appalachia, Northwest Georgia's rolling landscape is dotted with historical markers for Native American heritage sites and Civil War battlefields. In the early twentieth century, the area's accessibility by road and rail, ample water resources, proximity to the industrial city of Chattanooga, Tennessee, and large cotton mill (Crown Cotton Mill) in Dalton, Whitfield County, contributed to the region's rise to national prominence for its tufted textile industry. Specifically, Northwest Georgia became known for the production of candlewick coverlets, bedspreads embroidered with patterns made of fluffy tufts of yarn. These handmade spreads evoked the aura of the nation's colonial history and appealed to a purchasing public eager for connections to a preindustrial time. The huge demand for candlewick spreads led to Dalton being deemed the "Bedspread Center of the World," as well as to the eventual industrialization of the spreads' production. By the mid-1930s, this handcrafted emblem of the past became a machine-made product of the modern present. One often-overlooked aspect of the tufted textile industry is its foray into the world of American fashion. Employing the same technique used to make tufted bedspreads, individuals and companies in Northwest Georgia and beyond created tufted kimonos, aprons, dresses, coats, capes, and robes for over six decades.

Though the tufted textile industry has defined the region's economy for almost a century, its history is not simply a matter of local interest. The

OPPOSITE: "Making Hand Tufted Bedspreads—U.S. 41—Georgia" (detail), ca. 1940, postcard published by W. M. Cline Company, Chattanooga, collection of Bradley Putnam

Aerial view of Dalton, Georgia, 1932, showing U.S. 41 (also known as the Dixie Highway and the Battlefield Route), postcard published by W. M. Cline Company, Chattanooga, collection of David R. Stevenson

Crown Cotton Mills, Dalton, Georgia, 1935, postcard published by Curt Teich and Company, private collection

"Greetings from Dalton, Georgia, Bedspread Center of the World," 1943, postcard published by Curt Teich and Company, collection of Bradley Putnam

industry's regional growth depended on a widespread national desire for old-fashioned textiles. The history of the candlewick bedspread industry is not well known outside of Northwest Georgia, and within the region it has become so familiar through streamlined retelling that much of its context has been forgotten. The early history, largely based in oral tradition, is rife with vague and conflicting details. Even in one of the earliest published accounts of the industry's beginnings, the *Dalton Citizen* newspaper in 1925 acknowledged the scarcity of verifiable facts: "There is romance, pleasures and perhaps history threaded in the story, and we wish we had more accurate records of the progress springing direct from this one industry."[1] This chapter revisits that history, expanding the story to include accounts of the production and appreciation of candlewick outside of the region and bringing in stories from individuals who made the phenomenon possible through their diligent needlework.

Catherine Evans Whitener and the Birth of the Candlewick Industry

The story most closely linked with the origin of the tufted textile industry in northwestern Georgia is that of Catherine Evans Whitener, the key figure in the transformation of candlewick from an individual craft for home use to a marketable product.[2] The daughter of Nancy Nuckolls and William Evans, Whitener was born in 1880, in Walker County near the community of Reo, in Northwest Georgia. She moved to Dalton in 1909, married W. L. Whitener in 1922, and died in 1964.[3] Though her tale has been repeated innumerable times, two accounts in her own words survive, one as she told it to Stiles Martin in 1953 for the *Georgia Department of Commerce Newsletter* and one in an autobiographical essay she wrote around 1938.[4] These appear to be the most detailed and accurate versions of her story.

In 1892, when she was twelve years old, Catherine Evans visited the home of a neighbor and cousin, Milton Tate, in McCutchen, Georgia, and saw a bedspread that attracted her attention. She told Martin:

> The memory of the beautiful "counterpane," as we called a bed covering at that time, remained in my mind, and three years later (1895), when I was 15 years old, I again visited in the Tate home and examined the spread more closely. I observed that it was "tufted"; that is, the several strands of thread were pushed through the cloth, then clipped, the effect being a beautiful design.
>
> I was told that this bedspread in the Tate home was a family relic, or heirloom and that no one knew how old it was, who made it or when.

Catherine Evans Whitener with a candlewick bedspread, ca. 1960, courtesy of Bandy Heritage Center for Northwest Georgia, Carpet and Rug Institute Photograph Collection

It was the only spread of that kind I had ever seen and I decided to make one myself. It was tufted in squares on strips of cloth which were then sewed together to make a sheet large enough to cover the entire bed and hang down on the sides.

She went on to explain to Martin how she made her initial few spreads, the first two of which she kept for herself:

So, in 1895, I made my first tufted bedspread, using 12 strands of No. 8 thread doubled, which made 24 strands to be clipped. I wound the thread on a spinning wheel (which is still in the family) from skeins of yarn. I used a "bodkin" needle, about three or four inches long. One of these long needles usually came with each paper of needles and was used mostly to thread ribbons in girls' dresses.

My first spread was tufted in squares, with white thread and on white sheeting sewn together to make the "spread." When finished, I boiled it three times, it then being bleached white. . . .

In 1896, I made another spread, this time a star and circle design.[5] The designs were drawn or "laid out" on the cloth with chalk or a pencil, saucers or maybe plates being used to outline the circle designs. Later, other designs were drawn as fancy dictated.

It was through her sister-in-law that Whitener made her first commercial transactions involving candlewick spreads, as she recalled for Martin:

In 1900, I made my third spread, a star and circle design, and gave it to my brother, Henry Evans, and his wife, Lizzie, who married that year.

Mrs. John League, the former Miss Zella Creamer, a sister of my brother Henry's wife, and the wife of the superintendent of a textile mill at Trion, Ga., admired the spread I had given her sister as a wedding present, and asked me to make her (Mrs. League) one and she would pay me for it.

Also in 1900 I made my fourth spread, a star and circle design. The material (cloth and thread) cost $1.25. I valued my labor at $1.25 and sold the spread to Mrs. League for $2.50.

Whitener wrote, "This was the first sale of a tufted bed spread ever made in this section of the country," adding that Mrs. League moved to Summerville, Georgia, where other ladies "saw [League's] spread and began sending [Whitener] orders."

Whitener noted that for her first spread she marked off the design on a quilting frame and that "the task of marking off the designs with a pencil was a hard one." She then explained the easier process she developed for transferring designs to new spreads: "I recalled how I had stamped embroidery patterns by placing a piece of cloth over the design and rubbing it with a puter [sic] spoon or a box lid. But the tufts on the spread were so soft that this would not work. So I turned the bottom side of my spread up and placed the cloth over this and rubbed with a box lid. This made a clear outline for the stitches. This made the transfer of the design much easier."

Martin reported that requests for Whitener's candlewick spreads increased after "the spreads were first displayed in a New York department store in 1910."[6] She received such sizeable orders that she had to get other women to help her and teach friends and neighbors her method of tufting and transferring designs. Those women in turn taught others and shared designs. Eventually women from Dalton began traveling to department stores in major East Coast cities to sell bedspreads.

Mrs. H. L. Jarvis (née Eugenia Bitting, 1877–1966), a former insurance assistant in Dalton and wife of a local dentist, worked closely with Whitener to market her spreads, and in one early interview Whitener credited Jarvis's orders as the impetus for her to teach others to tuft.[7] A 1955 biographical sketch of Jarvis describes her as Whitener's agent (though Whitener simply mentions filling orders for Jarvis) and explains how she "stamped" (rubbed) the designs on the spreads, distributed them to be tufted, and wrote innumerable letters to businesses and individuals to promote them. Jarvis's first "large" order was for a dozen spreads for Wanamaker's department store in Philadelphia, and the *Dalton Citizen* reported that in New York, Jarvis gave Wanamaker's exclusive rights to sell the spreads.[8] Jarvis often is credited as being the first individual in Dalton to commercialize candlewick spreads, probably around 1915, though dates vary among historical accounts. Period newspaper advertisements confirm that Wanamaker's in New York offered "bed covers of unbleached muslin, tufted or with French knots; copies of Colonial designs" by 1915, and in October 1916 the store sold "charming old fashioned hand-tufted candlewick spreads of creamy bleached muslin."[9] In 1917 Wanamaker's described its candlewick selection as "the most interesting variety in the city" and noted that it had sold "a great many for Colonial rooms."[10]

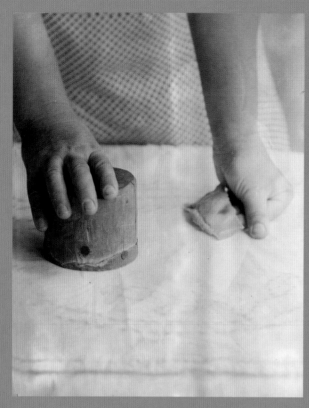

Ethel May Stiles transferring a pattern by rubbing a stamping block on an unwashed sheet of fabric that has been placed over an already-tufted sheet, Ringgold, Georgia, 1934, Doris Ulmann Photograph Collection, PH038-115-5-0567-002, Special Collections and University Archives, University of Oregon Libraries, Eugene, Oreg.

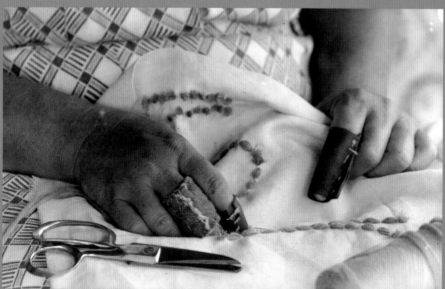

Ethel May Stiles tufting, Ringgold, Georgia, 1934. Wearing stalls to protect her fingers, Stiles is drawing her thick thread through the fabric with a large needle to create the stitches she will later clip with scissors. Doris Ulmann Photograph Collection, PH038-112-1-0045, Special Collections and University Archives, University of Oregon Libraries, Eugene, Oreg.

Murray E. Wyche (1904–75), chief of the Atlanta Bureau of Fairchild Publications (a leading fashion news publisher), writing in 1948, also reported that by 1910 "a number of Dalton women were making and selling bedspreads as a sideline to their housework," and that "these beautiful Colonial candlewick spreads were beginning to attract the attention of big stores in the North and Middle West."[11] Though the industry was started and run primarily by women for several years—needlework at the time was exclusively an activity for women, and the *Dalton Citizen* even described candlewick as "woman's work" in 1925—as the potential profits became apparent, more men became involved in the candlewick industry and began to establish formal companies.[12] The early leading companies included those owned by Addie Lee Cavender Evans (Whitener's sister-in-law), Mrs. M. W. Cannon, Mrs. C. B. Wood, Mr. Walter Kenner and Mr. G. H. Rauschenberg, Mr. J. T. Bates, Mr. J. M. Muse, and Mr. B. J. Bandy.[13]

The basic method of bedspread production, called tufting or "turfing" (a common colloquialism), used by hand tufters in Northwest Georgia followed Whitener's approach and began by "laying off" the design. This entailed spreading an unwashed cotton sheet over a pattern (an unwashed tufted spread turned fluff down so that the bumps of the stitches were facing up—a sort of master copy) and "stamping" it by rubbing it with a greased tin or a "stamping iron" (which took a variety of forms, including a wooden block with dye-infused wax on the stamping side) to transfer the design. The rubbing produced dots where the tufts were to go—like a relief rubbing with the side of a crayon. The tufter then used a large needle, sometimes with an added notch near the point to help the tufter measure even distances between stitches, to draw a thick yarn through the sheet. Next the tufter

Detail of hand-tufted stitches, showing clipped and unclipped stitches, photo by author

Detail of hand-tufted stitches, showing a single tuft in the center pulled apart to show how it was drawn through the material, photo by author

Unclipped stitches, clipped stitches, and clipped and fluffed stitches, illustration by Amanda Burk

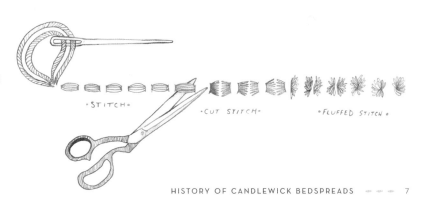

•STITCH•   •CUT STITCH•   •FLUFFED STITCH•

(or her husband or child) would clip the stitches on the top of the spread. Finally the spread was boiled to tighten the weave structure around the stitches to hold them in place, dried on a clothesline, and beaten to fluff the tufts.

As more and more people became involved in the tufting business, a system developed in which cotton sheets were stamped in a central location and delivered to home workers by "haulers" or distributed to women who came to pick them up. These central locations included private homes but increasingly came to be dominated by large companies with distribution points known as spread houses. Some companies paid haulers flat rates for their work, but often haulers earned income by taking a percentage of what companies paid per spread. Some families acquired larger batches of spreads and "let them out" to other tufting families. This distribution method, an outgrowth of Catherine Evans Whitener's efforts, lasted at least into the mid-1930s, throughout the hand-tufting era.

National and Regional Candlewick Production

William Secord of the Museum of American Folk Art provided a precise assessment of the complicated history of candlewick spreads in 1981 in an international textile journal.[14] He noted that the popularity of whitework bedspreads (white decoration on a white ground), including candlewick, reached its zenith in the United States in the Neoclassical era from about 1800 to 1840. He clarifies that the term "candlewick" derives from the similarity of the twisted cotton cording used in the spreads to wicks used by candlemakers, rather than being the same thing. Secord also explains that candlewick spreads could be created through two techniques: embroidery or weaving. According to Secord, the embroidered form (used in Northwest Georgia) became popular around 1825, "and is probably a descendant of seventeenth century English needlework." He further divides the embroidered spreads by three embroidery ornamentation techniques: tufting (in which the stitches are cut to make balls of fluff on the top of the spread), knotting (in which knots are formed on the top of the spread), and couching (in which a yarn is attached to the surface of the spread with tiny stitches). In his description of tufting, the embroiderer sewed large running stitches to the spread, passing them over a small twig that was later removed so that the stitch could be cut and the spread washed; the washing fluffed the tufts and caused the threads in the base fabric to shrink, holding the stitches in place.

Candlewick coverlet, 1793, made by Mary "Polly" Armistead in Bertie County,
North Carolina, cotton on cotton, 72 x 80 inches plus 6 1/2 inch fringe, courtesy of the
Museum of Early Southern Decorative Arts (MESDA), acc. 3173

When Phoebe Laing Mosley, writing for *McCall Decorative Arts and Needlework* in 1932, posed the question of where candlewick originated, she answered it with a quote from antiques authority Sarah M. Lockwood, from her book *Antiques* (1926): "It is extremely difficult to be definite about needlework, and foolish to try to be. . . . Better remember and revere the spirit that was behind the work than fuss about the dates."[15] Lockwood concluded simply that the candlewick spreads were "early." Mosley proposed that candlewick may be "truly an American art" and that its importance rested in the facts that it was a tradition that had been passed between generations since revolutionary days and that it could help homemakers beautify their homes. Mosley represents the popular period attitude: candlewick spreads, regardless of their specific history, should be appreciated for representing the beauty of our American past and need not be exact copies of antiques.

Catherine Evans Whitener's revival of the tufting technique was part of a larger interest in candlewick. Two examples from national publications of instructions for making candlewick spreads in the late nineteenth century attest to the widespread interest in and availability of information about this type of needlework. In 1893 *The Ladies' World*, a popular and inexpensive monthly women's magazine, suggested using a coarse darning needle with cotton yarn to sew stitches on unbleached sheeting, clipping each stitch as it was completed to create a series of tufts.[16] Also, a woman writing for the *Des Moines Homestead* in 1894 described a spread her mother-in-law had made for her by stretching heavy muslin in a quilting frame, marking off a design of concentric circles by tracing plates of varying sizes, and adding short stitches of candlewick that fluffed up after the spread was washed.[17] According to an article in the *Dalton Citizen* in 1925, Whitener employed a similar design method, tracing plates and bowls to create curves, and also took designs from quilts and incorporated floral motifs from carpets and wallpapers, showing that she generated many of her own designs rather than simply copying older textiles.[18]

Multiple areas in southern Appalachia besides Georgia and areas outside the South produced candlewick spreads as consumer products in the early twentieth century. Frances Goodrich's Allanstand Cottage Industries north of Asheville, North Carolina, included tufted spreads among its craft products by the 1910s.[19] Goodrich, in her book *Mountain Homespun* (1931), recalls selling tufted spreads and that the first one was copied by the great granddaughter of "Grandmother Duncan" who made the original around 1860, with a design based on flowers from her garden.[20] In a

1911 presentation of village industries from the historic town of Deerfield, Massachusetts, a woman showed tufted bedspreads "in quaint old time stitches," with patterns named "moonshine," "matrimony," and "barley corn."[21] Laura Riley, in Poughkeepsie, New York, founded Alnwick Industries around 1916 to market tufted bedspreads made in Appalachia, working with a contact in North Carolina. Her customers included Mrs. Alfred du Pont, Mrs. Andrew Carnegie, and Mrs. J. Pierpont Morgan, connecting modern candlewick textiles with some of the country's most prestigious homes.[22] Early advertisements cite additional locations as sources of spreads: Wanamaker's in Philadelphia offered spreads from Kentucky in 1920 and the Germantown Novelty Shop, also in Philadelphia, sold spreads from Virginia in 1922.[23] Stores in Pennsylvania advertised sheets stamped with patterns that buyers could embroider themselves, so candlewick spreads could have been made anywhere.[24]

The majority of spreads in the early decades of the twentieth century, though, were made in Northwest Georgia. The *Dalton Citizen* reported that in 1923–24 the sales figures for spreads sold from Whitfield County exceeded those of the cotton crop, a remarkable achievement for an industry operated largely from private homes.[25] In early January 1924, Gimbels advertised a new shipment of twenty-five hundred candlewick spreads made in Georgia, noting that they had sold thousands in the Christmas rush.[26] By 1929, the company of Kenner and Rauschenberg had grown from producing a few hundred spreads weekly to almost two thousand spreads daily. By 1932 that figure was over five thousand bedspreads daily.[27] By 1934 the region shipped about ten thousand spreads daily, and the *Dalton News* reported that half of the spreads sold in large New York stores were candlewick.[28]

Candlewick spread makers devised a variety of designs both traditional and modern. Many tufters took a communal approach to designs and generously shared them with friends, neighbors, and anyone interested in joining the business. A 1916 advertisement from Wanamaker's in New York offers "charming old fashioned hand-tufted candlewick spreads" on crinkly bleached muslin and states that orders would be taken for special designs, including "ostrich plume, circle and cross, lattice, shriner star in centre, circle in centre, doughnut, desert leaf, etc."[29] Spreads were made on a range of cotton sheeting thicknesses, and some had scalloped edges or handmade fringe. Also, the designs could vary from lightly tufted patterns to thick, all-over tufting. An advertisement from Wanamaker's in Philadelphia in 1920

praised the candlewick spreads as easy to launder, adding, "It is good to see things of such old-time charm are having a revived vogue."[30] Candlewick achieved such popularity that Bloomingdale's even sold printed fabrics "inspired by the beautiful old Colonial hand-tufted bedspreads," with subtle shadows on tuft edges to make them look three-dimensional.[31]

One important development often credited to Whitener is the addition of color to the traditionally white-on-white spreads. She sought color-fast yarns, eventually finding them from Franklin Process Company, of Rhode Island, which later established dye plants in Greenville, South Carolina, and Chattanooga.[32] In 1947 Evans received a letter from the president of the company expressing a desire to visit with her during his next trip to Chattanooga and recalling her first order, around 1920.[33] Most advertisements describe all-white spreads until about 1922, when colored sheeting and colored tufting became more widely available, though initially ads promoted just one or the other.[34] Gimbel Brothers in New York advertised "combination colors" (colored sheeting *and* colored tufts) in April 1924 "for the very first time."[35] The following year, the *Dalton Citizen* indicated that interior decorators encouraged this change through their requests for color.[36]

Other Early Tufters in Northwest Georgia

While Whitener is the best known figure in the growth of the candlewick industry in Northwest Georgia, other families in the area also have strong connections to candlewicking. In February 1937 William M. Sapp, a lawyer and prominent Daltonian, reported that Mrs. Alexander Heath (née Melinda Jane Roberts, 1841–1919), who learned to tuft from her Scottish grand-mother, had made the spread that inspired the tufted textile industry, and proposed that the town erect "a suitable memorial to her."[37] Sapp recalled that Heath had entered her spread in one of the first Whitfield County fairs, which he had helped conduct, and where he believed Whitener saw it and became inspired to make her own. Heath's daughter, Mrs. David Stewart, later exhibited her mother's spread numerous times in New York "as 'the first of its kind.'"[38] An article in the *Atlanta Constitution* in March 1937 acknowledged that there were two accounts—Whitener's and Heath's—of how the tufted textile industry began, and it said that the industry's "origin perhaps will remain buried beneath conflicting stories."[39] The Heath version quickly faded, though, and in later years the Stewart family, which operated a successful tufting business, stated that Heath's spread was in a fair in 1909, postdating Whitener's earliest spreads and resolving any contention between the stories.[40] Because the production of spreads centered around Whitener was still small in 1909, it is possible that each woman was unaware of the other's efforts and that multiple women in Northwest Georgia may have "rediscovered" the tradition independently.

In 1942 the *Dalton News* reported that J. T. Bates of Bates Bedspread Company owned an antique candlewick spread made by his great grandmother, Eva Deck, in 1789. According to the newspaper, Deck picked the cotton, spun the thread, and tufted the spread when she was sixteen years old. The newspaper considered it not as beautiful as the new ones her great grandson's company sold, but stated that he would sell "any other spread for much less than he would this old heirloom, in fact this one is not for sale."[41] The newspaper reported that Bates's antique spread had attracted much attention when displayed "some time ago at one of the national bedspread marts."

Daphne Caldwell, when interviewed in 1979 about her tufting business of the 1930s and 1940s, said that, according to her mother, Daphne's maternal grandmother had made tufted spreads in Marble Hill, Georgia, in Pickens County. Caldwell recalled, "[My mother] said that her mother made a bedspread by putting a stitch over a little stick, a little larger than a pencil and she would take a sharp knife and cut those threads on top of that stick which would meet together and form a ball [tuft]," and added, "I think that's where it really originated from."[42] These accounts indicate that the candlewick tradition had deep, branching roots in Northwest Georgia. Although the Whitener story came to represent the industry, for many makers and manufacturers the connections to candlewick were more personal.

Appalachian Craft Revival

Candlewick bedspreads of the early twentieth century were part of the Southern Appalachian Craft Revival, which began in the late nineteenth century and lasted until about World War II. The slightly earlier Arts and Crafts Movement and its ideas of the dignity of labor, reacting against industrialization and promoting the pleasure of working by hand, influenced many regional craft revivals including the one in Appalachia.

Anna Fariello describes the Appalachian Craft Revival as "impacting and reinforcing America's identity as a nation with its roots in rural living, an independent spirit, and skilled making."[43] She highlights woven goods as being particularly popular during the Appalachian Craft Revival because, especially when compared with heavy iron objects or fragile pottery, they were easy to transport—lightweight, durable, and made of inexpensive materials, characteristics also possessed by Northwest Georgia's tufted textiles.[44] Fariello explains that the handwoven coverlet "was considered to be an icon of individual and original expression, a piece of pure American culture" that "became a tangible symbol of tradition, preservation, simplicity, nature, and morality."[45] Candlewick bedspreads, which sold in huge numbers and were produced on a much larger scale than handwoven coverlets, similarly provided Americans with a chance to possess an example of a traditional craft with a connection to the nation's rural roots.

The Appalachian Craft Revival's popularity is reflected in First Lady Ellen Axson Wilson's decision in 1913 to redecorate a room in the White House with crafts from Appalachia.[46] The novelty of being handmade in Appalachia

Woodrow Wilson's bedroom at the White House, decorated with southern Appalachian textiles, 1917, glass negative by Harris and Ewing, gift of Harris and Ewing, Inc., courtesy of Prints and Photographs Division, Library of Congress, Washington, D.C.

was a selling point for many department stores, at least in the Northeast, where one store in 1922 described candlewick spreads as expressing "the quaint native art of the Georgia backwoods."[47] An advertisement in the *Atlanta Constitution* in 1926, though, likened the candlewick spread to "the prophet that has no honor in his own country," suggesting that its regional origins were more enticing to buyers in the North than in Georgia.[48]

In *Weavers of the Southern Highlands* (2003), Philis Alvic documents the histories of the leading weaving centers of the Appalachian Craft Revival. This important study provides a context for understanding the candlewick industry, which shares a history with southern weaving as regional hand-crafted textiles. Most of the schools and businesses Alvic discusses—includ-ing Fireside Industries of Berea College in Kentucky; Arrowcraft at the Pi Beta Phi Settlement School in Gatlinburg, Tennessee; Penland Weavers and Potters at the Appalachian School in Penland, North Carolina; and the Weavers of Rabun in Northeast Georgia—were started by mission-minded women who wanted to improve the lives of people in the mountains by helping them earn income and to better society by preserving and dissemi-nating examples of traditional Appalachian crafts. Alvic notes that the weav-ing centers emphasized "the revival aspect of their work" and "attempted to connect themselves with Appalachian weaving and weavers of the past." Each offered an origin story connected to a specific weaver or, more gener-ally, to "our grandmothers."[49] She states that the weaving centers "placed high value on their historical connections to people and places in the moun-tains" and that "some stories grew into legends, as retelling reinforced and sharpened connections," descriptions that aptly reflect Dalton's relationship with Whitener as well.[50]

These institutions primarily sold goods through women's and charita-ble organizations and eschewed commercialization of the crafts, adopting a moralistic stance and emphasizing the social good of their work. Berea College, for example, struggled with the desire to run a successful crafts business, Fireside Industries. Alvic explains, "The school wanted the sales but only if it could remain untainted by commercial motives."[51] The most business-oriented of the weaving operations was Churchill Weavers in Berea, and because of its commercial approach the Southern Highland Handicraft Guild initially denied it membership.[52] While much of the Appalachian Craft Revival was a reaction against industrialization, and the weaving centers maintained their emphasis on the importance of handcraft, the tufted textile industry in Northwest Georgia, due to the enterprising attitudes of the women involved and the ease of access to large markets via rail transportation, quickly embraced commercialism and mechanization.

The candlewick business straddled the line between craft and commerce. While the industry manufactured tufted textiles on an ever-larger scale, shipped goods across the nation, and marketed to major department stores, it also possessed rustic features like the haulers and hand tufters working in their homes. Especially as the industry mechanized in the mid-1930s, the connections to Catherine Evans Whitener and the industry's origins in traditional needlework became increasingly important to promote as a means to maintain a conceptual link between the tufted textiles and the country's colonial past.

Department of Labor Survey of Southern Appalachian Crafts Production, 1933–1934

Noted photographer Doris Ulmann (1882–1934) created images of craftspeople in Appalachia during the 1920s and 1930s, documenting the Appalachian Craft Revival. In 1934 she and her assistant, folklorist John Jacob Niles, stopped in Ringgold, Georgia, just north of Dalton, where she photographed members of the Stiles family. Frances Stiles Whitener (1925–2014), who married Catherine Evans Whitener's nephew, remembered Ulmann fondly.[53] Her mother, Ethel May Stiles, made both quilts and candlewick spreads and had a home where people regularly gathered to visit. Ulmann often posed her subjects with evidence of their work, and, in addition to the samples Ethel and her daughters are tufting, in some images there is a candlewick spread for the B. J. Bandy Company (for whom Stiles tufted) hung as a backdrop.[54] Some of the photographs of Stiles working focus on her hands and tools (see p. 6): the wooden stamping iron that her husband made and the fat that she rubbed on it, her needle and scissors, and the stalls—protective sheaths—that she wore on her fingers, ones of rubber inner tube to protect her index fingers and another of thick denim on a middle finger to help push the needle. Ulmann's images both document Stiles's process and emphasize the handcrafted and unmodern qualities of her work.

Ulmann's inclusion of Stiles, as well as Mrs. C. B. Wood, who operated a successful bedspread business in Dalton, and two younger tufters, Mrs. Blondin and Mrs. McConny, among her portraits of Appalachian craftspeople places the candlewick industry within the Appalachian Craft

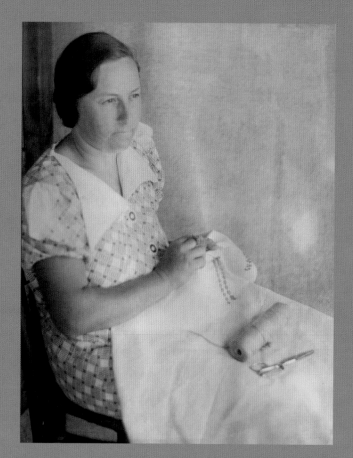

Ethel May Stiles tufting, Ringgold, Georgia, 1934, Doris Ulmann Photograph Collection, PH038-115-5-0491-001, Special Collections and University Archives, University of Oregon Libraries, Eugene, Oreg.

Frances and Wilma Stiles tufting, Ringgold, Georgia, 1934, Doris Ulmann Photograph Collection, PH038-112-1-0052-001, Special Collections and University Archives, University of Oregon Libraries, Eugene, Oreg.

Revival, but it was not a perfect fit. The scale, commercialism, structure, and success of the candlewick industry set it apart from other craft ventures in the region. Allen Eaton, noted scholar and promoter of traditional American folk arts, included a section on candlewick spreads in his seminal 1937 study documenting the Appalachian Craft Revival, *Handicrafts of the Southern Highlands*, but he focused largely on how the candlewick industry differed from the other crafts.[55] He described the candlewick industry as the home industry "employing the largest number of workers in the Southern Highlands," an industry "about which the business interests are enthusiastic," and "one of the few handicrafts that have been commercially standardized."[56]

Mrs. C. B. Wood marking off a pattern for a spread, Dalton, Georgia, 1934, Doris Ulmann Photograph Collection, PH038-115-5-1385-001, Special Collections and University Archives, University of Oregon Libraries, Eugene, Oreg.

Ulmann's portrayal of the Stiles family only hints at the reality of how the larger industry operated. Ethel May Stiles worked hard, riding the bus to B. J. Bandy's spread house to pick up spreads, filling a trunk on the back of the bus and stacking more on top, then distributing (or "letting out") some of the spreads to other tufters when she got home. She had to be mindful of all of the materials, since many distributors would weigh the sheeting and yarn when it left and again when it returned as finished spreads to make sure that no tufters kept leftover yarn for their personal use.[57] Similarly, three daughters in the Beard family in Cisco, Georgia, ages twenty-one, nineteen, and fourteen, tufted full-time at home for the candlewick spread company Kenner and Rauschenberg. They reported that they started working at 6:00 a.m. and worked until midnight, stopping for one hour for dinner and one hour for supper. One stated that while they preferred tufting to working in the field, "We don't work at this for pleasure, we'd be glad of a better job."[58]

By the early 1930s the candlewick industry was thriving. Huge shipments of spreads traveled to department stores across the country, where shoppers eagerly acquired the pretty and affordable textiles. Despite a steady stream of profits enjoyed by company owners, other aspects of the industry were less

Gimbels Basement, Milwaukee, Wisconsin, 1940, Bedspread Association scrapbook, Whitfield-Murray Historical Society, Crown Gardens & Archives, Dalton, Georgia. This photograph, from a scrapbook put together by an early tufted textile group in Dalton, shows shoppers at Gimbels Basement department store examining chenille bedspreads.

consistent and were subject to a variety of uncertainties. While hand tufting bedspreads undeniably allowed many families in the region to survive the Depression—Kenner and Rauschenberg, the largest candlewick business at the time, considered their payroll as "the salvation of the community"—the wages were low and the work was difficult.[59] Personal accounts from the often desperately poor families that tufted the spreads help to document the industry from their perspectives.

In 1933 and 1934, under the leadership of Bertha M. von der Nienburg (ca. 1890–1964), the Women's Bureau of the Department of Labor conducted a survey of southern Appalachian crafts production.[60] Nienburg and her researchers interviewed workers in a variety of crafts, including candlewick, and they often recorded details beyond the standard survey data.[61] These rare period accounts, preserved through transcriptions of tufters' comments and personal observations by the field agents, provide otherwise-undocumented details about the lives of candlewick workers. For example, after visiting a Mrs. Pack in Calhoun, Georgia, one agent reported that Pack was wearing "moccasins knitted from waste yarn" and that "many women were wearing these," while "some were barefooted."[62]

Many interviewees indicated that bedspread work provided their only income. Sally Jo Green of Chatsworth told the agent simply, "Bedspread money is all the money we have."[63] And Mrs. Mabel Watts of Chatsworth, who preferred spread work to fieldwork because she did not like working in the sun and could work spreads in the shade, told the agent, "We need the work. If we don't have spreads we'll starve to death."[64] Mrs. W. V. Sissin of Varnell went into greater detail about her family's situation. She worked ten hours a day at home, tufting spreads for the B. J. Bandy Company most of the year, making about two dollars a week (equivalent to thirty-six dollars in 2014). She had nine years of experience. The agent who interviewed her recorded her stating, "I just get up and milk and then works from milking time to sundown. Many times the oldest [daughter] too. Put the youngest one to housework and cookin'. . . . That's all we got to make our livin' on is spreads. Husband has a disease. Can't work so much. Didn't make nothin' on farming. Spreads is all we had to feed us and clothe us too. Took every cent we had to buy bread sometimes. Would like to set the youngest [daughter] to 'turfing' but her eyes ain't so good. Can't afford to buy glasses and food too. Just figure the glasses won't do her no good if she starves to death so give her the food instead.

. . . Whenever we'd get out of things and need food we'd sit up till midnight turfing."[65] Notes with the survey of the Godfrey family of Calhoun record the tufters as describing how all of the old houses near Calhoun were filled with families seeking spread work: "People all moving in from the hills. On Saturday evening you kin see dozens a women walking in, carrying sacks on their backs. They're women bringing in their spreads. Just means everything to country people."[66]

A few families, though, used tufting income to supplement their needs and elevate their status. Mrs. Webb Coffey, a widow in Eton, enjoyed spread work and used the money to educate her seven children, stating, "If I don't educate my children all they'll be fitten for is to make bedspreads or work on the farm." One of her daughters was a teacher and another studied at Berry College in Rome, Georgia.[67]

The survey interviews also suggest how physically demanding and debilitating the repetitive needlework could be. Mrs. Stella Bishop of Ramhurst stated that she liked tufting, but preferred fieldwork: "When I get to tufting, I get to hurting. In the field I can straighten up."[68] The agent who visited Miss Bonnie K. Dunn in Tennga wrote that her neighbors were concerned about her health because she tufted so much. Dunn explained, "You are bound to get nervous, you've got to get it finished on time. If you don't you'll be a long time getting another one to do," referring to the fact that if a tufter did not complete her allotment of spreads on time and with accuracy, the hauler would not bring her spreads the next time and she would lose that source of income. Dunn explained that she couldn't work all day any longer and that she rested in the afternoon because her shoulders and eyes hurt and that she was "about blind from it."[69] Mrs. Bradford of Fairmount reported, "Been 6 years at turfing. Worked myself sick. Got so now I can just work three hours and then I have to stop."[70]

Because only some of the sheets, often the more complex and expensive designs, were pre-stamped, home tufters sometimes had to "lay off" the spreads themselves. Mrs. Godfrey of Calhoun told the agent how hard that was: "Just get so hot and your back aches. Knees get black and blue and hurt so. . . . Takes a lot of strength to bring out the pattern. We lay it out on the parlor square. A lot of families don't have any rug."[71] Mrs. Bearden of Calhoun also described stamping a spread at home, and the agent noted: "Cracks in floor make it difficult to 'iron' smoothly. Nails in floor sometimes tear spread."[72] Some women preferred heavy patterns (with lots of tufting) because though those patterns took longer they usually paid more, while light patterns, though they took less time to tuft, paid little and required too much time to lay off and hem the edges. Others preferred light spreads because they took less strength to handle. Some women could hem a spread in just a few minutes, but others, without sewing machines, took up to an hour.

Families could earn more income if they hauled, distributed spreads to other families, or lived close enough to the company to pick up their own spreads. Mrs. Gertrude Caldwell's husband worked in Dalton as a stamper for Mrs. C. B. Wood, so he brought his wife the best designs, with no deductions for haulers' commissions. Mrs. Caldwell stated, "I was raised on the farm, and am used to hard work, but boy I'd rather work on the farm than tuft. This way you never get a chance to walk around and get any exercise." She liked Mrs. Wood, though, and believed that she paid the best of anyone in town.[73] Mrs. D. F. Woods in Cisco, who lived about nine miles down a dirt road from the nearest paved road, took in extra spreads and let them out to neighbors without charging a commission so that she would have a wider selection of spreads to choose from for her own work.[74]

While there were benefits to being a hauler, they faced challenges and risks as well. Mr. Edwards in Adairsville, who clipped spreads for his family on rainy days, hauled with his daughter, and they received five cents per spread, giving out and returning as many as 256 spreads in one week, with individual families tufting between two and twenty-five spreads each. Sometimes they could not get any spreads to distribute. Other times, such as during the "rush of hoeing and gardening," they couldn't give out all the spreads they had, as tufters tended to their crops first.[75] Mrs. MacDearis, a hauler in Adairsville, also encountered difficulty distributing spreads, stating, "Everybody's chopping cotton now. Hard to put out the spreads in a rush. Nobody got no time."[76] Another hauler, Mr. Fletcher in Adairsville, received five cents per spread but only if he distributed fifty or more, otherwise he received no commission from the company, a situation reported by the Teague family of Fairmount, as well, which had not received a commission in six months.[77]

Often there were multiple steps in the distribution of spreads. For example, the Women's Bureau field agent who interviewed Mrs. John Walker in Tennga noted that her spreads passed through two haulers before reaching her. The second hauler charged 10 to 20 percent of what the company paid per spread, "depending on how much he has to give out, where the person lives, etc." The agent described the family's house as "miserably poor."[78]

The survey interviews also document the participation of African American women in the hand-tufted spread business. When an agent interviewed two African American sisters in the Hill family in Calhoun, who worked spreads for the B. J. Bandy Company, they reported that they could always secure spreads and told the agent, "They say we do good work." The oldest, twenty years of age, had seven years of tufting experience.[79] Mrs. Henderson in Adairsville, whose family "let out" spreads to other workers, told a Women's Bureau agent that "some people fussed" at her for "letting out" to African American women, but she said that they were the best workers she had, with one family having worked twenty-three spreads for her the prior week.[80] Mrs. Chadwick in Calhoun also mentioned passing work to African American women but only because she was frustrated with a particularly difficult spread, indicating that African American tufters sometimes received the least desirable work.[81] One agent conducted a partial interview of an African American woman named Mrs. Scott in Calhoun, who was too ill, in the agent's opinion, to complete the interview. The agent noted that even though the woman had the measles and was pregnant with her fourteenth child, she had an in-progress candlewick spread rolled up with her bedclothes. During the agent's visit to the neighbor, Mrs. Scott sent her son to borrow scissors so she could clip stitches. The neighbor later told the agent, "We give all the hard work to the [African American women]," adding, "they take anything they kin get."[82]

Some of the large candlewick companies paid workers in trading chips to company stores, as did companies in other industries across the country, which was prohibitively challenging for families who lived far from the stores and lacked transportation. The Women's Bureau agent interviewing Mrs. E. Riddenberry of Folsom (in Bartow County) recorded that the family had "no means of transportation to city and so have repeatedly had to refuse work from companies who pay in trading chips. This troubles them because they need the work and if they had any way of reaching 'trading chip' stores, would accept. Recently they did not know they had done work for such a firm until hauler called for work. Had agreed to pay 20¢ for the spreads. When family refused to accept chips were told 'Well then I can only pay you 15¢ a spread.'"[83]

In 1935 Nienburg published a report on her findings through the surveys. In "Potential Earning Power of Southern Mountaineer Handicraft" she argued for the centralization of handicraft workers, stating, "The southern mountaineer craftswoman plying her craft in her home from sunup till sundown whenever work is available from any source, furnishing her own equipment, taking a material share of overhead expense off the shoulders of her employers, bearing the full burden of a poorly organized business, subject to every irregularity in market trends, at the end of her year's effort finds that her earnings have been about one-twelfth those of her lowest-paid factory sister."[84] Nienburg reported that of the handicraft centers surveyed, candlewick by far employed the most individuals and produced the largest sales.[85]

Nienburg conducted the survey just as the industry was beginning to transition from hand tufting to machine tufting. The sheer volume of the candlewick industry and the uncertainty inherent in the system of haulers and home tufters likely encouraged manufacturers to consider faster, more reliable ways of making tufted goods in factories. Fred Rosen, whose family owned LaRose Bedspread Company, believed that one reason the industry mechanized was the challenge of working with hand tufters during the cotton harvest season, which coincided with the biggest shipping time for candlewick.[86] However, the primary factor contributing to the shift was Franklin Roosevelt's National Industrial Recovery Act and the Federal Wage and Hour Law of 1932–33, which mandated a minimum wage of 32½ cents per hour. Industry leaders claimed that they could not make profits if they paid hand tufters that rate, and they turned to machinery to increase the speed of production.

Machine Tufting

The transition from hand tufting to machine tufting does not have a clear history. There are competing claims for nearly every mechanical development and technological innovation.[87] Some accounts indicate that companies experimented with machines in the 1920s. The *Wall Street Journal* mentions a mattress company in Chattanooga, Tennessee, thirty miles north of Dalton, that began making tufted bedspreads by 1922 using a machine of its own invention.[88] Later that year W. B. Moses and Sons, a large furniture and drapery store in Washington, D.C., advertised machine-made candlewick spreads that rivaled hand-tufted ones.[89] But it was not until the mid-1930s that the use of modified sewing machines became widespread in Northwest Georgia's tufted textile industry.

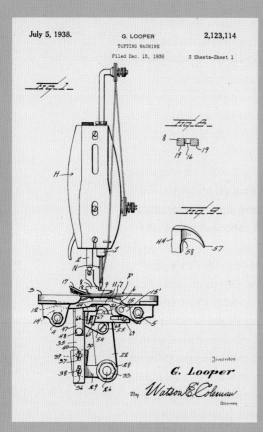

Tufting Machine, U.S. patent design by Glenn Looper, filed December 15, 1936, granted July 5, 1938, des. 2,123,114. The patent reads, "This invention relates to tufting machines . . . to be used in the decoration of articles such as bedspreads, pillow tops, rugs, dress coats for ladies, and other articles of like nature."

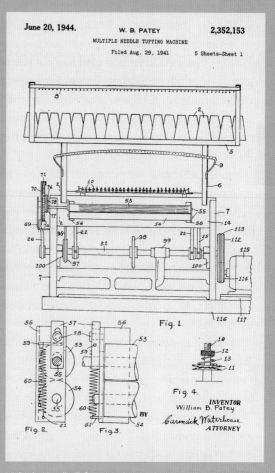

Multiple Needle Tufting Machine, U.S. patent design by William B. Patey, filed August 29, 1941, granted June 20, 1944, des. 2,352,153

The earliest tufting machines in the Dalton area were single-needle sewing machines converted to produce rows of tufting. Needles in the machines sewed stitches, and cutting elements clipped them from underneath. Zack Norville (1928–2013), whose family continues to be instrumental in the development of the tufted textile industry, recalled, "Many of our early machines came out of sewing lots in New York." These, he said, "had been used by the thousands to make overalls or shirts."[90] Similarly, in 1950 the Tufted Textile Manufacturers Association reported that in the 1930s "second-hand sewing machines were being bought . . . from the New York garment center," as the northern factories upgraded to higher-speed machines, and converted into tufting machines.[91] As the industry shifted to machine production, most tufting moved from private homes into centralized plants, and women often worked on line-shaft-operated tufting machines, with the workers in rows on both sides of long tables and their machines turned by one motor.[92]

The introduction of machine tufting presented the industry with a terminological quandary. "Candlewick" had a clear definition and a long history as handcraft, but as the new machine-tufted goods emerged, the industry needed a way to differentiate between the two. Despite the fact that "chenille" already had a textile-related definition (fuzzy yarn made of multiple core yarns twisted to hold short, perpendicular-pile yarns in place—the yarn equivalent of a pipe cleaner), it became the common term for machine-tufted textiles. For many years the industry used "candlewick" to denote hand tufting and "chenille" to denote machine tufting, and that is generally how those terms are applied in this book. The two techniques usually are easy to distinguish when the textile is viewed from the back. Chenille machines typically make neat, continuous rows of adjacent stitches, while the candlewick stitches often are less consistently sized and spaced.

In 1946 Henry C. Ball (1898–1959), executive director of the Tufted Textile Manufacturers Association from 1945 until 1959, expressed a preference for the terms "candlewick" or "tufted" instead of "chenille." *Georgia Progress* quotes him explaining, "We are advised that the word *chenille*, which means 'caterpillar' in French, was used [because] after the tufting had been made and the product had been fluffed, the tufting resembled a caterpillar's upper side or back, and the other where it had crawled upon the ground" and perhaps because "the tufting machines pull and work in the manner of a caterpillar crawling."[93] Though "tufted" is more precise, "chenille" already

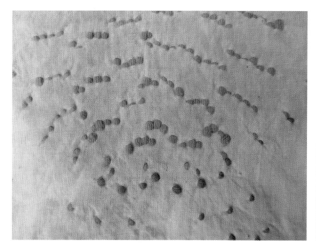

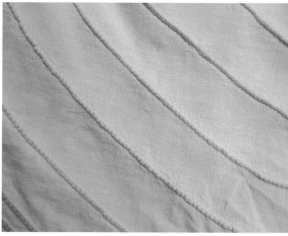

Detail of the back of a hand-tufted candlewick apron, photo by author

Detail of the back of a machine-tufted chenille child's cape, photo by author

was in wide use by the mid-1940s, and by the late twentieth century "chenille" generally was used to describe all tufted textiles, whether made by hand or machine.

As the industry matured, company leaders formed a series of influential trade associations, beginning with the Bedspread Association in 1933 and followed by the Tufted Bedspread Manufacturers Association in 1938, which became the Tufted Textile Manufacturers Association (TTMA) in 1945.[94] These groups focused on spreads, robes, and rugs, and they allowed company leaders to work collectively to promote industry interests. In 1963, the TTMA included in its activities "[compiling] industry statistics, [carrying] on an extensive public relations program, [disseminating] industry information to members, [and holding] an annual workshop meeting and a convention."[95] From a research standpoint, one of the TTMA's key projects was the annual publication of a directory with articles about tufted textiles, lists of tufted textile manufacturers, and advertisements highlighting tufted textile products.

In 1950, in its first annual directory, the TTMA included an article that begins, "Like a story-book romance reads the history of the colorful textile industry, a saga of American ingenuity, skill and success that is without precedent." What follows is a neatly summarized account of Catherine Evans Whitener's story.[96] In the 1953 directory, in an article on the promotion and sales of tufted goods, Frank Talley, a buyer for Rich's in Atlanta, advised stores to tell their sales forces "about the young farm girl, Catherine Evans, who made the first modern tufted spread in 1895 and launched a multi-million dollar industry."[97]

The industry continued to make technological advances, developing machines with increasing numbers of needles and experimenting with new yarns and backings, until it was possible to tuft wide widths of material, eventually leading to the production of wall-to-wall carpeting and the rebranding of Dalton from Bedspread Center of the World to Carpet Capital of the World. Even as the industry's mechanization ended handmade production, the frequent retelling of Whitener's story prolonged the sense of the industry's rural, rustic roots and of tufted textiles' handcrafted origins.

"Dalton Does Wonders" billboard on U.S. 41 and interior of a carpet manufactory, ca. 1980, postcard, collection of Bradley Putnam

Roadside chenille home business, probably on U.S. 41, 1940s,
unidentified photographer (possibly Ward's Photo Service,
Dalton, Georgia), courtesy of Betty Talley

Chapter Two

Bedspread Boulevard

— — — DALTON OFFERED A strategically enviable location for the development of the tufted textile industry, which grew hand in hand with the increasing ease of transportation through the area. Both the Southern Railway and the Nashville, Chattanooga, and St. Louis Railway (NC&StL, leased from the Western and Atlantic Railroad) served Dalton, and the *Atlanta Constitution* touted Dalton's growing trucking business in 1915, noting that the markets in Cincinnati, Louisville, Nashville, Knoxville, Atlanta, New Orleans, and Chattanooga were are all readily accessible, within a twelve-hour drive.[1] While railways and roads allowed for shipment of goods to stores across the country, the roadside itself developed a distinctive tufted textile culture. The roadside presence of tufted textiles drew individuals into production and sales, advertised the goods to travelers who then took souvenirs back to their homes, and served as a test market for tufted products. By the 1930s U.S. 41 through Northwest Georgia was widely known as Bedspread Boulevard and was lined with spreadlines selling spreads, rugs, bath sets (usually a matching toilet seat cover and bathmat), aprons, robes, capes, coats, dolls, scuffies (slippers), and novelties.

The Dixie Highway

The roadside presence of candlewick and chenille only became possible as the roads became passable. Residents of Northwest Georgia advocated for a good road from Chattanooga to Atlanta as early as 1903.[2] One of the first

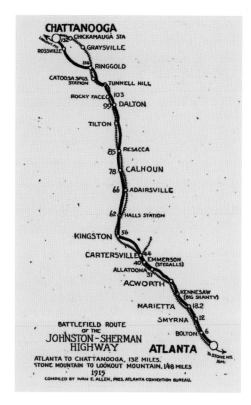

named automobile routes through the region was the Johnston-Sherman Highway (or Battlefield Route).[3] Plans for this highway, which roughly followed the Civil War campaign of Generals Joseph E. Johnston and William T. Sherman, began in 1909, and the road was completed by 1912. The local chapter of the United Daughters of the Confederacy erected a statue of Johnston in 1912 in downtown Dalton, ensuring the town's connection to the route.

A more widely familiar named route through the region is the Dixie Highway, which funneled tourists from the upper Midwest to Florida, specifically to Miami, and was conceived by Carl Fisher of Indianapolis, a leading advocate of the automobile industry and real estate developer promoting the new resort city of Miami Beach. The establishment of the Dixie Highway was fraught with so many competing interests that its founders could not settle on a single route, instead opting to designate two main routes in 1915, with the western route

Map of the Battlefield Route of the Johnston-Sherman Highway, March 28, 1915, *Atlanta Constitution*

going through northwestern Georgia. Numerous options existed within the two main routes, and Jeffrey L. Durbin, in a chapter on the Dixie Highway in Georgia in *Looking Beyond the Highway: Dixie Roads and Culture* (2006), details how the highway divided in Chattanooga. One branch, the Western Division, went through Fort Oglethorpe and Rome, while the Eastern Division followed the Western and Atlantic Railroad through Dalton.[4]

In 1915 the *Atlanta Constitution* praised Whitfield County's progress in building its section of highway, which it referred to as the Hoosierland-Dixie (and which was basically the already-built Johnston-Sherman Highway): "Not only in completing her share of the highway, but in her wonderful record of diversified industries, traceable to her county fairs, to her banks bulging with money, to her manufacturing and other industries, and, above all, the initiative and enterprise of her county commissioners, and her people, Whitfield blazes a trail each county in Georgia should follow."[5] While the specific path the route took was modified well into the 1920s as road conditions improved or deteriorated in various areas, Dalton stayed on the main thoroughfare.[6]

By the mid-1920s the system of named routes became so complicated in the United States that a newly formed Joint Board of State and Federal Highway Officials established a highway numbering system, giving east–west interstate highways even numbers and north–south highways odd numbers. By 1927 the Dixie Highway's route through the Dalton area was designated U.S. 41.[7] In 1965, U.S. 41's dominance was usurped by Interstate 75, which closely follows the route of U.S. 41 in Northwest Georgia.[8]

Automobile Tourism

As Howard Laurence Preston discusses in *Dirt Roads to Dixie* (1991), automobile travel shifted from a leisure activity of the wealthy to a middle-class pastime in the 1910s, and the incentives for improved road conditions in the South included ease of travel for farmers and economic boons from tourists.[9] In the *Atlanta Constitution* in 1915, Frank J. Reynolds wrote, "Whitfield [County] believes that during the next twelve months thousands of people will be traveling southward who never visited the South before." Reynolds explained, "The European war, practically barring foreign travel, has been the greatest stimulus to the 'See American First' movement since the advent of popular automobiling and good roads."[10] Reynolds's article conveys a clear awareness in Whitfield County of the importance of tourists and the highway to the local economy and documents efforts to make its stretch of the Dixie Highway especially enticing by adding shade trees and highlighting historic points of interest.[11]

People vying for the Dixie Highway, wanting it to pass through their towns, engaged in exuberant civic boosterism, touting every possible advantage they might offer over another location.[12] According to Durbin, after years of competition for the tourist trade between communities along both divisions of the western route of the Dixie Highway in North Georgia, by 1940 it was clear that the Eastern Division (Dalton's) was much more prosperous than the slightly longer Western Division. Durbin reports that a

Map of the Dixie Highway, from *Dixie Highway*, September 1919, courtesy of the Chattanooga History Center

review of highway maps for Catoosa, Walker, Floyd, and Whitfield Counties from 1940 shows thirty-nine gas stations and eleven tourist camps on rural areas of U.S. 41 (formerly the Eastern Division), with only six gas stations and four tourist camps on U.S. 27 (formerly the Western Division).[13]

Preston discusses the presentation of the South in automobile and travel publications as exhibiting "the same popular romantic imagery that had so characterized nineteenth-century books and articles about the South."[14] At the same time, writers promoted how increasingly easy travel through the South was becoming, combining reports of accessibility with "thick, syrupy romanticism."[15] Preston explains that travel through the South slowed during World War I because steel, iron, and rubber were needed for wartime manufacturing, halting the production of touring cars.[16] Tourism picked up again in the 1920s, and Preston notes that the increased flow of outsiders resulted in cultural changes along the automobile routes, making "the region less provincial and more like the rest of the nation."[17] He also notes that these changes were most visible in the 1920s and 1930s along the rural highways, "where the burgeoning new automobile tourist economy first developed."[18]

Tufted Souvenirs

For Dalton, tourism and the money it promised were strong motivators in the city's efforts to be on a major automobile route. Exactly when tufted goods appeared for sale on the roadside is unclear, though they were there at least by the late 1920s. It was probably earlier—likely developing with the post–World War I growth in tourism and the establishment of the popular Dixie Highway.[19] The marketing of candlewick along the highway may have been, at least in part, a calculated effort to make the area attractive to tourists and more desirable than alternate routes. While handmade souvenirs might not have been essential to travel, the colorful wares presented along the highway in the Dalton region must have contributed to its visual appeal.

The opening of the South to automobile tourism presented an opportunity to offer specifically southern experiences and goods to outsiders. Northwest Georgia met the challenge with a corridor lined by bright rows of flapping spreads, providing a unique driving experience and surrounding tourists with examples of Southern Appalachian handcrafts that they could purchase and take to their distant homes. Many tourists may have been familiar with the spreads from department stores but were attracted "by the

"Hand Tufted Bedspreads and Souvenirs, U.S. 41, GA," ca. 1940, postcard published by W. M. Cline Company, Chattanooga, private collection. This depicts the spreadline of Mrs. J. A. Greene of Adairsville and has a handwritten note and arrow drawing attention to "The Famous 'Peafowl' Pattern."

novelty of buying them 'off the line.'"[20] The *Dalton News* reported in 1929 that "tourists from every section of the United States utter exclamations of surprise as they drive through the county and see the beautiful spreads, in more than a hundred varieties of colors, as they hang from clothes lines around the country homes."[21] The spreadlines ranged from front porches hung with a few spreads and robes, to small buildings adjacent to homes with a wider variety of wares, to dedicated businesses with extensive signage and elaborate displays.

Because of its spreadlines, U.S. 41 through Northwest Georgia earned numerous nicknames, including Bedspread Route (in use by 1934), Bedspread Belt (1935), Bedspread Highway (1936), Bedspread Avenue (1938), Bedspread Land (1940) and, most popularly, Bedspread Boulevard (1936), which was still the preferred term as late as 1978.[22] Dalton itself has been called the Candlewick Capital (1938) and Bedspread Center of the World (1942).[23]

The constant interaction with tourists from other parts of the country meant that the region was far from isolated, and roadside retailers received immediate feedback about what items and styles tourists favored. Murray Wyche, writing in 1948, stated that as smaller manufacturers in the late 1930s experimented with new chenille garments, the items "first had to win their place on 'Bedspread Boulevard.'"[24] Since many travelers were headed to Florida, casual garments that they could wear on vacation found a ready market. Though the direct impact of this tourist trade on the development of

Roadside chenille business, probably on U.S. 41 between Adairsville and Cassville, 1940s, unidentified photographer (possibly Ward's Photo Service, Dalton, Georgia), courtesy of Betty Talley

Roadside chenille business, probably on U.S. 41 between Tunnel Hill and Ringgold, 1940s, unidentified photographer (possibly Ward's Photo Service, Dalton, Georgia), courtesy of Betty Talley

tufted garments is impossible to measure, it is a factor worth considering in light of the national popularity of tufted beach capes and sportswear in the 1930s, especially at southern resorts.

The spreadlines provided rich material for journalists and received adoring media attention. In 1935, Julian Haas of the *Hammond (Ind.) Times* wrote, "No markers are necessary to inform the motorist driving into North Georgia that the Tennessee boundary line has been passed," because "thousands and thousands of bedspreads flapping in the autumn breeze semaphore the northwestern Georgia stretch of the Dixie highway."[25] Phoebe Laing Mosley, writing for *McCall Decorative Arts and Needlework* in 1932, described the road as "bordered gayly with hand-tufted 'candlewick' . . . hung out to bleach and 'fluff' in the sun and wind," which she considered "a delightful change from the ubiquitous cigarette and soap billboards."[26] The managing editor of the *Oklahoma City Times*, Walter Harrison, wrote about his trip through North Georgia in 1935 on his way to attend a minor league baseball game in

Interior of a roadside chenille business, probably on U.S. 41 between Tunnel Hill and Ringgold, 1940s, unidentified photographer (possibly Ward's Photo Service, Dalton, Georgia), courtesy of Betty Talley

Bennett's Chenille Products

Mrs. J. H. Bennett (née Emily Mealer or Mealor, 1904–97) began hand tufting while her husband farmed.[a] Initially she sold her goods through a friend with a spreadline, then the family moved to U.S. 41 (where they had electricity) and she operated her own spreadline just south of the Gordon County and Whitfield County line. For her first tufting shop, in the 1930s, her husband built a log cabin near the highway and the Resaca Confederate Cemetery.[b] At this site Mrs. Bennett, who often wore a bonnet and usually worked alone, epitomized the popular notion of a southern Appalachian craftswoman.[c] The *Atlanta Journal* featured two photographs of her business on a page about Bedspread Boulevard in 1936. The paper referred to her log office and workshop as "picturesque" and captioned an image of her adding fringe to a spread "Early American Tableau." A photograph of a display of her pillows and aprons is labeled "Latest Wrinkle in Tufting," suggesting that her deviation from the traditional spread form was innovative.[d] Later, probably in the late 1930s, the Bennetts moved and she got a new little spreadline on U.S. 41.

As a hand tufter, Bennett made spreads, aprons, and pillows, and she began making robes after she bought a single-needle machine. Her daughter, Helen Johnson, also recalls that she made bath sets, capes for women and children, boleros, and short jackets, though the short jackets did not catch on like the robes. Johnson describes Bennett as a talented seamstress who often devised her own patterns, a skill developed of necessity because she had so many daughters. When Johnson asked her mother how she learned to sew so well, Bennett told her, "Well, I had to. We didn't have much money and I had you four girls. . . . People would give me clothes and I would take them apart and cut them down and make clothes for y'all." She sewed for other people as well.

Her daughter recalls, "She could fit. She could have different sizes. A lot of [tufters] just had one size, but I think because she was a seamstress that helped her."

To make a robe, Bennett first cut out the pattern and sewed the pieces of cotton fabric together, leaving the arms open. Next she spread the unfinished robe, if it was to have a complex motif like a peacock, on a large table over a pattern and rubbed it with a bar of wax infused with purple dye to transfer the design. Then she tufted the pattern and finished the robe. According to Johnson, Bennett used twisted cord ties with her robes, with loops at the waist to hold them in place, trimming the ends of the cords to make them fluffy. She started with a single-needle machine, later acquiring a double-needle machine and then adding a machine that sewed flowers. Her daughter recalls that she also had a hemmer for putting the robes together. Bennett's husband maintained her machines and machines for other people in the community.

Bennett used a lot of the same patterns for spreads as other people in the community, but she would sometimes alter the designs, especially the section

Two views of Mrs. J. H. Bennett's chenille business, with Willie Jean Chitwood, Helen Bennett (Mrs. Bennett's daughter), and Aveline Chitwood seated at left, ca. 1937, photographs probably taken by Iduma Chitwood, collection of Helen Johnson

below the break of the bed, on the part of the spread that hangs vertically. She favored a shell pattern of her own design. She made peacock robes and capes with the chenille lines forming chevrons in the back, and she also made ones bordered with abstract circular flowers.

Bennett had regular customers who would visit her when traveling U.S. 41 and who would write to her during the year to place orders. Some travelers placed orders with her when they passed through, and she shipped the items to them later. Mrs. C. R. McLaughlin of Chicago saw a robe belonging to a friend and wrote to Bennett asking her to make her one too, specifying all-white, heavy chenille, and providing measurements.[e] Bennett also sold spreads and possibly robes to a few buyers for department stores in Chicago. She shipped a lot of products to the Mackies (possibly Bill and Lucille), who had a spreadline in Crab Orchard, Tennessee. According to Bennett's account books, robes cost only slightly less than spreads. In a book recording transactions around 1940–41, robes are listed for between $2.75 and $3.25 and spreads are between $3.00 and $4.50. Aprons were only 33⅓ cents. She listed short coats and capes at $1.25 each.[f] Color increased the price. One typical shipment to the Mackies, recorded in another book from the same time, included thirty-three spreads, thirty-one robes, twelve coats, seven capes, twelve mats, thirteen aprons, six bed jackets, three baby spreads, and two baby robes.

Bennett's early business cards had her name, "Mrs. J. H. Bennett," and advertised handmade candlewick bedspreads in "many designs, all colors," and of the "best materials," as well as bath mats, aprons, and pillow tops. A later flyer lists chenille and candlewick bedspreads as well as coats, capes, and aprons, while an even later business card lists her as proprietor of Bennett's Chenille Products, nine miles south of Dalton on U.S. 41. Bennett continued her business,

Mrs. J. H. Bennett, Chenille apron, n.d., cotton, Whitfield-Murray Historical Society, Crown Gardens & Archives, Dalton, Georgia, gift of Helen Johnson, photograph by Michael McKelvey

tufting her own goods, including peacock robes, until I-75 opened and drew away the tourist traffic. Bennett tufted until she was eighty years old.

a Helen Johnson (daughter of Emily Bennett) and her husband Paul Johnson, interview by author, Dalton, Georgia, March 11, 2013; Bedspread Industry Material, "Clippings, History, Personalities" box, "Mrs. J. H. Bennett" folder, Crown Gardens & Archives.

b The Atlanta Chapter of the United Daughters of the Confederacy erected a historical marker at this cemetery site in 1938. "Atlanta U.D.C. to Unveil Marker," Atlanta Constitution, May 10, 1938.

c Usually Bennett worked alone, though at one time she had an assistant, and her daughters helped occasionally.

d "On Georgia's Bedspread Boulevard," Rotogravure Section, Atlanta Journal, October 18, 1936.

e Postcard, Mrs. C. R. McLaughlin, Chicago, to Mrs. J. H. Bennett, Resaca, Georgia, postmarked August 20, 1941, Bedspread Industry Material, "Clippings, History, Personalities" box, Mrs. J. H. Bennett folder, Crown Gardens & Archives.

f According to the Consumer Price Index Inflation Calculator, $2.75–3.25 in 1940 equaled about $47–55 in 2014, $4.50 equaled about $76, $0.33 equaled about $5.60, and $1.25 equaled about $21. Some of these may reflect wholesale prices.

Atlanta. Initially he was confused: "I thought I saw a washing strung on a line by the roadside. Soon another flashed past. Then they followed in regular succession. Funny that these Crackers should wash on Saturdays. And what in the world would they hang it by the highway for? Is it possible they get no breeze down here and they have to dry their sheets by getting the rush of wind from the passing cavalcade?" He learned more about the spreadlines when he visited Mrs. Gazaway in Adairsville, who had begun her spreadline five years prior and now had a successful filling station and two hundred men and women working for her candlewick business.[27]

While an amusement to tourists, the spreadlines provided important income to residents, though it was not always an easy venture. A feature on "Bedspread Boulevard" by William Boring for the Associated Press in 1938 quotes Homer McClure of Floyd County: "We used to farm all the time . . . but it got to where we couldn't do no good at it. Then we moved to the highway and strung a spreadline. We've lived better than we ever did."[28] Sometimes the income possible from spreadlines created difficulties for haulers and families that let out spreads for companies because, especially during high tourist season, tufters wanted to tuft for the lines rather than for companies.[29] Spreadlines also functioned as markets for slightly defective goods, as the entertainment of purchasing off the line might outweigh any imperfections in the eye of the buyer. For example, many home tufters working for large companies were forced to purchase any spreads damaged in their homes by errant clips that cut the sheet or by stray embers that burned holes, and one family reported sending damaged and repaired spreads to an aunt in Knoxville who had a spreadline.[30]

Mrs. Fletcher of Adairsville had eight years of experience tufting, when, in 1934, she was interviewed as part of the survey of southern Appalachian crafts conducted by the Women's Bureau of the Department of Labor. She talked about the demands of running a spreadline, and the agent noted, "Spreads have to be put out on line and taken off daily; also each time it rains. Takes much time with people who come to buy also." The agent recorded that the Fletchers sold the most off the line during tourist season, from December 31 to March 1. While the income from spreadlines was not steady, it often was higher than those of families who tufted spreads for companies, and Mrs. Fletcher told the agent, "Sometimes I sell 25 or 30 dollar's worth a week. Next week two dollars and a half." She and her sister-in-law made spreads for their line, and she also sold spreads for people who

did not live on the highway. She charged them fifty cents to sell a spread of any price, a quarter for a rug retailing for between $1.25 and $2.50, and a dime for tufted aprons selling for fifty cents. Mrs. Fletcher showed the agent spreads "made by 'people back off the highway,'" and the agent described the spreads as showing "very poor workmanship," being made on the "thinnest possible unbleached muslin," and of "uneven patterns and gaudy colors."[31]

The picturesque appeal of the roadside candlewick displays was not lost on regional entities, and in 1938 the *Atlanta Constitution* and Greyhound Bus Lines offered a four-hundred-mile photography trip to winners of an amateur photography competition and included as one of the scenic stops a spreadline south of Cartersville.[32] When the radio station WSB of Atlanta featured Dalton's tufted textile industry in 1947 as part of its *Forward Georgia* series, the broadcast included a dramatization of a tourist couple driving along the Dixie Highway and commenting on the spreads until they finally stopped to inspect and purchase some.[33]

As the industry grew, Dalton sought to bring even greater tourist attention to its bedspread industry with modern neon signage, though hand-tufted

Lawtex employees outside of the Lawtex building (with part of the neon sign visible), ca. 1947, Ward's Photo Service, Dalton, Georgia, courtesy of the estate of Leonard Lorberbaum

Put's Chenille Center and Colonial Craft

The Putnam family of Tunnel Hill owned numerous roadside chenille businesses from the 1940s to the 1960s. Georgia Lee Putnam (1925–2011) and Robert "Elbert" Putnam (1919–81) started their first chenille business, Put's Chenille Center, around 1943–45 on U.S. 41.[a] It had a tin building where they made spreads. In 1948 they built "the lodge," selling spreads downstairs and living upstairs. Elbert continued to add to the buildings, and the family later lived behind the store. At first they made their own spreads, and later they retailed spreads manufactured by others, including Ben Putnam, a relative who lived south of Dalton.[b] An undated brochure shows the buildings with a long row of rugs hanging just above the ground and a row of capes hanging above them. Other garments and rugs are visible inside the large front windows of the lodge. The brochure describes the center as a factory and showroom and invites customers to "Stop for Free Demonstration on How Chenille Is Made." In addition to spreads, rugs, bath sets, scuffies, and dolls, the brochure advertises robes with plain, floral, peacock, or waffle designs in all colors and a range of sizes; a waffle sport jacket with contrasting colors on the body and a single color on the sleeves, collar, pockets, and belt tie; and a beach cape with a geometric trim design.

In 1950 the Putnams opened Colonial Craft. The building was a riot of color and signs geared specifically to travelers. A large neon sign on the top of the building read "Where Your Friends Bought" and included a series of arrows that flashed in sequence arcing from the top of the sign down toward the store. The Putnams repurposed an old Shell Oil sign to advertise bath sets. Hand-painted lettering in the windows read "Buy direct from factory" and "Bring your camera." A friend of Elbert's built a round metal revolving display rack for housecoats, which sat outside, a feature the Putnams' son Bradley believes may have been unique. At Colonial Craft the Putnams sold housecoats, pillows, bath sets, spreads, children's robes, scuffies, dolls, and short jackets, both wholesale and retail, and Bradley recalls that they sold a lot of peacock chenille. The Putnams later moved into carpet, founding Dalton Carpet Jobbers.

The extended Putnam family owned and operated at least five or six spreadlines on U.S. 41. Of the eleven Putnam siblings, nine worked in chenille. Effie Collins (née Putnam, 1914–2007) and Bertie Collins (1907–84) ran South Bend Spread Company, a photograph of which shows children's robes hanging across the front under the roof overhang, a woman's robe on a mannequin, and a round display rack of robes outside, along with a row of rugs hanging on the front of the building and a line with bedspreads to the side. Oscar Franklin Putnam (1905–64) operated Lone Star Spread Company in Tunnel Hill. Photographs of it show spreads blowing in the breeze, dolls suspended in a row below a "Wholesale and Retail" sign, robes displayed in front, and coats hanging on the building. The busy spreadline is a marked contrast to the otherwise quiet two-lane road.

a Bradley Putnam, interview by author, Tunnel Hill, Georgia, December 21, 2012; Put's Chenille Center brochure and Colonial Craft postcard, collection of Bradley Putnam; Valerie A. Hoffman, "When Everybody Drove Peacock Alley," Progress Section, *Dalton Daily Citizen-News*, April 25, 1993.
b Benjamin Revis Putnam (1913–76) is listed in the 1940 U.S. Census as a chenille operator at home.

FACTORY and SHOW ROOM

PUT'S
CHENILLE CENTER

PHONE: COUNTY-2205   P. O. BOX 1   TUNNEL HILL, GA.

STOP FOR FREE DEMONSTRATION
ON HOW CHENILLE IS MADE

Located 25 Miles South of Chattanooga, Tenn. on U. S. Highway 41

ALL COLORS

SIZES 12 THROUGH 20

Plain, No Design $ 40.0

Flowered Design $ 450

Peafowl, as Pictured $ 500

Waffle Design $ 500

P-H 116 Chenille Robes

Selections from Put's Chenille Center brochure, Tunnel Hill, Georgia, ca. 1945, collection of Bradley Putnam

Colonial Craft, Tunnel Hill, Georgia, ca. 1960, postcard, collection of Bradley Putnam

Lone Star Spread Company, U.S. 41 in Tunnel Hill, 1940s, unidentified photographer (possibly Ward's Photo Service, Dalton, Georgia), courtesy of Betty Talley

signs likely garnered their share of attention as well, at least in the day-time.[34] Lawtex, a leading chenille manufacturer, in 1941 added a large neon sign with the company's name and "Dalton, GA" atop a plant on the Dixie Highway, visible to northbound tourists.[35] The city also erected billboards on the highway welcoming visitors to the Bedspread Center of the World.[36] In May 1941 the *Dalton News* described plans for another neon sign (sixteen by thirty feet), with the word "Dalton" in two-foot-high red letters and a six-foot-by-eight-foot bedspread cycling through four colors. This sign was to include seven hundred feet of neon tubing, and thirteen companies planned to share the $2,000 cost.[37] This sign likely was not built, as evidenced by the local newspaper again advocating postwar, in 1946, for proper signage to welcome tourists and celebrate Dalton's role as the "Tufted-Chenille Center of the World."[38]

During World War II, as restrictions on materials increased, the numbers and inventories of the spreadlines decreased; large manufacturers either ceased or limited production and many medium-sized manufacturers went out of business, while some of the smallest operations were able to cobble together enough sheeting and yarn to continue making chenille. In 1946, though, the *Saturday Evening Post* announced, "Bedspreads Bloom Again," with Minnie Hite Moody writing, "Now that gasoline has come back and the war plants are closing down, the 'spreadlines' are forming again along the ninety-mile stretch of highway between Atlanta and Dalton, Georgia." Moody explained, "Housewives brought the spreads in off the lines, which sagged lonesomely through the years between Pearl Harbor and V-J Day."[39]

The phenomenon of roadside chenille displays extended well beyond the Dixie Highway, and similar stands existed far outside the region. The Briggs Chenille Shop established by Helen C. Briggs in Shartlesville, Pennsylvania, in 1947 (and later moved to near the Delaware Water Gap) sold "peacock and other designs" and offered demonstrations of tufting well into the 1960s. Tufts Woodland Motel and Chenille Company in Wisconsin Dells, Wisconsin, around midcentury, featured colorful displays of chenille spreads, bath sets, peacock robes, and Mexican jackets, with a large sign reading "Genuine Southern Chenille."[40]

Wyche observed that in 1948 many roadside producers used machines that were antiquated in comparison to the newest models in the largest factories.[41] These simpler machines, combined with the smaller output and immediate feedback available to spreadline owners, allowed for greater experimentation in design. Big, bright peacocks and other designs easily

Tufts Woodland Motel and Chenille Company, Wisconsin Dells, Wisconsin, ca. 1955, postcard published by J. A. Fagan Company, Madison, Wis., private collection. Printed on back: "Tufts Woodland Motel . . . Welcomes you to visit our Sales Room of Beautiful Genuine Southern Chenille Gifts. BED SPREADS, BATH ROBES, RUG SETS, MEXICAN JACKETS, ETC." Oliver and Ann Tufts owned Tufts Woodland Motel.

recognizable when viewed through car windows appealed to the rapidly moving consumers. R. E. Hamilton, who served as president of the TTMA from 1954–55 and executive vice president from 1959–69, discerned a difference between the goods sold by the roadside and those marketed by department stores. He praised the chenille wares intended for stores and offered this unflattering description of the roadside goods: "Generally they are flashy designs in clashing colors."[42] Fred Rosen, whose family owned LaRose Bedspread, similarly said, "You never sold one of those [peacocks] in a [department] store, people wouldn't buy them. It was a big joke. I mean they looked 10 times better hanging on the line than they did once laid out on a bed."[43] Hamilton, however, noted that as peacocks became the best-selling tufted motif along the highway, customer requests led larger manufacturers to make the peacock products as well, demonstrating the influence of the spreadlines on the production decisions of major companies.[44]

Though the peacock motif was hugely popular with tourists, many Georgians disparaged the brightly colored designs as tacky and undesirable. Chenille designer Eathel Stewart recalled, "There was also a joke told about so many of those gaudy bedspreads being sold on the line: It was said

Beckler's Chenille

Burch Beckler (1907–75) and his wife Claudell started one of the largest roadside chenille businesses.[a] Claudell, at age thirteen, hand tufted spreads at home for the company Cabin Crafts, and Burch worked as a mechanic in the local hosiery mill. After living and working in Detroit during World War II, the Becklers saved enough money to return to Georgia and purchase a single-needle machine, which they taught themselves to operate and maintain. The Becklers began by making spreads and selling them to larger companies, with Burch hauling to private homes in Whitfield and Murray Counties.

Around 1944 or 1945, the Becklers went into business with R. C. "Clarence" Thomason, building a small factory with twenty machines on U.S. 41 at Hill Top, and also working with home tufters, loaning them machines. Their partnership, Thomason and Beckler Chenille, lasted until around 1949 or 1950, when the Becklers went into business on their own. They bought property from Thomason on U.S. 41 next to Valley Point School in 1949, and in 1950 they built a house and a store, which opened in either late 1950 or early 1951 as Beckler's Chenille. (Randy Beckler explains that his father often had multiple ventures going simultaneously, making it difficult to determine precise dates.) The wide single-story building featured windows along the front—each large enough to display a spread—and an open space in the back for manufacturing, which they only used briefly, soon turning it into an apartment. Beckler's sold spreads, robes, rugs (especially Smoky Mountain rugs by Roy Kinsey), scuffies made by J. W. Bray, pillows made by the Bumgarners of Summerville (filled with lint, floor sweepings from the chenille plants), and dolls made by local barber Henry Hall and his wife, as well as bath sets, capes, boleros, aprons, and coats.[b] The peacock motif was by far their best seller.

Randy Beckler remembers using clothespins to hang rugs back to back on the fence north of their house (the side closest to Beckler's Chenille) so that travelers from both directions could see them. He used a long pole with a hook to hang capes in front of the windows outside the building. He also described a long clothesline running from the north side of the business, which was set about one hundred feet off of the road, almost to the highway. They hired a young man who would stop by before and after school to put out the spreads and take them down. Burch Beckler believed in the power of signage and had numerous consecutive roadside signs similar to the famous Burma Shave ads, although less elaborate.

In addition to selling to tourists, the Becklers also sold chenille to other retailers.[c] One way Burch developed contacts with potential customers was by paying a friend at the post office to copy names from packages mailed out by larger chenille businesses in town. Then he would contact those companies and send them samples.

Beckler's Chenille Products, with Claudell Beckler modeling a chenille robe by Ben Putnam, Dalton, Georgia, 1950 or 1951, postcard, collection of David R. Stevenson

Beckler's Chenilles, Dalton, Georgia, ca. 1953, postcard published by W. M. Cline Company, Chattanooga, private collection

The Becklers continued to manufacture chenille goods for a while, then retailed products from individuals and firms in the area, including Ben Putnam, Gordo Bedpreads, Log Cabin, and Art-Rich. Randy explains that his father decided that even though he could manufacture his own chenille, the larger companies could manufacture it at much lower cost, so it was more profitable just to retail their goods.

At the height of their chenille business, the Becklers owned eight spreadlines between Tunnel Hill and Cartersville. Most were run by relatives or close friends, including Claudell's brother Earl Howell and his wife Ruth, who ran Howell Chenille House in Resaca; old family friends Edith and Ralph Galloway, who ran Galloway Chenille Shop about a mile south of Valley Point; Burch's sister Olma Smith and her husband Colonel Smith, who ran Smith's Gift Shop; and Emma ("Tot") and William Stocks, who operated Chastain's Gift Shop in Resaca.[d] The Becklers also furnished inventory for Belle Holcomb, Burch's double first cousin, who ran Holcomb Gift Shop in Resaca. The Becklers provided the money and stock to these shops, and every evening Burch visited each business, often accompanied by his son in the 1950s. Each had a legal pad with handwritten columns

labeled "sold," "selling price," "cost," and "net profit," and they would total the figures, and Burch would take half of the profit in cash. Burch Beckler's extensive use of signage helped all of the businesses. If tourists passed one of the Becklers' stores without stopping, the repeated reminders of chenille wonders might entice them to eventually stop at another.

In 1964 the business changed from Beckler's Chenille to Beckler's Carpet, which still operates today. The Becklers remain committed to roadside advertising and now have the largest billboard on I-75 between Chattanooga and Atlanta. Their oversized ad stands among a host of other signs for a concentration of carpet outlets easily visible and accessible from the interstate. Claudell, when interviewed in 1996, recalled the busses of tourists stopping to buy chenille and said, "I never thought I'd see the day we didn't have chenille."[f]

a Randy Beckler and his mother Claudell Beckler, interview by author, March 13, 2013, Dalton, Georgia; Randy Beckler, telephone conversation with author, September 12, 2013; "About Beckler's Carpet," Beckler's Carpet website, http://www .becklerscarpet.com/about; Cheryl Wykoff, compiler, Peacock Alley, ed. by Lydia Stevens (Dalton, Ga.: Prater's Mill Foundation and Whitfield-Murray Historical Society, 1992), 20–23; Miriam Longino, "Chenille Spreads Were Warp, Woof of a Region," Atlanta Journal-Constitution, October 20, 1996; Thomas M. Deaton, Bedspreads to Broadloom: The Story of the Tufted Carpet Industry (Acton, Mass.: Tapestry Press, 1993), 167–70.
b Advertisement, Beckler Chenille Co., Georgia Capitol Directory and State Guide (Atlanta: DXE Directory Publishers, 1956), 317. Randy Beckler recalls that they also sold woven handbags made by Dolly Parton's family.
c Randy Beckler recalls that one business Beckler's Chenille sold to was located in Wisconsin Dells, Wisconsin.
d John Willis, "'Our Children Would Bag up Red Georgia Dirt and Sell It for 10 or 15 Cents a Bag.'—Emma Stocks," Rome (Ga.) News-Tribune, August 26, 2007.
e Wykoff, Peacock Alley, 20–23.
f Miriam Longino, "Tuft Love: Fuzzy, Fanciful Chenille Finding Fans Once Again," Atlanta Journal-Constitution, October 20, 1996.

Hamlin's Chenille Shop,
Dania, Florida, ca. 1945,
postcard published by
Beals, Des Moines, Iowa,
private collection

WORLD'S FINEST CHENILLES

1000's & 1000's To Choose From

Patterns of Peacock, Florals, Solids, Etc.

Peacock Spreads	$7.98 Up
Cowboy Spreads	8.98 Up
Floral Spreads	5.98 Up
Solid Spreads	3.97 Up
Little Girls' Spreads	8.98 Up
Peacock Robes	8.98 Up
Other Robes	3.98 Up

ALL WEIGHTS

Attention: Hotels & Motels

We carry seconds - Exporting - We Ship

DIXIE CHENILLE & POTTERY, Inc.
4699 N.W. 7th Avenue
Miami, Florida

Pub. by T. N. Gilbert & Associates,
P. O. Box 861, No. Miami, Fla.
49128

Genuine Natural Color Made By DEXTER PRESS, Inc., West Nyack, N. Y.

POST CARD

PLACE
STAMP
HERE

Postcard, Dixie Chenilles and Pottery,
Miami, Florida, ca. 1955, published by
T. N. Gilbert and Associates, Miami,
private collection

that salesmen that had been off on a trip and maybe gotten 'high as a kite' would buy one of those gaudy bedspreads to take home to his wife."[45] Henry Nevin, secretary of Dalton's chamber of commerce, writing for the *Atlanta Constitution* in 1935 explained, "After passing two or three lines loaded with spreads, the tourist usually stops his car to find out what it's all about—and a sale is made. Nine times out of 10, if the prospect is a man, he will buy the colorful peacock design, while women almost invariably pass this up for something more subdued to match the color scheme of the bedroom at home."[46]

In the late 1980s, Ann Hamilton (Mrs. R. E. Hamilton), shared her opinion of the peacocks: "It was a great joke around Dalton . . . that so many of the tourists bought those flamboyant Peacock bedspreads. . . . We thought they were not pretty and . . . weren't very well designed."[47] Claudell Beckler, who with her husband owned the roadside business Beckler's Chenille, explained pragmatically, "As long as they were selling, they were pretty to us; if they didn't sell, they got ugly."[48] Writing for the *Tampa Morning Tribune* in 1947, Lucy O'Brien also disparaged the peacock motif as "the acme of bad taste," saying, "Most of the roadside crafters admit that they themselves would not have a peacock spread as a gracious gift, but they turn them out in quantities because the peacock outsells all other patterns 12 to one!"[49] Even Allen Eaton in his 1937 book *Handicrafts of the Southern Highlands* described the peacock as "perhaps the least tasteful of any of the designs, because of its elaborate form and its variegated colors."[50] By the 1990s, though, these colorful tufted souvenirs started becoming prized collectibles and appreciated for their folk art aesthetic.[51]

Interstate 75

As Henry Nevin observed in 1935, despite the impression tourists might gather, less than 10 percent of the industry catered to the roadside market, with the majority of manufactured wares going to department stores.[52] But the road would become an important element in the telling of the tufted textile industry's history. The *Southern Israelite*, a Jewish periodical based in Atlanta, described in 1950 the tourist traffic on U.S. 41 "carrying caravans of people to Florida and then funneling them back to their homes." "Soon," the article went on, "Mr. and Mrs. America . . . slowed down out of curiosity. Many stopped to admire, examine—and buy. They bought with a vigor

Morgan Manufacturing Company

Willene Morgan and Jack Morgan (1927–94) opened their spreadline, Morgan Manufacturing Company, on U.S. 41 in Tunnel Hill in 1952, with the help of Burch Beckler, who supplied them with inventory to get started but would not let them repay him for a long time, allowing them to have funds to reinvest in their business until it was secure.[a] In the early years, the Morgans were surrounded by spreadlines, and Willene Morgan remembers that from her driveway she "could look each way and there were ten of them open." Willene's parents worked in candlewick, and she learned to operate a single-needle machine, the tool she used for the entire forty years her business existed.[b] They made many of their own items but also retailed products made both by larger companies and by home workers specifically for them. They sold chenille robes from manufacturers including Duchess, Lawtex, Art-Rich, and Sparks, and then from a company in Alabama after the Dalton companies stopped making chenille. They also offered chenille dolls that were made in Acworth, Georgia; bib aprons made by "a little old lady from Ringgold"; and old-fashioned (nontufted) bonnets, made by the same woman. Willene recalls with amusement that the bonnets sold well. "Of course, the northern people thought that was something great."

With a creative inclination and the flexibility allowed by a small business, Willene often came up with her own patterns or embellished items manufactured by larger companies, sometimes adding peacocks to plain robes. She described one of her original spread designs as having a cross in the center with dogwood flowers along the top, and another with a heart: "When people came in, if they wanted me to, I would put their names on it [across the heart]." Willene also made handbags from carpet. By the late 1950s, even with the mass production of tufted goods, handmade articles (which likely at this time would have included the goods made by individuals using outdated single-needle machines), like those offered by the Morgans, still found a ready market among tourists. A report in 1959 noted, "Those who have continued to make fine quality hand-tufted products have continued to prosper on 'Bedspread Boulevard.'"[c] The Morgan Manufacturing Company was one of the last surviving spreadlines, remaining open until 1992.[d]

Morgan Manufacturing Company, Tunnel Hill, Georgia, 2013, photograph by author

a Willene Morgan with Janet McKinney, interview by author, July 26, 2013, Calhoun, Georgia; Cheryl Wykoff, compiler, *Peacock Alley*, edited by Lydia Stevens (Dalton, Ga.: Prater's Mill Foundation and Whitfield-Murray Historical Society, 1992), 18; Thomas M. Deaton, *Bedspreads to Broadloom: The Story of the Tufted Carpet Industry* (Acton, Mass.: Tapestry Press, 1993), 166–67. Willene Morgan noted that Mrs. Fred Caldwell (highlighted in chapter 5) was her mother's cousin.

b Willene Morgan's mother, Katie Bagley, and older sister are listed in the 1930 U.S. Census as bedspread tufters. According to the 1940 census, while Willene was still a child, her father worked as a janitor in a spread house and one of her older brothers and one of her older sisters worked as machine operators in spread houses.

c Ray G. Jones Jr. and Claude A. Campbell, "The Development of Georgia's Tufted Textile Industry," Research Paper no. 12, Bureau of Business and Economic Research, School of Business Administration, Georgia State College of Business Administration, March 1959, 40.

d Nancy Carney, "Last 'Peacock Alley' Vendor to Close," *Dalton Advertiser*, December 30, 1992. Gertha Lee Painter's chenille stand still existed in 1996. Miriam Longino, "Chenille Spreads Were Warp, Woof of a Region," *Atlanta Journal Constitution*, October 20, 1996.

that spread the quaint tufted articles through the width and breadth of the land."[53] Driving through the region and seeing the spreadlines became a collective memory for Georgians and for Florida-bound tourists. The *Georgia Journal* in 1996 quoted an Atlanta resident, Frank Wood, happily remembering, "You would go up 41 and see even chenille underwear and bathing suits hanging on the lines."[54]

The industry's shift from chenille to carpet, the general change in popular taste, and the increasing presence of lesser-quality goods made of synthetic materials contributed to chenille's roadside decline. When the new interstate bypassed the highway in 1965 the vibrancy of Bedspread Boulevard quickly diminished, and only a handful of stands survived into the 1970s and 1980s. Tot Stocks of Calhoun, who owned or operated six gift shops on U.S. 41 between 1956 and 1976, recalled: "When that final section of I-75 opened near Cartersville in [1977], it was like turning a light out for U.S. 41."[55]

Chapter Three

Handmade Beginnings
Candlewick and the Colonial Revival

– – – IN ADDITION TO being part of the Southern Appalachian Craft
Revival, Northwest Georgia's candlewick bedspreads also fit neatly within
the larger, national Colonial Revival. This style gained momentum in the
1870s, as the United States approached its centenary, and lasted well into
the twentieth century. The Colonial Revival influenced all areas of design,
from architecture to flatware, and reflected a growing reverence for history and the material culture of the nation's past. It was a flexible style and
included objects that were faithful reproductions of specific items, as well
as objects loosely based on a general idea of the antique. By the 1920s, companies that made reproductions of eighteenth- and early nineteenth-century
furniture proliferated, and museums began adding American antiques—
furniture, silver, textiles, and pottery—to their collections.

OPPOSITE: Candlewick
apron with peacock
design, ca. 1950, cotton,
private collection,
photograph by
Michael McKelvey

Northwest Georgia's candlewick textiles epitomized the image and values
of the Colonial Revival in part through their connection to antique needlework. While the designs of twentieth-century candlewick spreads ranged
from copies of early textiles, usually quilts, to modern geometrics, their construction made each design traditional. The industry frequently reinforced
the new spreads' connection to earlier textiles through the retelling of the
story of Catherine Evans Whitener and how she had taken inspiration from
an heirloom coverlet.

As architectural historian William B. Rhoads explains, the Colonial
Revival style was in part a reaction against increasing immigration. By
turning to forms and techniques used by the country's founders, some

Sale of Hand-tufted
Candlewick Spreads
$3.96

At An Unusually Low Price!

A new collection has arrived from the Georgia
mountains, where generation after generation
has perfected this quaint old craft. And what
spreads may more charmingly fit into an early
American room than these of American origin?

Unbleached muslin, single and full sizes
Hand-tufted in rose, orchid, blue or gold

MACY'S—*Second New Floor, West Building,*
Rear Escalators Are Convenient.

Advertisement, Macy's,
New York City, from
New York Sun, October
7, 1925.

Americans, especially white Anglo-Saxon Protestants,
sought to evoke the Founder's patriotism and morals, both
to reinforce their own American-ness and to educate others
about the country's heritage.[1] This desire to proclaim their
national pride and indoctrinate their beliefs into others
found fervent expression between World War I and World
War II.

Popular literature of the 1930s and 1940s often linked
the southern Appalachian mountain region to colonial
America. Its inhabitants were perceived as direct descen-
dants of English settlers, especially as compared to regions
with increasingly ethnically diverse populations. When
describing the workers in bedspread plants, the *Dalton
News* stated in 1940 that they were "from substantial families of pure Anglo-Saxon stock—'All American' blood, if
you please—characteristic of farm homes throughout the mountain regions
of this part of the state," and the *Helena (Mont.) Independent* carried an article that described the inhabitants of Dalton as "nearly all pure-born Anglo
Saxon mountain people."[2] Though some journalists proclaimed an ethnic
and racial purity among the industry's factory workers and the majority of
the population were WASPs, there was some diversity within the industry.
As documented in the Women's Bureau surveys, African American women
tufted spreads, and by 1940 notable numbers of tufted textile companies
were owned by Jewish families (discussed in chapter 5), drawn to Dalton by
the industry.

The candlewick industry certainly embraced the idea that its products
were Colonial Revival style. For example, Blue Ridge Spread Company used
a silhouette of a woman working at a spinning wheel (a common Colonial
Revival image) in its logo, and Mae Weatherly Cannon (ca. 1878–1940),
who established her own candlewick business in Dalton in 1921, called her
spreads "Colonial Candlewick Spreads." Department stores often linked
candlewick spreads with Colonial Revival objects and ideas. Wanamaker's
in New York advertised candlewick spreads in conjunction with Wallace
Nutting's reproduction furniture, and Macy's in New York asked rhetorically
in an ad, "What spreads may more charmingly fit into an early American
room than these of American origin?"[3] The *Dalton Citizen* touted the
colonial nature of candlewick spreads too, saying that "many of them are

replicas of lovely coverlets of Martha Washington's day and, in appropriate settings, bring to mind colonial homes rich in history."[4]

Often women giving demonstrations of hand tufting in department stores, to promote candlewick bedspread sales, would wear colonial-style costumes. Fashion historian Beverly Gordon, in an article on Colonial Revival dress, explains that by the interwar years this practice was increasingly associated with entrepreneurial ventures such as colonial-style tearooms with costumed waitresses.[5] Historical accuracy in these costumes was less important than conveying a charming and picturesque sense of a golden past. Gordon also notes that marketing "colonial-looking products" was popular among some women at this time, and that though in previous decades the Colonial Revival had high moral associations, by the interwar years it was used more often to increase profits. She writes, "Their businesses were based on mass marketing and reproduction, and, although the images they sold looked 'old,' they were based on up-to-the-minute design principles."[6]

Tufted textiles' national credibility as a specifically southern Colonial Revival item received a significant boost with the premiere of *Gone with the Wind* in 1939. Joseph B. Platt, a noted industrial and interior designer, created interiors for the film. He had the company Cabin Crafts in Dalton, for whom he designed, create two tufted spreads for the film, an all-white "Rosette" spread used in Scarlett O'Hara's bedroom at Tara and a spread described as a "Henry Clay" spread used at Twelve Oaks, the Wilkes family plantation.[7] Some of the supporting cast members who attended the premiere in Atlanta received chenille bedspreads as mementos.[8]

1920s Candlewick Dresses

Though the candlewick industry clearly is related to the Southern Appalachian Craft Revival and the Colonial Revival, some of its first garments are difficult to classify. Early candlewick dresses and kimonos, despite the historical roots of tufted spreads, often were associated with exoticism as well. Until at least the mid-1930s, with the introduction of chenille, candlewick garments were novelties.

One of the earliest illustrations of candlewick-like tufted decoration in connection to fashion appeared in the Spring/Summer 1921 issue of the

Anna Q. Nilsson, screen actress, wearing a beige silk cape-suit designed by Faber & Hein and made of Mallinson's "Roshanara" crepe, with navy blue embroidered dots, for the International Silk Exposition, from *Blue Book of Silks de Luxe*, Spring/Summer 1921, published by H. R. Mallinson and Company, Inc.

Blue Book of Silks de Luxe, a promotional publication of the American silk giant H. R. Mallinson and Company. The publication includes a photograph of the screen actress Anna Q. Nilsson wearing a "cape-suit of beige Roshanara Crepe embroidered in navy blue chenille dots designed by Faber & Hein."[9] Though the use of the term "chenille" is early, its combination with the word "embroidery" and the appearance of the dress strongly suggest that it is candlewick.[10]

Another early mention was by the department store Wanamaker's in Philadelphia in December 1922, in an ad for girls' dresses of cotton crepe with "fluffy embroidery . . . of white cotton, like the wick of a candle" that "dots the bodices or is used all over the frocks."[11] The following month, Frederick Loeser, a department store in Brooklyn, offered similar children's dresses, describing them as "the most charming novelty that we have seen for a long time," with an illustration of a drop-waist dress with a grid of dots, on a young girl in a casual beachside setting.[12] In February 1923 Wanamaker's in New York advertised women's candlewick frocks with leather belts. The department store offered these alongside muslin dresses with Ukrainian cross stitch, peasant blouses from southern Europe, and simple frocks with silk patchwork designed by Léon Bakst for Sergei Diaghilev's Ballets Russes, firmly associating candlewick with exotic fashion choices. The prices for these dresses were high, the girls' dresses ranging from about $20–$38 and the women's dresses $45, though Lord and Taylor in New York also offered inexpensive women's and children's dresses with designs stamped on them that customers could stitch with candlewick embroidery at home.[13] None of these ads for garments suggest any connection to Appalachia or the South, but the popular association between southern states and candlewick spreads was increasingly widespread at the time.

Candlewick Kimonos

In November 1923, several department stores in New York offered candlewick kimonos, including Gimbel Brothers and Abraham and Strauss, which ran ads with illustrations of a kimono with a double row of tufts along the border and four tufted butterflies on the front, two near the waist and two in the lower corners.[14] At Gimbels the reduced price was $3.95 (about $55 in 2014), only slightly less than the average cost of candlewick bedspreads at that time. Abraham and Strauss noted that the illustrated kimono featured seven butterflies in all, and described the kimonos as "charming gifts for any woman who adores pretty, unusual things, or who appreciates good, practical things." An ad for the Joseph Horne Company in Pittsburgh from the same month provides a more detailed description of the candlewick kimonos: "Solid-color Japanese crepe with great chenille-like butterflies and conventional designs in candle-wick cotton" in a variety of color combinations ("gray with rose designs, orchid with lavender, orange with blue, pumpkin with white, black with rose, old blue with white, yellow with yellow, leaf green with green") for $5.05 each.[15] These candlewick kimonos were part of a larger vogue for Orientalism in fashion, epitomized by French designer Paul Poiret's creations, and specifically for Japanese embroidered kimonos during the late 1910s and early 1920s.

Though the kimono ads do not mention Georgia or the South, the illustrated kimono in the Gimbels ad and the description of the ones in the Horne's ad appear strikingly similar to one worn by Mrs. Ralph Haney (née Exzene Carter, 1894–1962) of Calhoun, in a photograph documented in Vanishing Georgia, a collection of historical images of Georgia assembled by the Georgia Archives.[16] Possibly the same individual or company made them. Haney's robe, seen from the back, features candlewicking along the edges and a large monochromatic peacock atop stairs in a trellis setting with a vase of flowers, a popular early peacock composition used in Northwest Georgia.[17] The black-and-white image also suggests a two-color design like those described in the Horne's ad, a solid-color background with a single color of tufting. The image's original documentation notes that the peacock was tufted on crepe, again linking it to the Horne's ad.[18] A brief mention of tufted kimonos in the *Dalton*

Advertisement for Gimbel Brothers department store, New York City, November 9, 1923, *Sun and Globe*

Citizen in 1925 also describes them as made of crepe.[19] The peacock on this kimono and the butterflies of the ads are appropriate motifs considering their context within a vogue for Japanese design. As women from Dalton traveled to department stores along the East Coast to promote candlewick bedspreads, they likely observed other popular products, including embroidered kimonos from Japan, which may have inspired them to make candlewick kimonos.

The candlewick kimono worn by Haney introduces the most iconic motif used in tufted textiles, the peacock (or peafowl), which appeared on a variety of tufted wares, including bedspreads, rugs, aprons, robes, jackets, and capes, and came in a variety of designs. Generally the peacocks are shown from the back or side with their heads in profile and their tail feathers fanning out below. Some are depicted on steps with a vase under a trellis, some appear in pairs, and many are the sole design. Peacocks were executed in candlewick, on single-needle machines with the peacock worked into the overall tufted pattern, on single-needle machines tufted over chenille yardage (as overlay designs), and sometimes on machines with several needles, typically in five or six colors. Tails range in size, with some spreading extravagantly over the fabric and some contained in neatly defined bunches not much larger than the birds' bodies. On robes, peacocks generally are centered on the back, with the tail spilling across the wide skirt, though sometimes a series of three small peacocks are spaced evenly above the hem.

J. A. Keller Chenille Company, Dalton, Georgia, ca. 1955, postcard with handwritten prices added, collection of David R. Stevenson. Handwritten notes and stamps on related Keller postcards indicate a connection between the company and Wisconsin Dells, Wisconsin.

#1053

Mrs. Ralph Haney wearing a candlewick kimono with a peacock design, ca. 1923, courtesy of Georgia Archives, Vanishing Georgia Collection, gor466

The most common explanation given today for the origin of the peacock motif in chenille is that tufters developed it as a way to use leftover bits of multiple colors of thread. Henry Nevin suggested this as one of the reasons for the motif's popularity as early as 1935, adding that using all leftovers meant higher savings and profits for roadside sellers.[20] Eathel Stewart, a noted spread designer, shared her understanding around 1992 of the origins of the peacocks: "They said, and this was gossip among bedspread workers and bedspread haulers, that these peacocks were made from scraps of yarn that people didn't turn back in and the people themselves originated those peacock bedspreads and made them."[21] Fred Rosen, whose family owned LaRose Bedspread Company, explained that many smaller makers of peacocks bought inexpensive skinners, "pieces of yarn that had been snipped off of the tufted bedspreads being manufactured in the area," and mixed them together to make the peacocks, showing how the production may have shifted from a way to use up materials to a design-driven activity.[22] Allen Eaton addressed the peacock motif too, describing how the families that tufted the designs sometimes devised their own patterns, citing an example of a grandson who drew a peacock for a child's apron after watching his grandmother draw a design for his mother to execute. Eaton cites the peacock as a favorite motif, adding, "Where the design originated no one seems to know, but almost everyone uses it and presumably sells it."[23] Haney's kimono, though, with a monochromatic peacock design, suggests that the motif is earlier than traditionally believed and may predate the production of wares with multicolored tufts.

OPPOSITE: Back of chenille robe with peacock design, ca. 1950s, cotton, 57 inches long, collection of Peter and Sandy Loose-Schrantz, photograph by Michael McKelvey

Kimonos were a short-lived facet of tufted fashion production. Though few individuals can be connected with their production, they are linked to the most famous tufter: Catherine Evans Whitener wrote that in addition to spreads, she made "kimonas," aprons, and mats.[24] From the beginning kimonos were considered just one of several companion pieces or "specialty lines" offered by the industry to accompany the primary product, bedspreads, along with valances, scarves (probably dresser scarves or bureau covers), and curtains.[25] Memory of the candlewick kimonos quickly faded in the Dalton area as the industry shifted to machine production and as housecoats and bathrobes came to be the dominant tufted garments. R. E. Hamilton, executive vice president of the TTMA for many years, when asked in 1972 about Whitener making kimonos, explained that while she used the word "kimono," the industry used "robe," "housecoat," or "beachcoat," indicating that he was unaware of the earlier production of the distinct garment

form.[26] Fred Rosen joked about how the robe industry started: "We put three holes in the bedspread so that the woman was able to put the thing around her and wrap herself in [it]."[27] Rosen's humorous comment highlights the simplicity of the candlewick kimono's design; with no fasteners, cuffs, collars, belts, or other complex details, the creation of this garment did not vary significantly from making a spread.

Mary McBryde Sims (1878–1942) included kimonos in the inventory of her company Tennoga Hooked Rugs ("Tennoga" comes from "Tennessee and North Georgia") in Dalton. An undated company brochure, probably from the early to mid-1920s, includes illustrations of candlewick bedspreads and hooked rugs and descriptions of the colors and designs available, with just a brief listing for "Kimonas (hand-tufted)." Tennoga sold through women's organizations and to gift shops, camp craft shops, and individuals. Sims promoted her company's products as the work of "southern mountain women, to whom the art has been handed down through generations since colonial days." The brochure explains how important the work was to the women who made the products, that they "have been shut off from the world's activities," and that the money they earned provided many new opportunities to them and their children. The designs for the spreads included "Martha Washington" (described as "a copy of a spread at Mt. Vernon" and the company's "exclusive design"), "Colonial Star," "Mountain Lily," "Snowdrop," and "Dewdrop," and the hooked rugs provided a similar balance of titles based on patriotic and regional floral themes. The brochure also notes that Tennoga's goods "have recently been featured and won distinction in national magazines devoted to the promotion of beautiful house furnishings."[28] A subsequent brochure, which does not list kimonos, provides a longer description of the company's hooked rugs, linking them to the Pilgrims and explaining how Sims found women to craft the rugs and taught them how to use colors that would appeal to modern consumers.[29]

Tennoga's approach to promoting regional crafts was more aligned with other southern Appalachian craft organizations than with the majority of candlewick businesses in the immediate region, and it drew heavily on colonial associations. Like the weaving centers highlighted by Alvic in *Weavers of the Southern Highlands*, Tennoga sold through women's organizations and promoted how the purchase of the goods would improve the lives of the makers, advocating moral reasons to purchase the regional crafts. While candlewick kimonos, through their connection to Tennoga, existed within a traditional Appalachian Craft Revival framework and a Colonial Revival context, they represent an intersection between those influences and the cosmopolitan commercial settings of leading department stores in big cities.

Tufting Demonstrations and Colonial Costumes

From the late 1920s (if not earlier) through the mid-1930s women traveled from the Southeast to department stores throughout the United States to show customers how candlewick spreads were crafted, presenting a picturesque vision of the industry. An early demonstration took place in Atlanta, at M. Rich and Brothers (later Rich's) department store in 1927. A newspaper ad invokes state pride, claiming, "The Candlewick Spread Vogue is more than a revival—The love of this traditional art of Georgia has always remained in our hearts!" The ad offers contrast to the rustic, historical aspect of the spreads by noting that they "are enjoyed by Modern American housewives."[30] Women from Georgia also demonstrated tufting at Abraham and Straus in Brooklyn, which promoted the spreads as having patterns descended "for generations" in the families of the mountain girls who made them, even though such direct multigenerational lines of instruction and transmission were rare and many women learned techniques and designs from their contemporaries.[31] In 1929, Sibley, Lindsay and Curr Company in Rochester, New York, announced an upcoming demonstration by women from "the Kentucky mountain country," stating that they made the spreads in the same manner as their great-grandmothers and that the "colonial days will live again in this unique . . . Candlewick Demonstration."[32] According to Phoebe Laing Mosley, writing in 1932, one firm sent "two young women up to the Northern markets every spring on a demonstration trip." She explained, "These women carry with them a representative exhibit of the various hand-tufted products, and sitting in the midst of the display in a department store show-window, they work on a spread and tell the onlookers how it is done 'way down in Georgia.'" Mosley added, "This is of unfailing interest, as anything Southern, from accent to waffles, carries a glamour for Northerners."[33]

A 1928 ad for a demonstration at Jordan Marsh Company in Boston includes illustrations of a cotton field and hands tufting, with the heading, "From 'way down South in the fields of cotton.'" The ad appeals to teachers, promoting the demonstration as "a unique educational opportunity, never before provided in this part of the country, for your class to observe a regional occupation both interesting and instructive." The text describes how the "folk art" was growing in popularity among people of Georgia and Tennessee, how the tufting was done by hand, and how the spreads were "wind-blown for days by mountain breezes and warmed by the golden sun," again presenting an idealized image of the spreads' creation.[34] Macy's advertised a tufting demonstration in 1931 by stating that shoppers would "have to imagine the log cabin and the cotton fields background," but that the girls would be wearing cotton frocks and sunbonnets, "tufting the spreads by hand, just as they do in their native Georgia."[35] Paradoxically, some of the later vignettes of the colonial past presented by these tufting demonstrations included both traditional hand tufting as well as more modern machine tufting.[36]

While the names of most of the women who gave demonstrations are not recorded, a few, often with close ties to the industry's leaders, are. Mrs. G. H. Rauschenberg and Mrs. W. T. Kenner, whose husbands established one of the first large candlewick companies, Kenner and Rauschenberg, gave demonstrations in Washington, D.C., and New York. One undated photograph shows Mrs. Rauschenberg in a Colonial Revival costume with Georgia congressman Malcolm C. Tarver at a demonstration at Palais Royal (a department store) in Washington, D.C. A hand-tufted sign in the background of the photograph has an image of a log cabin and reads, "Candlewick Bedspreads Made by Hand Expressly for Palais Royal."[37] Christine Bandy (McCutchen; 1916–2003) and her aunt Lois Bradley Fuller, respectively the daughter and sister-in-law of B. J. Bandy, who was remarkably successful in the candlewick business, traveled together in 1934 giving demonstrations while wearing attractive, old-fashioned costumes. When they visited Lion's department store in San Jose, California, the local newspaper described them as "charming Southern girls" and quoted Fuller sharing the history of the candlewick technique. The article emphasized that the spreads were made by hand and that many of the designs were colonial but that there were modern designs as well.[38] Christine Bandy's brother, Jack, recalls that the women did not do a lot of demonstrations, but that on the trip to San Jose they probably also visited other cities such as Chicago or Dallas or New York. Christine attended Shorter College (in Rome, Georgia) at the time, and her aunt, who was divorced, worked for B. J. Bandy.[39]

Often the candlewick demonstrators wore Colonial Revival costumes. Genung's in Mount Vernon, New York, in 1929 hosted the daughter of Mrs.

Mae Weatherly Cannon, who is credited in the advertisement with having "originated the modern Candlewick spread."[40] Cannon's daughter and her assistants "in Colonial costumes" spent three days at the department store giving demonstrations of hand tufting.[41] Two unnamed Georgia girls "from the land of cotton" offered demonstrations at Sibley, Lindsay and Curr Company in Rochester, New York, in 1931 wearing "cotton frocks and sunbonnets."[42] A small illustration accompanying an announcement of a demonstration at Gimbels in New York

Advertisement, candlewick demonstration at Gengung's Department Stores, Mount Vernon, New York, from the *Mount Vernon (N.Y.) Daily Argus*, December 4, 1929

City by "clever Georgia women from the foothills of the [Cohutta] mountains" shows a woman wearing a bonnet and a dress with full sleeves, tufting a spread covering her lap.[43] Most of the women giving demonstrations would not have worn bonnets and old-fashioned dresses daily. These were costumes put on for the enjoyment of potential customers—providing an appealing antebellum spectacle.

One company that regularly sent young women to department stores to conduct "advertising demonstrations" was Polly Prentiss of Sumter, South Carolina. In 1934 Anne Milling and Virginia Warren traveled north to tuft and sing traditional songs.[44] Stops by the "Polly Prentiss Cabin Girls" that year included the Sisson Brothers–Welden department store in Binghamton, New York, which supplied a "suitable atmosphere" by creating a setting of a "typical cabin of plantation days."[45] In 1935 Anne Milling, joined by Frances Kolb, traveled to Rutland Brothers in St. Petersburg, Florida; Joske's in San Antonio, Texas; and the Wallace Company in Poughkeepsie, New York.[46] Joske's advertised that the two young women would "sing folk-songs of the mountain people, still current among the families of those who make the wide variety of candlewick spreads shown at Joske's," even though Sumter is not in the mountains and traditional country, folk, and bluegrass music had been broadcast on national radio for nearly a decade. Kolb returned to San Antonio the following year and gave demonstrations at Wolff and Marx, where she wore "a quaint costume" and sat in the bedding department in front of a replica of a "typical Log Cabin found in the mountainous regions of the Southeast." When she appeared in 1936 at Whitney's

in Albany, New York, she sat in the department store's window to give her demonstrations, and at Barney's in Schenectady she gave a demonstration in the Art Department wearing "native costume."[47]

While few of the demonstrations involved the making or promoting of candlewick garments, they may have included garments in the associated displays (note that in Mosley's description the women carried "a representative exhibit of the various hand-tufted products"), and some of the "quaint" Colonial Revival costumes demonstrators wore may have been tufted. In the image of Mrs. G. H. Rauschenberg at the Palais Royal, she appears to be wearing a dress and bonnet of a dark fabric covered with light-colored tufts about an inch or two apart. A surviving dress from the 1930s, with an unknown history, probably is an example of what tufting demonstrators would have worn. The cotton dress is homemade, hand tufted, and dyed pink. An accompanying bonnet is not tufted but matches in material and color. The dress is composed of a long straight skirt, tufted only where it will show, and a top that snaps in the front, with short ruffled sleeves, and a long, ruffled overskirt that is open at the front and gathered at the sides to suggest eighteenth-century panniers. The design is simple, befitting a modern woman, pretty with its ruffles and feminine form, and only vaguely colonial. The costumes hand-tufting demonstrators wore needed to suggest colonial America, but they did not have to be exact replicas of what colonial women wore.

OPPOSITE: Candlewick dress, ca. 1930s, cotton, collection of Bradley Putnam, photograph by Michael McKelvey

Mrs. Carl Hall's chenille business, customers with peacock and butterfly aprons, U.S. 41, Kennesaw, Georgia, early 1940s, collection of Joanne Hall Garner, courtesy of Abbie Tucker Parks

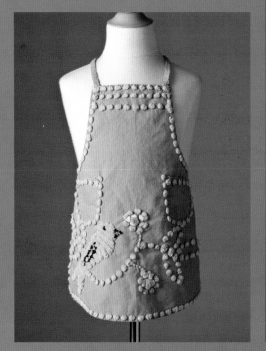

Child's candlewick apron with a bird on a branch, ca. 1950, cotton, private collection, photograph by Michael McKelvey

Candlewick apron with flower motif, ca. 1930, cotton, private collection, photograph by Michael McKelvey

Tufted Aprons

Of all the tufted garments, aprons probably were made for the longest period of time, but these inexpensive, functional, and modest items receive relatively little attention. Aprons appeared on spreadlines at least by the early 1930s and probably earlier, and they survived until the end of Bedspread Boulevard.[48] Tufted aprons span the periods of candlewick and chenille, though even then they typically were executed with nothing more advanced than a single-needle machine. Their small scale and minimal material investment provided easily manageable canvases and allowed for creative expression by their makers. More often than other tufted garments, aprons exhibit the incorporation of both clipped and unclipped stitches. For example, with peacock aprons, details like the beak, legs, and head crest often are executed with unclipped running stitches, providing contrast with the fluffy areas.

Tufted aprons sold in department stores as well, and often these show more-refined designs and include colored trim. Kann's of Washington, D.C., offered a variety of candlewick aprons in November 1934 for $0.49–$1.59, including simple cocktail or tea aprons, pinafore aprons with floral "peasant designs," and Hooverettes (or Hoovers or Hooveralls, dress-like aprons), all with multicolored hand tufting.[49] And Filene's in Boston offered candlewick aprons in 1936 for sixty-nine cents. Their princess-line aprons were tufted with a floral design in red, blue, green, and yellow on a natural ground.[50] Tufted aprons, however, were spreadline staples and, though infrequently mentioned, appear in numerous images of roadside stands.

Popular motifs for tufted aprons included peacocks, flowers and flower baskets, butterflies, bows, and birds. Even though these feminine motifs are not specifically colonial, the aprons' evocation of domesticity connects them to the Colonial Revival. Tufted aprons in many ways epitomize the tufted textile industry's ability to be both traditional and modern and to be both a regional folk art and a department store commodity.

Chenille apron with peacock design, ca. 1950, cotton, collection of Peter and Sandy Loose-Schrantz, photograph by Michael McKelvey

Chapter Four

Depression-Era Fashion
Tufted Dresses, Coats, and Capes

THE TUFTED GARMENT INDUSTRY flourished from the mid-1930s until the beginning of World War II. These tufted garments rose to prominence during the latter part of the Great Depression as American women sought novel and glamorous clothing that was reasonably priced and easy to care for. The transition to machine production in the tufted textile industry in the mid-1930s increased the speed and volume of tufted garment output, and this period of quick growth resulted not only in affordable prices but also in an expanded variety of chenille garments. Manufacturers eagerly experimented with new forms in order to sell more products. Norman Reints (1911–94), who established Mason Chenille in Dalton in 1938 with Mason Treadwell, recalled the somewhat haphazard nature of coming up with designs as the number of companies and competition in the small town increased (Dalton's population in 1940 was about fifteen thousand): "Everybody was looking for something new. . . . We'd lay [on these old design tables] all night trying to think of something new. We'd think let's make capes for the beach, make children's wear, like little sacks or little wrappers, crib spreads, or just anything that was different."[1] Later, in 1946, a writer for the *Atlanta Journal Magazine* reported that one chenille executive in Dalton had remarked "that he used to say they could put chenille tufts on everything but brassieres—and now they've done that," and explained that "he had been looking at one of the new tufted halter playsuits."[2]

Journalists frequently noted that tufted garments were priced reasonably and as simple to clean as their bedspread counterparts—just wash and dry,

OPPOSITE: Model wearing a chenille coat, March 20, 1938, photograph by H. Armstrong Roberts / Classic Stock / Corbis

no ironing necessary. Their novelty came from their unexpected needlework ornamentation—common for bedspreads but uncommon for apparel—and their glamour through association with Hollywood actresses, America's style icons. Also, chenille garments were part of a burgeoning American ready-to-wear market, especially for casual sportswear, that gained strength as French fashion influences waned with the onset of war in Europe. The department store Best and Company on Fifth Avenue in New York praised chenille robes as "inspired by, and made for, the American scene."[3]

As chenille came to dominate the tufted textile market, some advertisers persisted in using the word "candlewick" to describe tufted garments, even when the accompanying illustrations clearly depict the distinctive machine-made rows of chenille. Though perhaps hesitant to abandon a familiar term in favor of a new one (especially one with multiple definitions), advertisers may have sought to bestow the new chenille garments with the aura of tradition conveyed by the term "candlewick." Though of modern design, tufted clothing provided a reassuring comfort—donning a tufted garment felt like wrapping up in a bedspread.

1930s Candlewick Dresses

Long, bias-cut candlewick dresses experienced a brief vogue during the mid-1930s and were available in a range of prices. In May 1934 Best and Company advertised "Candlewick Muslins" in the *New York Times*, describing the line as "a whole series of delightful Summer fashions." The illustration depicted an elegant light-colored dress, fitted at the waist, with narrow straps over the shoulders, and covered in dark tufts in a regular grid (or "popcorn") pattern, with a matching fringed shawl.[4] The Candlewick Muslins collection included sports frocks ($15), a dance frock named "Carioca" ($29.75), "shorts costumes" ($12.75), and a "fur" coat ($17.50).[5] Best's promoted them as "completely different, so gay and decorative and amusing," and suggested their versatility: "We can see them being worn in the country, against a tapestry of green. We can see them on the beach, colorful 'confetti' in that ever-changing scene. We can see them on an ocean liner, looking very chic and expensive and old-world. For each of these fashions has a character all its own." The ad does not mention Georgia, but period descriptions note the obvious connection between the garments and candlewick spreads, which *were* regularly promoted as from the South.

Reviews of the candlewick trend were mixed. Eileen Earle, for the *New York Sun*, derided the new practice of making dresses out of bedspread material, writing, "We used to think that a girl outgrew tricks like that at fourteen or thereabouts," while Phyllis-Marie Arthur of the *Lowville (N.Y.) Journal and Republican* expressed only minor hesitation about the new trend, describing it as "a very startling innovation . . . one that takes a flair to wear."[6] Some journalists expressed amusement. In an article on the popularity in 1934 for dotted fabrics, Mollie Merrick described candlewick garments as "one of the newest and nuttiest variations of the dotsy mode," while Rhea Seeger in the *Chicago Daily Tribune* praised the "counterpane costumes," reveling in their "goofy" unexpectedness.[7] Evelyn Bolton, writing for the *Syracuse Journal*, told readers that "lifted eyebrows may return to their normal level," saying that candlewick muslin "is acquitting itself very nicely." Bolton described how the new candlewick dresses often employed "smaller and more carefully made" tufts and "finer, sheerer muslin" than the related bedspread, crediting the fashion with a higher level of sophistication than the spreads. She also noted the practical benefit of the candlewick fabric's durability and ease of care: "If its owner sits on the grass or falls overboard there is no harm done. Simply run the gown into a washing machine." She considered the material appropriate for pajamas, beachwear, or camping clothes, describing it as "tough as a longshoreman and pretty as a Follies girl."[8]

Virginia Pope, fashion editor for the *New York Times*, took a favorable view and described candlewick dresses as "very pleasing."[9] In an illustrated article on easily washable summer fashion, Pope also provided evidence of the connection between the South and the new candlewick fashions, describing how they originated: "Down to the mountains of Tennessee went expert designers from New York. Armed with measurements, patterns and instruction, they directed the women who for years had industriously tufted bedspreads in the adjustment of designs to fit 12s, 14s, 16s, and 18s." She also listed the available colors: "white with tufts in two shades of blue, or yellow and burnt orange," and "brown on a yellow ground." Pope discussed garments made from Czechoslovakian tablecloths and Mexican boleros as well, conveying the novelty of candlewick as a clothing fabric.

In June 1934, the Specialty Shop at Rich's department store in Atlanta claimed to be the first to present the "'Candlewick' Frock" (for $13.95).[10] Rich's offered dresses tufted in red, green, navy, or rose and described them as "quaint as an old-fashioned bouquet," adding a hint of the Colonial

Advertisement for Best and Company, May 10, 1934, *New York Times*

Fireside Handcrafts Company

The extensive Bedspread and Manufacturers' Edition of the *Dalton News* dated February 29, 1940, hails Mrs. Anne Brown, founder and president of Fireside Handcrafts Company, as one of the leaders in the chenille garment industry.[a] The article describes a talented and innovative designer and successful entrepreneur.

Though much of Brown's personal history is difficult to trace, it appears that she was born in Illinois about 1891 and lived for a period in Miami, Florida, with her husband Arthur Patey, who was born in England, and their son William, who was born in Florida in 1906. The family appears in the Miami city directories in 1925 and 1926. By 1927 Arthur was living with William and another woman, Alma, a dressmaker, in Miami, indicating that Arthur and Anne had separated. At some point Anne married J. T. Brown, though his name does not appear in city directories during her time in Dalton.

According to the *Dalton News*, Brown began her business in Dalton with "only herself and 65 cents capital," and in 1935 she made candlewick coats of her own design by hand, discovering "that she could sell all that she could turn out."[b] Then, as orders began to exceed her production capacity, she turned to the new machines to make her garments, described by the *Dalton News* as the *first* chenille garments. The newspaper explains:

> In 1936 she made the first chevron designed coat and also the first cross-chevron. In her spare time, when she had any, she studied styling and designing and soon her models had the same stylish flair and modes turned out by big fashion houses.
>
> The beauty of her coats, robes, and jackets soon began to attract the feminine eye and in no time she had more orders than she could fill[,] necessitating the expansion of Fireside and increased quarters. She also experimented with bathrobes and made the first solid chenille tufted coat to appear on the market.

Continuing the study of the modern trends in styling, Mrs. Brown created her own designs as well and now her trade-mark 'Fluffy-anne' can be noticed in some of the smartest shops of the land. Recently she has trade-marked a summer evening jacket and coat of closely tufted chenille under 'Summer Ermine' and this winter it too is expected to be seen in the smartest circles.

By 1940 Fireside had sixty-five operators, and Brown spent much of her time designing. The company manufactured evening wraps, coats (including beach coats), sports jackets, boleros, robes, housecoats, and bed jackets. Fireside's ad in the *Dalton News* reads, "We manufacture CHENILLE PRODUCTS, both Bedspreads and Wearing Apparel, that possess quality—also noted for appearance and wear. They have that chic look that differentiates them. This means greater sales and more profit. Our HOUSE COATS are striking and most attractive. They are smartly styled and designed by a well-known consultant." The consultant is not named but may have been Brown herself.[c]

Brown had formed a partnership with her son, William B. Patey, in 1939.[d] Patey was an ideal business partner for Brown, because, while she was skilled in design, he had extensive experience with sewing machines. In 1930, according to the U.S. Census, he worked in Miami as a manager of a retail sewing machine shop, and the 1932 and 1934 Miami city directories list him as a salesman for the Singer Sewing Machine Company. When he first moved to Dalton, he was listed in the city directory as a sewing machine manufacturer.[e] Patey built Fireside's tufting machines and held several patents on chenille machines. According to the newspaper, Fireside's inventory of machines included "his famous 'skip-stitch' machine which turns out candlewicking that only experts can detect from that done by hand." Instead of creating a continuous row of tufts like a typical chenille machine, skip-stitch machines sewed a single tuft, then moved

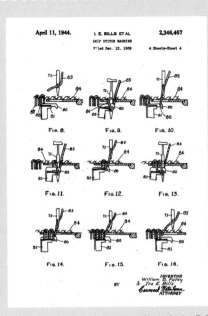

April 11, 1944.   I. E. BILLS ET AL   2,346,467
                                   SKIP STITCH MACHINE
                                   Filed Dec. 12, 1939   4 Sheets-Sheet 4

FIG. 8.   FIG. 9.   FIG. 10.

FIG. 11.   FIG. 12.   FIG. 13.

FIG. 14.   FIG. 15.   FIG. 16.

                              INVENTOR
                              William B. Patey
                         & Ira E. Bills
                    BY
                              Carmod ....
                                     ATTORNEY

Skip Stitch Machine, U.S. patent design by Ira E. Bills and
William B. Patey, filed December 12, 1939, granted April 11,
1944, des. 2,346,467. The patent reads, "Our invention
relates to tufting machines and more particularly to tufting
machines of that character which incorporate yarn into
fabric at intervals to form dots over the upper surface of
the fabric very much in the manner or style of handmade
'candlewick' spreads."

the fabric forward a few steps before making another stitch, mimicking the look of candlewick.

In the patent for a multiple-needle tufting machine (which tufted chenille yardage; see p. 26), filed in 1941, Patey explained that this invention had "particular reference to piece goods from which chenille garments of various characters may be made," although it could also be used for spreads or mats. He described how chenille garments had been made until that time: "It has been the general practice to cut out the parts of the garments from the backing, apply the chenille to those parts and sew them together. This work is ordinarily done with a single needle machine due to irregularities in the shapes of the pieces that go to make up the garment, although in rare instances chenille has been

applied to the backing before it is cut or to the backing after the garment has been made up therefrom." This likely detailed the process Brown had used before Patey developed his new technology.[f]

Neither Brown nor Fireside appears in the 1943 Dalton city directory. Possibly her business was a casualty of the war—it likely was not large enough to convert to war production. An Anne Brown, possibly the same person, is listed in the 1951 Dalton city directory as a textile worker at National Chenille. In the 1953 directory she is a forewoman at National, and she is gone by 1955. The Patey family disappears from the Dalton city directories by 1950.

When asked in 1940 about the future of the chenille industry, Brown replied, "In the garment production industry especially I think that we have hardly started. . . . It has wonderful possibilities which I believe will be brought out much more fully during the coming year."

a "Fireside Handcrafts Specialize in Coats, Robes, Novelties," Bedspread and Manufacturers' Edition, Dalton News, February 29, 1940.
b Ibid. The 1936 Dalton city directory describes Fireside as a "women's clothing manufacturer." The 1940 U.S. Census lists Anne Brown as owner of a coat factory in Dalton.
c Advertisement, Fireside Handcrafts, "Chenille Products," Bedspread and Manufacturers' Edition, Dalton News, February 29, 1940.
d Brown and Patey hosted a Labor Day barbecue for the employees and friends of Fireside at Fort Mountain in 1939. "Fireside Handcraft Employees Entertained at Barbecue," Dalton Citizen, September 7, 1939.
e The 1940 U.S. Census indicates that he lived in Dalton by 1935, though he does not appear in the city directories until 1938.
f William B. Patey, Multiple Needle Tufting Machine, U.S. Patent 2,352,153, filed August 29, 1941, issued June 20, 1944. Patey is not the only individual credited with inventing the skip-stitch and yardage machines. He does receive mention in Deaton's book, though, for helping Albert Cobble build his first yardage machine in 1945. Thomas M. Deaton, Bedspreads to Broadloom: The Story of the Tufted Carpet Industry (Acton, Mass.: Tapestry Press, 1993), 33. A particularly early patent, from 1932, for a multi-needle tufting machine belongs to Erskine E. Boyce, whose company was purchased by B. J. Bandy. Erskine E. Boyce, Multiple Needle Sewing Machine, U.S. Patent 1,984m330 A, filed January 12, 1932, issued December 11, 1934.

Detail from an illustration for an article on washable fashion, May 13, 1934, *New York Times*

Revival to the contemporary style. A newspaper ad for the dress showed an elegant, long, narrow silhouette, with an allover candlewick pattern alternating between single large dots and groups of five smaller dots. The dress had a boat neckline and cap sleeves and was tied at the waist with a cord belt with large pompoms on the ends, a detail echoed at the neckline. The ad declared that the style for candlewick cotton dresses also was popular in Paris and New York, though it does not mention where they were made.

R. H. White Company in Boston offered inexpensive unbleached muslin frocks stamped with patterns, similar to the dress offered by Rich's, that women could tuft at home.[11] White's advertised that women did not need to be expert dressmakers and offered instruction free of charge. Ruth Wyeth Spears, who wrote numerous books on dressmaking and home decorating, offered detailed instructions for making a candlewick dress (also nearly identical to the one offered by Rich's) that ran in multiple newspapers in 1934. She wrote, "There is gay informality with a dash of daring about those candlewick bedspread frocks that strikes just the right note for summer. . . . It is the simplicity and the handmade look that give the costume its piquancy."[12] Spears's comments reflect how the style blended modern and traditional qualities. A writer for the *Christian Science Monitor*, discussing a hand-embellished dress of unbleached muslin, observed, "The delightful thing about these candlewick dresses is that you are given the opportunity to become your own designer," another feature appealing to Depression-era readers.[13]

Candlewick dresses continued to be novel in 1936, when Janet Treat wrote in the *Christian Science Monitor* about a candlewick dress at Plotkin Brothers in Boston: "It really is tufted! And trimmed with fringe. Entirely different."[14] This dress, available in the fall rather than the summer (unlike the previous candlewick dresses), cost about $30 (approximately $511 in 2014). And in the fall of 1937, a store in Boston offered less expensive candlewick dresses ($10.95—about $181 in 2014) "in beige with wine, green or black blops of the candlewick, or oxford with gray dots," with high necks, rows of buttons along each shoulder, and "plenty of width to climb into." Treat suggested that these were for "the younger set."[15]

Candlewick Beach Togs

Tufted fashions became increasingly associated with sports and casual wear. Dorothy Roe, writing for the *Syracuse Journal* in 1934, stated, "Candlewick sun suits and beach slacks and coats are blossoming out on our best beaches, the quaint charm of the tufted muslin bedspreads having caught the eye of the canny designers."[16] Arnold Constable, a prominent upscale department store in New York, offered a line of candlewick beach togs in 1935, including a two-piece playsuit ($1.98), a long robe ($1.98), a matching bag ($1.00), and an ensemble of slacks, halter, and coat ($4.98).[17] Most of the embroidery on these garments was in geometric designs along the edges, except on the halter. An ad highlights their novelty, durability, and easy care: "They're new, they're colorful and . . . You'll be proud of your smart appearance in them and proud of yourself, too, for selecting these perfect vacation affairs that wear so well and require no ironing."[18] Bloomingdale's in New York promoted a similar set of candlewick beach togs in 1936, offering a two-piece playsuit with shorts and a halter on sale for $1.29, a full-length beach robe for $1.98, and a three-piece beach suit with robe, slacks, and halter for $2.98 (about $51 in 2014), shown in an ad. The copy reads, "They're fascinating togs—patterns hand-embroidered and tufted on natural colored . . . cloth—which is washable and pre-shrunk."[19] They came in red, blue, or brown, and featured wavy lines of tufted dots and simple flowers along the edges of the pants and robes and on the front of the halter.

The candlewick beach tog fad also extended to children's wear.[20] Diana Merwin wrote in the *Kingston (N.Y.) Daily Freeman* in 1936 about children's sunsuits and matching hats "inspired by grandmother's candlewick bedspread," available in yellow, pink, red, or blue on white or natural, or yellow on brown or pink on wine.[21] Again, the ease of care for the material is touted, an especially attractive quality for children's clothing. Dorothy Gentry, writing for the *Daily Boston Globe*, highlighted the new children's candlewick garments as well, describing them as the "cutest sun suits and play costumes with matching hats."[22]

Tufted Coats

One of the most popular forms executed in tufted materials before World War II was the coat or jacket. These were made in both candlewick and chenille, varied in length from fingertip to ankle, and came with an extensive list of names. Boxy, fingertip-length coats sometimes were

Advertisement for Arnold Constable department store, July 1, 1935, *New York Sun*

Feb. 4, 1941.   C. SHAPIRO   Des. 124,983
CHENILLE JACKET
Filed March 13, 1940   2 Sheets—Sheet 1

FIG. 1

CHARLES SHAPIRO   Inventor

By   Edwin Leviska
    Attorney

Chenille jacket, U.S. patent
design by Charles Shapiro,
filed March 13, 1940, granted
February 4, 1941, des. 124,983

Two women on a dock, one
wearing a short chenille
fitted coat dress, ca. 1940,
found photograph, private
collection

Youth's chenille hooded jacket,
ca. 1940, cotton, made by
Esther Baxter (1893–1962) for
Mrs. C. B. Wood, collection
of Bradley Putnam, photograph
by Michael McKelvey

referred to as jigger coats, bush coats, or lumberjack-style coats.[23] Longer ones (knee-length or falling just below the knee) often were called swagger coats. Sometimes the terms for coats overlapped with other forms. For example, an ad in the *Albany (N.Y.) Knickerbocker News* in 1940 notes that long beach coats could double as housecoats, and an ad illustrating a short dress-like garment (fitted at the waist with an A-line skirt, as in the photograph to the left) calls it a "fitted coat."[24] Chenille coats were promoted for both day and evening wear, with Janet Treat, for example, reporting for the *Christian Science Monitor* on a summer chenille jacket "that can be worn at the beach in the morning, on the clubhouse porch if you find a coolish afternoon, and then on into the evening to top your sheer white evening gown."[25]

Most jackets were free of fasteners, though some did have a single button at the top, several buttons down the front, or a tie closure at the neck. Some had hoods and many had patch pockets. For most chenille coats, the linearity of the monochromatic tufted rows provide the only design, while others had multicolored stripes, waffle patterns, or checkerboard created from overlapping perpendicular rows, flowers, or borders of abstract round flowers. A few even feature peacocks, though the sale of these may have been limited to spreadlines.[26] Gilchrist's in Boston offered girls' chenille jackets with button fronts and special tufting: on the top halves of the front and back were musical staffs and notes, and on the lower half of the back were the words "SWING IT!," referring to the era's popular swing music.[27] Chenille coats in the late

Elaine Mulligan (*left*), wearing a chenille jacket, and Lois Larson at the National Wash Apparel Show in Chicago, February 8, 1939, Acme Photo, private collection. Caption on back: "Elaine Mulligan . . . wearing a parka-hooded beach jacket of rainbow hues, and Lois Larson in an equally brilliant 'Jitterbug Costume' for the skating rink or informal dancing. They are two of the summer styles shown at the National Wash Apparel Show in Chicago."

1930s and early 1940s typically sold for between about \$2 and \$5, the equivalent of about \$35–\$85 in 2014.

A rare, hand-tufted, three-quarter-length coat from 1931 surviving in the collection of Crown Gardens & Archives in Dalton is densely covered with irregularly arranged black tufts. It has long sleeves rolled at the cuffs, a wide notched collar, and no fasteners. The coat belonged to Lucille Hall (1914–2001) and was made by her mother, Dessie Hall (1891–1983), both workers at Crown Cotton Mill in Dalton.[28] The lush texture of the allover tufting on this coat suggests a thick pelt, and it clearly demonstrates why advertisers sometimes described tufted coats as fur-like. One newspaper described a candlewick coat as having tufting so thick that it "looks at least a little like ermine."[29] Also, when Jack Bandy recalled the tufted housecoats that the B. J. Bandy Company made, he described the tufting as being so close together that it resembled a fur coat.[30] For Depression-era consumers who could not afford real fur coats, these cotton versions would have been welcome alternatives.

The *Chicago Tribune* in 1934 ran a photograph of a woman wearing a "spectator sports ensemble" of a mid-calf-length slim dress and three-quarter-length loose swagger coat with a lattice pattern of tufts in navy and white on a salmon-pink ground. In the accompanying article Rhea Seeger praised another candlewick coat, writing, "What you will lose your heart to is this swagger coat of all white. . . . It is the best looking summer sports coat you ever wore."[31]

Short, finger-tip-length chenille coats became popular in the late 1930s, and *Life* magazine ran a photograph by Alfred Eisenstaedt of a model wearing a short white chenille jacket with three-quarter sleeves in an article on cotton in 1939. "Cotton chenille, a bedspread fabric, broke into the sportswear field last winter at southern resorts," the accompanying text read.[32] Mary Hampton, writing for the *Bakersfield Californian*, described a white chenille jacket in a young woman's trousseau as a "shortie . . . short with [a] very flared back," also noting that the jackets were commonly known as "sugar coats."[33] Peggy Townsend, a popular debutante, when asked by the *Washington Post* to suggest summer holiday outfits, included in her list "a chenille beach lumberjacket which is as short as a chorus girl's skirts," making it sound both fashionable and a little daring.[34]

Another jacket form popular in chenille, the bolero, appeared by 1935.[35] In 1938 the fashion department of the *New York Times* described a chenille bolero, in vertical stripes of yellow, red, and blue on white, as appropriate to

Candlewick coat, 1931, cotton, made by
Dessie Hall (1891–1983) for her daughter
Lucille Hall (1914–2001), Whitfield-
Murray Historical Society, Crown
Gardens & Archives, Dalton, Georgia,
gift of Lucille Hall, photograph by
Michael McKelvey

ABOVE: interior view

Model wearing a short chenille coat, illustration from an article on cotton, *Life*, May 8, 1939, photograph by Alfred Eisenstaedt (1898–1995), The *Life* Picture Collection / Getty Images

wear over a bathing suit or with summer daytime or evening frocks.[36] Seeger, in the *Chicago Daily Tribune*, explained that new chenille boleros had smaller ridges and daintier tufts than typical robes and spreads and praised the colors ("off-white maize, luscious bonbon pink," or multicolored stripes) as "exceptionally good."[37]

Couple on the beach, the woman wearing a chenille bolero, summer of 1941, found photograph, private collection

Unlike other chenille jackets, bed jackets were intended specifically for indoor wear. The T. D. Whitney Company in Boston advertised chenille bed jackets as "coquettish and comfy" and described them as "soft, cozy, just the thing to slip on for breakfast or reading in bed," adding, "lovely, too, for invalids."[38] Like other chenille garments, these short jackets, often with cord ties at the neck, were promoted as inexpensive and easily washable. Based on a review of period advertisements, production of chenille bed jackets was limited primarily to just a few years around 1940.

Child's chenille bolero, ca. 1940, cotton, made by Esther Baxter (1893–1962) for Mrs. C. B. Wood, collection of Bradley Putnam, photograph by Michael McKelvey

Polly Prentiss, Inc.

One of the leading manufacturers of chenille garments was Polly Prentiss, Inc., of Sumter, South Carolina, founded by Mr. and Mrs. O. C. Moore—Otis Corcoran Moore (1893–1939) and Annie Norine West (1896–1995). O. C. Moore graduated from the Citadel in Charleston and served in the coast artillery during World War I, and Mrs. Moore graduated from Winthrop College in Rock Hill.[a] In 1932 O. C. Moore worked as a salesman for the Dalton-based Kenner and Rauschenberg candlewick bedspread company.[b] He sought additional items to sell and added maid's aprons and caps to his stock, overseeing their production. During one of O. C. Moore's business trips, his wife, while recovering from an illness, learned to hand tuft. They became interested in starting a candlewick business and established Polly Prentiss—named after their daughter (Ann Prentiss), the "Polly" added for alliteration—in South Carolina in 1933, making aprons, caps, and candlewick bedspreads.[c]

When Polly Prentiss incorporated, T. H. Clark of Sumter was president, Mrs. Moore was vice president and general manager, and O. C. Moore was sales manager. They sought to work exclusively with citizens of Sumter. Mrs. Moore taught local women how to hand tuft spreads, which they did in their homes, while the aprons and caps were made in the factory. Mrs. Rob Warren of Sumter, along with the Moores, developed many of the early designs for Polly Prentiss.[d]

O. C. Moore had established Asbury-Prentiss, Inc., "a pioneer company in the use of chenille process for making wearing apparel" in connection with Asbury Mills in New York by 1938.[e] Asbury Mills manufactured beachwear from at least the 1910s through the 1940s, and one of its two owners, Leonard C. Asch (1885–1959), was a noted bathing suit designer.[f] In 1938 Asch patented a beach coat

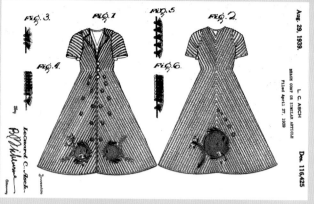

Beach coat, U.S. patent design by Leonard C. Asch, filed April 27, 1939, granted August 29, 1939, des. 116,425

on behalf of Polly Prentiss and Asbury-Prentiss. The form resembles a dress, with short sleeves and a long wide skirt, a plunging neckline, small lapels, and three buttons at the waist. The chenille runs in diagonal rows, forming chevrons in the back.[g] A patent by Asch from the following year has the same form, with a fish-and-bubbles motif added on the front and back.

By 1939 Polly Prentiss advertised robes, beach coats, jackets, and beach bags as well.[h] A columnist in Florida's *Sarasota Herald-Tribune* praised: "Polly Prentiss is the gal who put the style in candlewick sports clothes. Check me on this! You'll find them shown at HELENA's charming accessory shop in the Mira Mar. Inspired by the Hollywood stars, designed in California, made in Dixie, they are gay, ultra-smart, have a patented hydro-velvet finish, and carry such amazing designs as lobsters, jack tars [sailors], and fish."[i]

Though residing in South Carolina, O. C. Moore was deeply involved with the tufted textile manufacturers in Georgia. He helped establish the Tufted Bedspread Manufacturers Association (the predecessor of the Tufted Textile Manufacturers Association), and served as its first president, a position he held at the time of his death in 1939.[j]

In February 1941 the owners of Polly Prentiss decided to liquidate the company, although in April, in a special announcement, the *Charleston (S.C.) News and Courier* reported that M. G. Scher, John F. Fitzgerald, and Harry Berger of New York had joined Mrs. Moore in the management of the company. Production and employment numbers decreased after the initial announcement, but following the management change, production resumed "with a full force in the beach wear department and a limited force in the spread department."[k] The importance of this company to the town of Sumter is reflected in the *News and Courier* reporting the resumption of production: "The announcement comes as good news to Sumter, as practically every business in the city is affected."[l] Mrs. Moore, according to her family, was not pleased with the new arrangement, though, and later started a career with Shaw Air Force Base in Sumter.[m]

By 1950 Polly Prentiss beach and house robes were advertised as part of M. G. Scher and Associates.[n] One of Polly Prentiss's notable postwar contracts was with Roy Rogers Enterprises. As part of a large merchandising program that included costumes, toys, lunchboxes, and pajamas, Polly Prentiss manufactured Roy Rogers–themed bedspreads (with matching drapes and rugs) and children's robes by the mid-1950s.[o] Robe motifs included Roy Rogers riding his horse Trigger (with his name and a double R), a double R with a pistol and decorative scroll, and Dale Evans riding her horse Buttermilk (with her name and the double R), all executed in overlay on narrow-gauge chenille yardage. The labels on these robes read, "Roy Rogers / by / Polly Prentiss / Originals." Polly Prentiss went out of business sometime before the early 1970s.[p]

a Chlotilde R. Martin, "Product from South Carolina Finds Favor in White House," *Charleston (S.C.) News and Courier*, September 16, 1934.

b Ibid.; "Passing of Moore Is Deplored," Bedspread and Manufacturers' Edition, *Dalton News*, February 29, 1940.

c Chlotilde R. Martin, "Product from South Carolina Finds Favor in White House," *Charleston (S.C.) News and Courier*, September 16, 1934. An article published in 1940 indicates that Polly Prentiss either had an earlier name or that the company absorbed an already existing business, stating that in 1933 Home Crafts, Inc., became Polly Prentiss, Inc. "Polly Prentiss, Inc., Builds Big Plant in Sumter, S. C.," Bedspread and Manufacturers' Edition, *Dalton News*, February 29, 1940.

d Chlotilde R. Martin, "Product from South Carolina Finds Favor in White House," *Charleston (S.C.) News and Courier*, September 16, 1934.

e "Passing of Moore Is Deplored," Bedspread and Manufacturers' Edition, *Dalton News*, February 29, 1940.

f Saul Pett, "It's Yard Down, Half Yard to Go in Swim Suit World," *Kingsport (Tenn.) Times-News*, June 6, 1948. A 1915 New York business directory lists Asch with Asbury Mills, a bathing suit company. That company still designed bathing suits in the 1920s and 1930s, in particular swimsuits named after Annette Kellerman, a famous Australian swimmer. *Trow's New York Partnership and Corporation Directory, Burroughs of Manhattan and Bronx* (New York: R. L. Polk, 1915), 59. The 1940 U.S. Census lists Asch as a beachwear sales manager. Asch was the godfather of Carolyn Cook, granddaughter of the Moores. She remembers hearing that Asch shocked residents of Sumter by walking around town with a model who wore a two-piece swimsuit well before that style was common. Carolyn L. Cook, e-mail to author, October 21, 2013. Asbury-Prentiss is listed at the same address as Asbury Mills and Asch in the New York city directories from 1940 (if not earlier) to 1946 (1410 Broadway and then 1350 Broadway), and is not listed by 1949. It is listed as a beachwear company until 1946, when it is listed as a robe company.

g Leonard C. Asch, Beach Coat or Similar Article, U.S. Patent 111,827, filed August 2, 1938, issued October 18, 1938.

h Advertisement, William S. Frankel Company, "Beach and Sports Wear Reduced for Clearance," *Sandusky (Ohio) Star-Journal*, July 17, 1939.

i "Ambling with Miss Sarasota," *Sarasota Herald-Tribune*, January 8, 1939.

j "Passing of Moore Is Deplored," Bedspread and Manufacturers' Edition, *Dalton News*, February 29, 1940.

k Polly Prentiss did not take on military contracts during World War II. Seymour Seidman, "Chenille Men Working on Defense Production," *Dalton News*, February 13, 1945, reprinted from the *Daily News Record* of New York.

l "Sumter Industry Not to Be Closed," *Charleston (S.C.) News and Courier*, April 3, 1941.

m Carolyn L. Cook (granddaughter of the Moores), e-mail to author, November 5, 2012; "South Carolina Deaths," *The State* (Columbia, S.C.), June 12, 1995.

n Advertisement, M. G. Scher and Associates, *Textile Manufacturers Association 1950 Directory and Yearbook* (Dalton, Ga.: Tufted Textile Manufacturers Association, 1950), 18.

o Advertisement, Roy Rogers Enterprises, "Roy Rogers Dreams of Santa," *Life* (November 15, 1954), 55–58.

p Van King, "Council Rejects Planning Recommendation," *Sumter (S.C.) Daily Item*, April 12, 1972.

Chenille Slacks

Manufacturers also produced chenille slacks, probably intended as beach-wear, and two examples survive in a group of garments made by Esther Baxter (1893–1962) for her aunt, Mrs. C. B. Wood, at her spread house in Rocky Face, Georgia, in the late 1930s or early 1940s. Baxter's son, Sidney, recalls that a man from New York came to Georgia and drew up the patterns for Wood's garments.[39] One pair of pants is pink with diagonal rows of che-nille on the wide legs, forming broad zigzags, and multicolored horizontal stripes along the cuffs and waist, with a zipper at one hip. The other pair,

Chenille harem pants, ca. 1940, cotton, made by Esther Baxter (1893-1962) for Mrs. C. B. Wood, collection of Bradley Putnam, photograph by Michael McKelvey

Chenille pants, ca. 1940, cotton, made by Esther Baxter (1893-1962) for Mrs. C. B. Wood, collection of Bradley Putnam, photograph by Michael McKelvey

cinched at the bottom like harem pants, also with a zipper at the waist, is of heavy, dark pink chenille in thick vertical rows, with wide burgundy stripes down the sides and burgundy horizontal stripes at the cuffs and waist. A designer named Melvin D. Brod patented a design for chenille pants in 1940, with wide legs, thick vertical rows of chenille, contrasting stripes at the waist and pockets and down the sides, and laced at one hip for closure.[40] The surviving examples of chenille pants are remarkably heavy and must have been challenging to wear if they got wet.

Chenille Capes

Chenille capes present an especially striking contrast between the historical needlework traditions associated with their production and their use by women wearing modern swimsuits and engaging in a twentieth-century leisure activity. Capes appeared as the tufted textile industry transitioned from hand to machine production, and some advertisers highlighted their connection to tradition as a selling point, although they were primarily made by machine. In 1937 the *Schenectady Gazette* mentioned "candlewick" capes as popular beachwear, though these almost certainly would have been *chenille*, the writer perhaps intentionally using a word that had a stronger association with familiar, historical needlework.[41] Capes and bedspreads typically occupied different spheres, but at least one advertisement shows them together: a promotion from Hopkins Brothers of Kokomo, Indiana, offered a free chenille cape with the purchase of a chenille spread, providing a clear connection between the domestic textile and the modern garment.[42]

Woman wearing a chenille beach cape, Miami Beach, Florida, April 1939, found photograph, private collection

Chenille capes fulfilled the practical functions of protecting skin from too much sun, providing warmth, and serving as beach towels. They also allowed women wearing modern swimsuits easy access to modesty; as swimsuits became more revealing in the 1920s, beach capes became an essential swimwear fashion accessory. Capes also increased in popularity as the nation experienced a rising interest in physical fitness in general and swimming in particular in the 1930s.[43] In 1921 Eleanor Gunn of the *Washington Post* claimed that "beach cape" had "become an absolute necessity in the lexicon of the smart summer girl."[44] The next year Gunn again stated that any woman who planned to sun "on any fashionable beach" needed a cape, and she wrote that capes could be

Beachcomber Fashions

for Ocean, Beach and Pool

You needn't go in the water to be the glamour girl of water sports . . . as long as you're wearing one of these eye-catching suits. However—if you swim like a champion, you'll relish their excellent fit and freedom—giving comfort.

Rayon Jersey — Satin Lastex Wool Jersey

Dressmaker Suits of fine cottons and pretty satins.

1.98 to 3.98

Satin Lastex suit in princess silhouette, halter neckline.

2.98 up

Over any swim suit—throw a chenille cape. We have a selective group of capes and coats for your beach ensemble.

1.98 up

Wool Jersey suit in princess silhouette, evening decollete.

2.98 up

Headquarters for Smart Beach Wear

Tristram & Fuller

104 Wall Street   NORWALK

Advertisement for Tristram and Fuller, Wilton, Connecticut, June 20, 1940, *Wilton (Conn.) Bulletin*

OPPOSITE: Mrs. Frederic W. Howe Jr., Sea Spray Beach, Palm Beach, Florida, February 3, 1940, Acme Photo, private collection. Caption on back: "Among fashionables seen on the exclusive sands of Sea Spray Beach following the return of normal temperatures, was Mrs. Frederic W. Howe, Jr., of Boston, Mass., Charlotte, N.C., wearing a smart ensemble consisting of a wine-colored bathing suit of rubber, a Bahaman straw hat, and a chenille cape."

made of a wide variety of materials, from crepe de chine or rubberized silk to terrycloth.[45] As fashion historians Richard Martin and Harold Koda explain in *Splash! A History of Swimwear* (1990), swimming pools and beaches became more accessible to nonelite Americans in the 1920s, and by the 1930s swimming and swimwear became widely acceptable for women (not just men), significantly increasing the market for inexpensive swimwear and accessories.[46] As stylish, affordable, and easy-to-care-for garments, chenille capes became a popular option for middle-class women seeking comfortable, quick-to-put-on swimsuit coverups.

Like other tufted garments of the 1930s, capes offered fashion flexibility and, while primarily used for the beach, were also promoted as appropriate as evening wear. Newmans department store in Oshkosh, Wisconsin, advertised this versatility, saying of a chenille cape, "Slip it over your bathing suit, wear it over your evening gown."[47]

When sold in department stores, chenille capes fit in with other popular swim accessories. For example, in 1939, the new swim shop at Gilchrist's, a Boston department store, featured chenille capes along with sunshade hats, "play togs," goggles, beach shoes, bathing caps, and rubber-lined beach bags.[48] Chenille capes were also sold in roadside shops, where they were displayed among other chenille items and souvenirs. Murray Wyche, writing in 1948, noted that beachwear garments initially found favor in the roadside market, "particularly with Florida-bound tourists," and then appeared in stores and resort shops.[49] His observance that new tufted garments "first had to win their place on 'Bedspread Boulevard'" raises the possibility that Florida-bound tourists significantly influenced the tufted textile industry's decision to produce beach capes.[50]

Chenille capes came in a variety of styles, though most were semicircular with cord ties at the neck. Generally they cost about $1–$2, which equaled approximately $17–$34 in 2014. Lengths varied from fingertip to knee to ankle. Capes were made for both women and girls, and some featured collars or hoods. Some higher-end capes included small

A group at Long Beach, California, with a woman wearing a chenille cape, August 1940, found photograph titled *Hamburgers*, private collection

Two women at the beach wearing chenille capes, ca. 1940, found photograph, back stamped "Newark, N.J.," private collection

pockets on the inside. Capes were simply draped over the body, fitted at the shoulders, or gathered at the neck with a drawstring, and the gathered capes could also be worn as skirts.[51]

Due to the basic construction technique of chenille, which resulted in rows of tufts, chenille capes appealed to those who liked another element of style then popular for resort wear: stripes. Caroline Rennolds Milbank, in *Resort Fashion: Style in Sun-Drenched Climates* (2009), attributes this trend to the influence of striped awnings and Breton fishermen's sweaters.[52] Stripes on chenille capes typically ran horizontally or in diagonals forming a chevron pattern in the back. Still more creative designs included slight curves that swooped across the fabric or scalloped rows that seemed to ripple from swirls along the bottom. The emphasis on line in chenille, especially for capes with their uninterrupted expanses of machine-tufted rows, hints at the "speed lines" popular in American streamlined design at the time and creates a sense of movement, appropriate to the athleticism of swimming.[53]

The most common color for chenille capes was white, although the base fabric also came in other colors, including blue, burgundy, yellow, and pink. Milbank notes the popularity and practicality of white resort wear—white is relatively cool, for one thing, reflecting the sun's rays instead of absorbing them—and adds, "The craze for suntans that started in the 1920s further enhanced the chic of white."[54] Jordan Marsh Company in Boston praised white for its

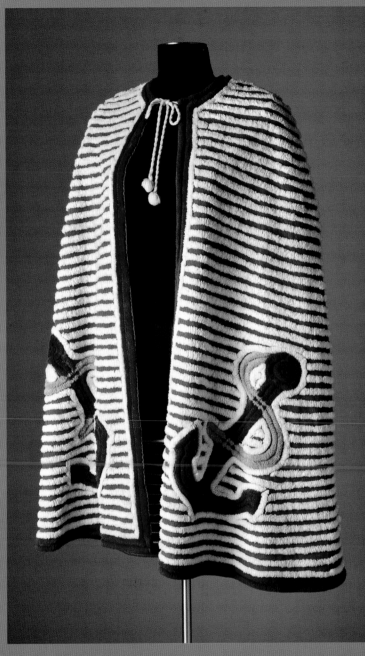

Chenille cape with anchor design, ca. 1940,
cotton, 38 inches long, private collection,
photograph by Michael McKelvey

ABOVE: interior view

Back of a chenille cape with a shrimp design, ca. 1940, cotton, 31 inches long, collection of Peter and Sandy Loose-Schrantz, photograph by Michael McKelvey

Back of a chenille cape with a sailboat design, ca. 1940, cotton, 31 inches long, collection of Peter and Sandy Loose-Schrantz, photograph by Michael McKelvey

beauty in beach fashion—shining in the sun, complementing tanned skin—in an advertisement in the *Boston Globe*, with an illustration of a white chenille cape with a sailboat motif in the front corners and a mock sailor collar.[55]

Many capes used chenille rows, sometimes in multiple colors, as decoration, while others featured simple designs at the borders or shoulders and still others featured novelty motifs. Often the latter were nautically themed and executed patriotically in red, white, and blue. Images included anchors, helms, sailboats, fish, shrimp, seahorses, seagulls, waves, stars, palm trees, and peacocks. The back of a white cape available during the 1939 New York World's Fair featured a red-and-blue depiction of the fair's iconic Trylon and Perisphere structures and the words "New York World's Fair" below them.[56]

Chenille Glamour

Hollywood actresses wore tufted coats and capes, lending glamour and charm to them. In 1934 Kay Francis, a popular and highly paid actress with Warner Brothers, wore a candlewick coat that tapered to a straight skirt.

The coat had raglan sleeves, a "bulky turn-over collar," and broad lapels, and Mollie Merrick described it in the *Boston Globe* as "something to make a Summer's day perfect."[57] Also that year, newspapers reported that actress Ann Harding wore a new summer sports coat in white with green tufts, and actress Ann Dvorak donned a sports ensemble with a belted candlewick jacket of red and white.[58] In 1938, while working on *Sally, Irene and Mary* for Twentieth Century Fox, Louise Hovick, better known as Gypsy Rose Lee, appeared in a promotional photograph wearing a white full-length chenille coat that she wore over a floral playsuit. A description reads, "When Louise Hovick finishes a game of badminton or tennis she bundles herself into this cotton chenille coat that falls to the floor." The young leading actress Deanna Durbin sported a fingertip-length striped chenille coat in red, white, and blue over her bathing suit in 1939. Her star power is reflected in an ad from Efird's Department Store in Danville, Virginia, which offered "exclusive" chenille garments described as "Deanna Durbin 'Fluffy-Tuff' chenille Coat and Cape."[59] Not least, both Susan Hayward and Virginia Dale were photographed wearing chenille capes with swimsuits, and the *Atlanta Constitution* described a chenille bathing suit with a flying fish design and matching cape worn by Priscilla Lane in 1939.[60]

Chenille also made appearances on stage. The Classic Players from Bob Jones College in Greenville, South Carolina, performed *King Lear* in 1939 wearing costumes crafted from chenille spreads. The costume designer described the "brilliant colors and exotic design" of the bedspreads hanging along the roadside in north Georgia and wrote, "I have never driven along the road and noticed these spreads without thinking how beautiful they would look under stage lighting, and finally I determined that the first time I did a play which they would at all fit, I would use them for my costume material." She explained that she sought to capture a mood rather than a specific historical period and required material that "draped well and had a rough pile and texture and barbaric color and design." She believed that tufted spreads "met the need admirably."[61] Chenille appeared later, in 1958, in *My Fair Lady*, starring Julie Andrews, Rex Harrison, and Stanley Holloway at the Apollo Theatre on London's Drury Lane, with costumes by Cecil Beaton, the noted costume designer and photographer. Some members of the chorus wore skirts made from chenille bedspreads, and just as spreads provided eye-catching attractions to motorists driving along the highway, the same textiles provided vivid contrast and pattern on stage.[62]

Julie Andrews and Stanley Holloway in *My Fair Lady*, with some chorus members wearing chenille skirts, costumes by Cecil Beaton, photograph by Cecil Beaton, courtesy of Bandy Heritage Center for Northwest Georgia, Carpet and Rug Institute Photograph Collection

The Decline of Chenille Coats and Capes

The production of chenille garments like jackets and beachwear thrived in the late 1930s and very early 1940s, but the U.S. entry into World War II cut short the apparently healthy business. While all chenille garments faced production decline with the increasing restrictions on materials during the war, beachwear faced the additional challenge of new, dark associations with the ocean. Martin and Koda eloquently explain, "In the 1940s, the swimmer entered deep and treacherous water, now populated with submarines, guarded coasts, and the harbingers of America in the war that brought long, ponderous shadows to the beach and to the delights of swimming that had seemed unmixedly joyous so few years before."[63] The decline in popularity may have had practical reasons as well. Wyche suggested that the heavy chenille used for these early garments, compared with the lighter weights that became popular less than a decade later, "were not so adaptable to the hot Southern sunshine."[64] Also, the garments were bulky and took up a lot of luggage space, making them less than ideal for vacation travel.[65] Though chenille capes and coats continued to be made following World War II, their popularity never again reached the prewar heights.

OPPOSITE: Louise Hovick (Gypsy Rose Lee) wearing a chenille coat, February 17, 1938, Twentieth Century Fox

Chapter Five

The Rise and Decline of Chenille Robes, an American Fashion Staple

AS THE TUFTED GARMENT INDUSTRY matured, the item that achieved greatest popularity and longevity was the robe. Along with coats and capes, robes grew in popularity during the 1930s, but unlike their fashion companions they increased in desirability during and after World War II. The boom in chenille garments by the late 1930s encouraged several large tufted textile manufacturers to establish robe departments and drew many new manufacturers into the business.[1] Martin Richman, whose father started Art-Rich, one of the leading chenille robe companies, described the early commercial success of chenille robes: "In 1939 large chain store volume buyers saw the possibilities of this item, and by the time Fall of 1940 rolled around a tufted robe was to be found in every department store, whether it be upstairs or basement, mail order house, chain, specialty shop or the smaller retail or dry goods store."[2] Murray Wyche included a section on chenille robes and housecoats in his 1948 essay on the tufted textile industry in the South, listing robes, housecoats, beachwear, capes, and toppers as the garments made of chenille but highlighting robes as having "emerged as the favorite of the group."[3]

After World War II, chenille robes became "a staple garment," according to Wyche.[4] Though the items were popular throughout the country, some early ads continued to link chenille robes to Georgia. Davison's Basement in Atlanta advertised a chenille beach robe in 1940, describing it as "genuine Georgia-made," and in 1941 Gimbels in New York touted the origins of their robes, advertising candlewick housecoats as "tufted in Georgia, famed home

OPPOSITE: Model wearing a chenille robe, ca. 1950, courtesy of Bandy Heritage Center for Northwest Georgia, Carpet and Rug Institute Photograph Collection

Playing card with image of Art-Rich chenille robe tag, ca. 1955, collection of Joy M. Richman, PhD.

Lady Pickwick

The Very New
CANDLEWICK ROBE

Illustration from an ad for Smartwear Emma Lange, Inc., Milwaukee, Wisconsin, April 13, 1934, *Milwaukee Journal*

of fine candlewicking!"[5] Art-Rich in Dalton added paper tags to their robes that featured a cotton boll and a message that shows the commercial importance of highlighting the robes' regional origin: "This CHENILLE ROBE is made where the Candlewick Tufting Industry Originated." Manufacturing of chenille robes extended well beyond Northwest Georgia, though the majority of companies remained concentrated in that region. By 1947, according to the *Washington Post*, 320 of the country's 400 chenille plants were in Northwest Georgia.[6] The well-trained work force and ever-evolving specialized machines, which required frequent maintenance by mechanics familiar with their idiosyncrasies, limited the easy expansion of the industry beyond the region.

Prewar Robes

Candlewick Robes

Some of the earliest mentions of candlewick robes (or bathrobes or housecoats) date to spring 1934. In April that year, Smartwear Emma Lange, a department store in Milwaukee, advertised a candlewick robe. The illustration depicted a robe with wide three-quarter sleeves, a bias-cut fit, a long cord tie with tassels at the waist, and an allover honeycomb-and-dot candlewick pattern, similar in style to the candlewick dresses made at the same time. The ad described the "Lady Pickwick" robe as "very new" but said that it "quaintly matches your bedroom." It came with tufts in rose, blue, or green, and its price was $5.98 ($106 in 2014).[7] Another robe was mentioned in May that year in an ad for Abraham and Straus in New York City. This ad's two columns illustrated an old-fashioned woman in a wooden rocking chair and then a modern woman in a streamlined metal chair, with these words: "Is She Lavender or Is She Lipstick?" The candlewick bathrobe was included in the modern column, along with "naughty 'thin' stockings," shorts, makeup sets, and pastel alligator handbags.[8] Though the department store sought to sell the items on both lists and presented them both positively, it is notable that the candlewick bathrobe, even though executed in a traditional needlework technique, was considered modern.

Virginia Lee Warren, writing for the *Washington Post* in July 1934, also mentioned candlewick robes, describing the new dressing gowns as being made of "the same heavy, closely woven material" used in bedspreads, with "the same little tufts sprinkled around in circles, stars, serpentines and

other wavering designs."[9] An August 1934 Gilchrist's ad in Boston described "gorgeous hand tufted candlewick robes," adding that some of them were hand-painted, an unusual detail.[10] The accompanying illustration shows a robe with a large, allover candlewick lattice pattern with dots in the center of each diamond. As mentioned in chapter 4, Arnold Constable in New York offered hand-tufted long robes with its other beach togs in 1935, and these were unbelted and featured a simple pattern along the edges of dots and lines that end in spirals.[11] Dalton's Everwear Candlewick Corporation made robes by 1935, and Bloomingdale's in New York sold candlewick robes in 1936.[12] Saks in New York also illustrated a "hand-tufted candlewick" robe worn over a swimsuit in a 1936 ad, describing the unbelted, vertically striped robe as a "Joseph's coat."[13]

Changing Image

For their first few years, tufted robes lacked a consistent image. Were they candlewick or chenille? As with tufted jackets and capes, some robes continued to be described as candlewick well after the advent of chenille machines, even as late as 1945.[14] Were they robes or coats? The terms "robe" and "coat" were used interchangeably until at least 1943.[15] Were they for the beach or the home? In 1940 Sylva Weaver described a chenille robe as "a perfect summer garment" with varied informal uses, including "for vacation wear, mornings and evenings at the beach home or in the mountains, [or]

Daphne and Fred Caldwell

Daphne Cleo Sloan Caldwell (1903–79) of Resaca, Georgia, worked with tufted textiles in the 1930s and 1940s.[a] An interview with her from 1979 and remembrances of her son Calvin reveal her to have been an intelligent, resourceful, and kind woman and suggest that she played an influential role in the early development of the chenille robe industry. The daughter of a prominent farmer, James "Jim" Lewis Sloan, Daphne in 1922 married her childhood sweetheart Fred Greenberry Caldwell (1901–75). In 1923 she graduated from Young Harris College, where she and her sister both studied to be teachers, and she taught for a while beginning in 1924. As a young married couple, Daphne and Fred Caldwell worked as farmers, and the 1930 Census lists them as farmers with two sons, Calvin and Alfred.

Starting in 1936 Daphne worked as a hauler for the B. J. Bandy Company, delivering one hundred or so spreads at a time, usually weekly, to private homes to be hand tufted.[b] Fred purchased a 1936 Ford with a trunk on the back, and Daphne stuffed bundles of spreads inside, each marked with the name of the family that was to receive it. Their son Calvin recalls that his father received seven cents per spread. Daphne stopped hauling when payments decreased. She felt that the tufters were not making enough money, saying, "It wasn't fair to them."

In 1938 the Caldwells moved from the country to the highway, to a former filling station on U.S. 41 with an adjacent house, both with electricity, and started their own spreadline, with Daphne hand tufting. She operated the spreadline for three or four years, and, unlike most spreadline owners, she offered garments. Daphne noted the eagerness with which her goods were received: "I made things so different to what other people were making. I was cutting my own patterns for coats and housecoats and things, capes and shawls and things. They just stood at my door

begging for it." Calvin recalls that the peacock was by far their biggest seller on the spreadline but that his mother didn't have a special design, she "just picked it up from somewhere." He also remembers selling "more to people from Ohio than all the rest of [the other states] put together."

Daphne explained how she came to make her first robe: "A lady from North Carolina wrote she had bought something at my place. . . . she wanted a chenille housecoat and drawed a picture of it, just a skeleton picture of how she wanted it and what color she wanted it in." Then Daphne studied the drawing and cut a pattern, adding, "And from that so many people that saw it wanted it and from that I just went to making them." Daphne also recalled that she wasn't aware of other people making robes when she started: "I cut the pattern and made the first one I ever saw." Calvin does not know how she learned to sew but was always impressed by her ability to see a garment in a store and then go home and make one like it. The *Southern Israelite*, when recounting the history of the chenille industry, mentioned bedspreads, then added that "the most skilled of the women perfected the art for robes and rugs," acknowledging the talent required to make these items and the important role played by women like Caldwell.[c]

Daphne worked briefly for H. F. "Super" Jones, president of a cotton mill and owner of a chenille company called Hy-Way Arts, which is where she learned to operate a chenille machine. She worked for him for about six months around 1940 and helped him set up his chenille business. Then her father became too ill to take care of his farm and risked losing it, and she determined that they would find a way to pay off the $12,000 owed on it. She explained: "I was so worried, that's the reason I got the machine, and getting my own business was to try to pay off the loan on this farm." She told Jones

Man cutting pieces for chenille robes, Sparks, Inc., Dalton, Georgia, early 1950s, collection of Alice Sparks Young

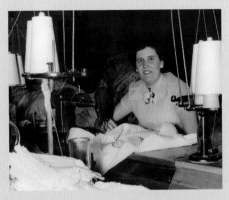

Woman sewing a chenille robe, Sparks, Inc., Dalton, Georgia, early 1950s, collection of Alice Sparks Young

that she was going to quit and was having her own machine made; she knew where to get sheeting but did not know where to get yarn, and he agreed to let her have some if she would "make herself some money" and spend it wisely.

Daphne bought a single-needle machine, one of the first in her area, and focused on making housecoats and crib spreads. She described how just after she got her machine, in addition to her father being sick and in danger of losing his farm, her husband's crops were destroyed by flooding: "We were just desperate as to what we would do[,] and I just got it in the back of my head that this is what I would do." So with the filling station building and her own machine, she "went to work." She recalled, "Fred and the boys would come down and stay with me 'til bedtime or late at night, I'd be working so hard and they'd wait to carry me home." She paid off the loan on the farm in three years, "and had [pin] money in the bank."

During and just after World War II, the Caldwells operated the chenille business in the gas station building and lived in the little house next to it. Fred stopped farming after Daphne sold a week's worth of work for the significant amount of $65, and he learned to maintain the machines. Their business grew to have fifteen machines, all arranged on a

line and turned by one motor, and around thirty-five to thirty-eight employees. The additional fourteen machines were installed by a chenille company, O'Jay Mills (or Ostow and Jacobs). For the first three months, the Caldwells worked for that company, but it was not able to get material during the war, so the Caldwells continued on their own.[d]

Calvin recalls that his father "loved to cut" and explained that he would put the pattern for the robe parts on top of a stack of fifteen to twenty sheets of fabric and cut them by hand, with a large knife (similar to the technique demonstrated by the Sparks employee above). Then the women would serge the pieces of the robes together, with each woman responsible for a different section, such as collars or sleeves. They primarily made robes with simple, straight rows of chenille, although later they added overlay designs. They had the robes dyed at a laundry, then brought them back to the business to be inspected and packed. They made some chenille robes with peacocks, but, as Calvin recalled, those were "more for fun, if someone wanted them."

The Caldwells continued to sell a little to tourists but focused on selling to department stores, which provided a larger and more consistent business than spreadlines. Their easily accessible location

Women using sergers to make chenille robes, Sparks, Inc., Dalton, Georgia, early 1950s, collection of Alice Sparks Young

them set up a robe department, offering her three thousand dollars to spend two months with the company, which she did. She explained, "They wanted me to go over there and teach them how to make housecoats. And I says, 'Well, I'm not no teacher, but if they've got any brain to make a bedspread, they can chenille a housecoat.' And he [Mr. Winkler] said, 'Well, I've spent ten thousand dollars trying and we failed,' and says, 'Now I've got an option on a big plant in Dalton and if you'll teach us how to make these, I can get Sears and Roebuck's business.'" She replied to Winkler: "Well, I'll come under one condition; they tell me you're real rude to those people over there and . . . I work on a level basis and . . . if I'm not doing what you want done, you come tell me, but don't you come cursing and jumping up and down thinking you're gonna scare me . . . because if you do, I'm gonna knock you down." Dixie Belle became a major manufacturer of robes, and Daphne and Winkler came to think highly of each other. Mr. Jacobs, co-owner of O'Jay's, also asked her to help them set up after the war, but she declined.

benefited relationships even with distant customers, and Daphne recalled a buyer from Cincinnati who traveled through the region going from spreadline to spreadline. She explained that they had open accounts with the local bank, he put five thousand dollars in an account for her, and she drew money out as she sent him merchandise. They shipped so much merchandise to one address in New York City that even sixty years later Calvin recalls it—398 Broadway—and adds that the business there "would take whatever we could make." At the height of their business, the Caldwells daily shipped out eight to ten boxes, each with one hundred robes, and their customers included J. C. Penney and Sears, Roebuck.

The Caldwells' chenille business was limited during World War II and ended soon after, and while their son is not certain of the exact year, he knows they had stopped making chenille by 1950. As the Caldwells were getting out of the manufacturing business, Ben Winkler and Nathan Snow from the chenille company Dixie Belle asked Daphne to help

a Calvin Caldwell (son of Daphne Cleo Sloan Caldwell), interview by author, November 23, 2012, Calhoun, Georgia; Calvin Caldwell, Calhoun, Georgia, letter to author, July 16, 2013; Mrs. Fred Caldwell and Calvin Caldwell, interview by Thomas Deaton, December 10, 1979, transcript, Fred Caldwell Folder 012, box 2 of 4, Dr. Thomas Deaton Collection, Bandy Heritage Center for Northwest Georgia, Dalton State College, Dalton, Georgia; Thomas M. Deaton, *Bedspreads to Broadloom: The Story of the Tufted Carpet Industry* (Acton, Mass.: Tapestry Press, 1993), 25–27. When interviewed by the author in 2013, Calvin Caldwell played a recording of Deaton's 1979 interview; the audio included more detail than the transcript. All of the quotations here from Calvin Caldwell are from my interview of him, and the quotations from Daphne Caldwell are from Deaton's interview.
b The Caldwells also hauled occasionally for a Mr. Moore, probably the S. Z. Moore Spread Company of Calhoun.
c "Dalton's Chenille Industry," *Southern Israelite*, December 8, 1950.
d Calvin Caldwell, Calhoun, Georgia, letter to author, July 16, 2013.

Lawtex Corporation

One of the large manufacturers that had a housecoat division was Lawtex Corporation, which grew out of a business first called the Newport Trading Company, founded in 1898 and renamed Laurel Textile Company in 1912, owned by the Lorberbaum family in New York.[a] The Lorberbaums bought and sold candlewick spreads from Dalton by 1930, especially from the Stewart family, which operated Stewart's Bedspread Company. Seymour Lorberbaum (1912–83) moved to Dalton in 1935 and started Lawtex Corporation ("Lawtex" from "Laurel" and "Textile"), and the Stewart family helped him set up the factory and provided patterns.[b] The company transitioned from candlewick to chenille in 1937. Lorberbaum's brother-in-law, Morris William "Bill" Wiesen (1916–2008), moved to Dalton in 1938 and ran the housecoat division.[c] Wiesen later served as president of the TTMA, from 1956–57. In 1963 the local newspaper credited Lawtex with helping to "develop and promote acceptance of the chenille robe." Lorberbaum's brother Leonard (1917–2013) joined the company after serving in World War II and was TTMA president in 1963–64. Leonard recalled that the company's first machine designed to accept material forty-eight inches wide was used to make yardage for chenille housecoats.[d] Lawtex used the name "Candlewick Washenille" to promote some of its garments, drawing attention to the material's easy care.

According to Leonard, the company hired a piece goods maker from New York to design robes, while Eathel Stewart (1901–2003), an in-house designer who worked at Lawtex from 1948 until 1973 (she worked for LaRose for six years before that), designed spreads.[e] Lawtex stopped making chenille bedspreads around 1963, quit making robes by 1968 (1967 is the last year the company is listed as a robe manufacturer in the TTMA directories), and then, after experimenting with carpet, focused on room-size rugs.[f] Spring Mills acquired Lawtex in 1979.[g]

a "Lawtex First Operated on W. King Street in Dalton," Progress Edition, *Dalton Daily-Citizen News*, March 30, 1963.
b Cheryl Wykoff, "Lawtex Corporation," Wykoff's chenille bedspread oral history notebook, Crown Gardens & Archives.
c Leonard Lorberbaum, interview by Thomas Deaton, April 21, 1981, transcript, p. 1, Leonard Lorberbaum folder 041, box 2 of 4, Carpet History 2010.1, MSS 1, Dr. Thomas Deaton Collection, Bandy Heritage Center for Northwest Georgia.
d Ibid.
e Wykoff, "Lawtex Corporation."
f Lorberbaum interview, 2–3.
g Ibid., 5; *Heritage of Gordon County, GA, 1850–1999* (Waynesville, N.C.: County Heritage, 1999), 38.

Lawtex employees outside of the Lawtex building, ca. 1947, Ward's Photo Service, Dalton, Georgia, courtesy of the estate of Leonard Lorberbaum

Child wearing a chenille robe
on the beach, ca. 1950, found
photograph, private collection

general household activities around a city home."[16] Were they
traditional or modern? Chenille robes, which reached the height
of their popularity in the 1940s and early 1950s in the United
States, came to be viewed as modern domestic garments during
that period, breaking with the Colonial Revival emphasis associated with the earlier candlewick bedspreads. Weaver described
a robe with a large V neckline, padded shoulders, a full bias-cut
skirt, and large circle designs in the tufting, favoring it in white
because, "In white, this robe will make you look quite as modern
and streamlined as your smartest new bedroom with Venetian
blinds and white candlewick spreads."[17] A later robe description
also highlights the streamlining effect of the tufted rows, emphasizing how flattering they could be, with the long, vertical lines
allowing the wearer to "look your tallest, slimmest self."[18]

Like other tufted garments, robes benefited from their practical attributes of affordability and ease of care. Janet Treat, in a
column about shopping in Boston, praised the chenille robes she
found at the Jordan Marsh department store for their combination of beauty (they had "enough sheen to them to make it look
almost like silk") and practicality: they were inexpensive and did
not need to be ironed, just shaken out like a chenille bedspread.[19]
Weaver, in the *Los Angeles Times*, described a robe as something
that would "bring happiness and chic to every member of the
fairer sex whether she lives on a movie star's income or a relief
worker's salary."[20]

The tufted textile industry again benefited from associations
with Hollywood actresses, and in 1938 the *Atlanta Constitution*
included a photograph of Katharine Hepburn wearing a yellow
chenille robe designed by Robert Kalloch for her to wear in the
film *Holiday*. The newspaper noted, "The high, shaped collar,
loose raglan sleeves and sweeping circular skirt make it a garment not only for the bedroom, but useful for bathing or perhaps
an informal dinner at home."[21] Tufted robes appeared in numerous other Hollywood films, including *Only Angels Have Wings*
1939 (worn by Jean Arthur), *In Name Only* and *Made for Each
Other* in 1939 (worn by Carole Lombard), *Remember the Night*
in 1940 (worn by Barbara Stanwyck), and *The Ghost Breakers* in

1940 (worn by Paulette Goddard). Stanwyck also wore a chenille robe in ads for Lux Toilet Soap.[22] One particularly popular line, Adrian Evans by the Walter M. Gotsch Company, frequently advertised chenille robes or housecoats as made and styled in Hollywood.[23]

By 1939 chenille robes were more strongly associated with domesticity. Several factors likely contributed to this shift. First, there was a general move away from promoting beach activities as the war approached. Also, as larger manufacturers came to dominate the production of chenille robes, the messaging became more consistent. Perhaps chenille robes just found their niche, as well. The *Los Angeles Times* featured a traditional wraparound robe in 1939, with Weaver advocating that with this item a woman could be chic not only at nightclubs and luncheons but also "at the breakfast table, in the boudoir, [and] around the house all day."[24] A year later Weaver promoted another robe as perfect for wearing while the family gathered around the Christmas tree, especially when in red, again emphasizing its domestic appropriateness.[25]

Promotions of robes began noting how women could coordinate their robes and their bedspreads, firmly tying the garments to indoor settings. The Wallace Company in Poughkeepsie advertised robes "to match your bedspread" in 1940, calling it "the newest idea in ensembleing," and an ad in the *Atlanta Constitution* read, "It's now possible to 'key' yourself to the harmony of your bedroom scheme by wearing a chenille robe to match the bedspread."[26] The TTMA repeatedly used a photograph (p. 109) of a model wearing a chenille robe, standing next to a bed with a chenille spread and a vanity with a chenille skirt, touching chenille drapes, and standing on a chenille rug, illustrating the extreme to which coordinated tufting could be carried.

While a variety of robe styles were produced concurrently for decades, the typical early chenille robes were manufactured on single-needle machines and had widely spaced rows of tufts. When they had designs other than straight lines, those designs were worked into the overall tufted pattern. Early robes, wraparound in style, often had V-necks or shawl collars, shoulder pads, three-quarter or long sleeves, cord ties at the waist, a single pocket for the right hand, and flowing skirts. Many robes were monochromatic, tufted in a natural color on a natural base and then dyed. One atypical design featured white tufting in a swirl pattern on gingham, sold through Sears, Roebuck in 1944 as "Swirlaway, chenille-gingham robes."[27] Prewar chenille robes typically cost between $2 and $7, or about $34–$119 in 2014.

Child wearing a chenille robe, ca. 1943, found photograph, private collection

G. H. Rauschenberg

One of the companies to manufacture robes on a large scale was the G. H. Rauschenberg Company of Dalton.[a] Mrs. G. H. Rauschenberg (née Beulah E. Swick, 1888–1972) and her sister Mrs. W. T. Kenner (née Mary Jane Swick, 1872–1953) started hand tufting bedspreads probably in the late 1910s.[b] Encouraged by their success and by the increasing numbers of packages he observed leaving Dalton while he worked with the railroad, Gerhardt Henry Rauschenberg (1890–1957) joined with his brother-in-law Walter Tibbs Kenner (1868–1953) around 1920 to form Kenner and Rauschenberg.[c] By 1932 their company produced five thousand spreads a day, making it "possible for the entire world to consume an article that is strictly Georgian."[d] Following a fire in the Kenner and Rauschenberg plant in 1937, the two men established separate businesses. Kenner started Ken-Rau (which was purchased by Belcraft Chenilles in the late 1940s), and Rauschenberg started G. H. Rauschenberg Company.[e] Rauschenberg soon quit producing candlewicks and focused on chenilles.[f]

Henry Nevin, secretary of the Dalton Chamber of Commerce and assistant secretary of the Tufted Bedspread Manufacturers Association, reported that G. H. Rauschenberg Company began making chenille robes in June 1939 by transferring two machines from bedspread to robe production.[g] The company made a handful of robes the first day, he reported, and 6,730 on April 16, 1942. In 1939, Rauschenberg hired A. H. Nicholas, a designer in New York, to run the new robe department. In 1940 the *Dalton News* offered this praise: "Still the pioneer, Mr. Rauschenberg was the first to experiment with the making of beautiful robes, house-coats, jackets, and beachwear from chenille material. So successful has he been that in a few short months since he started the garment department of Rauschenberg's, it has grown and the demand has become so great that now he is unable to fill all orders received for the coats and robes."[h] The *Dalton Citizen* further explained in 1941, "This company, whose product is known as 'The Pride of Georgia,' makes, in addition to their high quality line of chenille spreads, a very high type line of ready-to-wear chenille housecoats, robes, etc." that "are sold in every leading store throughout the country." The paper reported that the company was "sold up," saying that "they are now guaranteed full production throughout this year."[i] The company's main robe line was "Lady Beth," with "Miss Beth" and "Baby Beth" for children and infants.[j]

The G. H. Rauschenberg Company focused on robe production and military contracts during World War II. Afterward the company resumed full production, and by 1947 it had sales offices in New York, Chicago, Boston, Dallas, Denver, and Los Angeles.[k] In the early 1950s, the company began producing carpet as well. James Calhoun, plant manager, stated that they quit making spreads by 1953 and only made rugs and robes after that.[l] The last year the company is listed in the TTMA directories as a manufacturer of robes is 1955.

A leader in the tufted textile industry, G. H. Rauschenberg served as vice president of the TTMA in 1951–52 and as president in 1952–53. Rauschenberg died in 1957, and his son-in-law, Arthur Linton Zachry Jr. (1915–85), took over the company and continued its move toward carpet.[m] Zachry served as TTMA president from 1960–61. Columbus Fiber Mills bought the company around 1960.[n]

a Murray E. Wyche, "The Tufted Textile Industry in the South," 1948, 15, Bedspread Industry box, Articles on History, Companies, and Machinery folder, Crown Gardens & Archives.
b Cheryl Wykoff, "Kenner and Rauschenberg," Wykoff's chenille bedspread oral history notebook, Crown Gardens & Archives.
c. Wyche, "Tufted Textile Industry," 10. The founding date for Kenner and Rauschenberg is uncertain. A handwritten page of notes with the Women's Bureau of the Department of Labor surveys records that Kenner and Rauschenberg started fifteen years earlier, which would be 1919, with $150 in capital, while

Rauschenberg's obituary indicates that it officially incorporated in 1925, though it had been operating for several years prior. Kenner and Rauschenberg handwritten notes, Candlewick folder, box 232, Records of the Women's Bureau, Department of Labor, National Archives; "G. H. Rauschenberg Is Laid to Rest Friday in West Hill," *Dalton News*, February 17, 1957.

d "Kenner and Rauschenberg Ship Bedspreads to Far Corners of Globe," Anniversary Edition, *Dalton Citizen*, August 25, 1932.

e The G. H. Rauschenberg page in the Centennial Edition of the *Dalton Citizen* in 1941 states that the company was organized in March 1929, but the fire was in 1937, and the business split between Kenner and Rauschenberg was reported in the local newspaper as completed in March 1938. Also, 1938 is the first year the Dalton city directory lists the new company. G. H. Rauschenberg page, Centennial Edition, *Dalton Citizen*, October 16, 1947; "G. H. Rauschenberg to Open Up Factory," *Dalton News*, March 10, 1938.

f Wykoff, "Kenner and Rauschenberg."

g Henry Nevin, "Robes Chenille Have Oomph Appeal," *Dalton News*, May 5, 1942.

h "G. H. Rauschenberg Helped to Develop Bedspread Industry," Bedspread and Manufacturers' Edition, *Dalton News*, February 29, 1940.

i "Rauschenberg Company Raises Pay of Machine Operators to 40 Cents Hour," *Dalton Citizen*, April 10, 1941.

j Advertisement, Henderson-Hoyt Company, "The New Chenille Robe Ensemble," *Manitowoc (Wis.) Herald-Times*, December 3, 1942.

k G. H. Rauschenberg page, Centennial Edition, *Dalton Citizen*, October 16, 1947.

l Wykoff, "Kenner and Rauschenberg"; advertisement, G. H. Rauschenberg Company, *Polk's Dalton City Directory* (Richmond, Va.: R. L. Polk, 1953), 111.

m Gerhardt H. Zachry (Arthur Linton Zachry Jr.'s son), telephone conversation with author, October 29, 2013.

n Wykoff, "Kenner and Rauschenberg."

Blue Ridge Spread Company (Blue Ridge Manufacturing Company)

Adolph Rosenberg, writing for the *Southern Israelite* in 1950, credited Ella Hurowitz (1898–1975) and Samuel B. Hurowitz (ca. 1897–1968), both born in Russia, with being among the first to recognize the commercial possibilities of candlewick, explaining that they ordered as many candlewick spreads as they could acquire to display and sell in the store they ran in downtown Dalton.[a] Sam Hurowitz then founded Blue Ridge Spread Company in 1933, and he added a garment department by 1939, hiring Arthur Richman, an experienced garment designer from New York, to serve as production manager and stylist.[b] The robe and spread departments of this large company had separate showrooms in New York in 1941.

In the 1941 Progress Edition of the *Dalton Citizen*, Blue Ridge offered a full-page tribute to the company's personnel, stating that all employees "have full knowledge of their craft" and asserting that the skilled craftsmanship played "an all-important part in making Blue Ridge 'Chenille Robes & Candlewick Beach Wear' so popular."[c] By 1950 Blue Ridge had sales offices in New York, Chicago, and Minneapolis, and it sold both lightweight and heavier chenille robes.[d] The founding couple's son Irving Morton Hurowitz (1929–2008) also worked with the company, which last appears in the TTMA directories as manufacturers of robes in 1956 and in the Dalton city directory around 1961 (with A. B. Tenenbaum as president).

a Adolph Rosenberg, "The Dalton Story," *Southern Israelite*, June 18, 1948, 13.

b Blue Ridge page, rotogravure section, Progress Edition, *Dalton Citizen*, October 2, 1941.

c Ibid.

d Advertisement, Blue Ridge Spread Company and Blue Ridge Manufacturing Company, *Textile Manufacturers Association 1950 Directory and Yearbook* (Dalton, Ga.: Tufted Textile Manufacturers Association, 1950), 3.

LaRose Textiles (LaRose Bedspread Company)

Louis Rosen (1882–1960) of New York founded LaRose Bedspread Company in 1935 with his sons Frederick (1917–2003) and Ira (1909–60). Louis, who emigrated from Russia in 1904, worked in New York as a textiles importer with his business LaRose Importing Company, traveling to Europe once a year to select merchandise. According to family history, while attending a trade fair in Frankfurt in February 1934, Louis Rosen heard a speech by Adolph Hitler, realized that his business would not be able to continue, and immediately returned home. As his son Fred recalled when interviewed in the 1980s, "Several of his business friends told him about a growing bedspread industry in Dalton, Georgia. He arrived in Dalton in early 1935 and liked everything he saw but knew that this sort of operation could not be run by remote control. He knew someone very responsible had to be here. In June 1935 my eldest brother Ira and I came to Dalton with my father and started La Rose Bedspread Company."[a] The company first worked with home candlewick tufters, then added machines in 1937, maintaining their candlewick business concurrently for a while. LaRose began making garments by 1939. Fred explained that "we had to bring people in that understood the ready-to-wear business" and that the robes were made of tufted yardage: "We laid the machine-tufted rolls on tables and cut the material by patterns, the same method as regular garment plants."[b] The last year the TTMA directories list LaRose as a robe manufacturer is 1951, and the company switched to making carpet around 1954.[c]

a Cheryl Wykoff, "La Rose Bedspread Company," based on interviews of Fred Rosen by Ellen Thompson in 1982 and Cheryl Wykoff in 1987, Wykoff's chenille bedspread oral history notebook, Crown Gardens & Archives.
b Helen Shope, "From Pin Money to a Cottage Industry," unpublished manuscript, February 9, 1994, in notebook marked "Bedspread Articles," Crown Gardens & Archives.
c Thomas M. Deaton, *Bedspreads to Broadloom: The Story of the Tufted Carpet Industry* (Acton, Mass.: Tapestry Press, 1993), 160.

OPPOSITE: Model wearing a chenille robe, standing beside a chenille curtain, bedspread, rug, and table skirt, ca. 1950, Kaufmann and Factory, Commercial Photographers, Chicago, courtesy of Bandy Heritage Center for Northwest Georgia, Carpet and Rug Institute Photograph Collection

Designers

Designers are often overlooked in the tufted textile industry, both regarding spreads and garments. Their roles are particularly important with clothing, and several industry leaders noted that with the significant growth of chenille garment production in the late 1930s, it became necessary for the large companies to hire individuals familiar with the ready-to-wear clothing industry to create successful designs. For example, Polly Prentiss joined forces with an established beachwear designer in New York to develop tufted beach garments.

One designer mentioned during the candlewick era was Mrs. W. L. McWilliams (née Nell Manly, 1871–1965), who is listed in the 1930

Two children wearing chenille robes, ca. 1943, found photographs, private collection

Youth's chenille robe, ca. 1945, cotton, 39 inches long, collection of Peter and Sandy Loose-Schrantz, photograph by Michael McKelvey

U.S. Census as an art teacher married to a sewing machine salesman.[28] Designers noted in the 1940 Dalton city directory who worked at companies that made chenille garments include Helen D. Mau (1917–77) and Bettye Kirksey, who worked at Blue Ridge; Mary Lou Hilley for Everwear Candlewick Corporation; and Walter Smith, Robert Beavers, and Fred L. Buckner Jr., for San-Rog Spreads. The names of other designers associated with chenille fashion are recorded through patents for chenille garment designs. Murray M. Taradash, president of Monarch Textile Corporation, a large chenille manufacturer in Fall River, Massachusetts, patented two designs in 1940 for chenille robes.[29] Frances Schaeffer of Los Angeles patented a design in 1940. Charles Shapiro of New York (possibly the brother of Phil Phillips who ran Everwear Candlewick in Dalton) patented two designs in 1940, one modern composition with columns of concentric circles down the front and back, and one with a vermicelli and floral pattern above the waist and vertical lines below. Irving Weiser of New York patented a robe design with the Roman numerals I–XII along the bottom hem in 1941, perhaps suggesting that the robe was appropriate to wear around the clock. George H. McLaughlin of New York patented two robes in 1948 each with a scrolling overlay design around the hem and near the ends of the sleeves.[30] Even more designers' names appear in the 1940 census in Dalton but not in connection with specific areas of design or tufting businesses. More designers' names appear too in later Dalton city directories.

One designer about whom something more is known was Camille Cronk, who designed spreads, rugs, and robes for B. J. Bandy in Cartersville. She worked in the design room, just off an office with modern furnishings, "[evolving] the new and intricate patterns for the different articles put out by this company."[31] The *Dalton News* in 1944 reported: "Upwards of 2,000 designs are stored on shelves along the wall, and plenty more [are in] repose in the clever consciousness of Miss Cronk, who specialized for her work at a Philadelphia art school for commercial designing." Previously Cronk worked in Gastonia, South Carolina, at Boysell Manufacturing, one of the earliest and leading companies to develop tufting machines and patents. She moved to Cartersville when Bandy purchased Boysell in 1934, remaining with the company until after Bandy died in 1948.[32] The 1955 and 1957 Dalton city directories list Cronk as a designer for J. T. Bates Candlewicks.

A. G. Andre, described as a "well-known designer for Chenille products," enumerated the many challenges faced in his field in an article for

Chenille negligee, U.S. patent design
by M. M. Taradash, filed March 19, 1940,
granted July 9, 1940, des. 121,428

Chenille robe, U.S. patent design
by Charles Shapiro, filed August 22, 1940,
granted October 8, 1940, des. 123,021

Chenille robe, U.S. patent design by
Charles Shapiro, filed August 22, 1940,
granted October 8, 1940, des. 123,022

Chenille robe, U.S. patent design by
Irving Weiser, filed June 6, 1941, granted
August 26, 1941, des. 129,195

Aug. 13, 1940.　　　F. SCHAEFFER　　　Des. 121,932

CHENILLE ROBE

Filed June 1, 1940

FIG. 2.

FIG. 1.

FRANCES SCHAEFFER
INVENTOR

BY Crosby Gauthier
ATTORNEY

Chenille robe, U.S. patent design by Frances Schaeffer, filed
June 1, 1940, granted August 13, 1940, des. 121,932

the Bedspread and Manufacturers' Edition of the *Dalton News* in 1940.[33] Andre arrived in Dalton around 1938 from Calhoun and had seven years of experience. He lamented that "too many factors act as a check to keep the hand and mind of the artist from running riot with a blaze of display such as would put to shame the talents of a Van Gogh, or a Rembrandt." He highlighted the various day-to-day concerns he faced: "Consider then the plight of the Chenille artist who works with sheeting for his canvas, multi-colored thread for his paints, and a singing, throbbing machine for his brush—there is one on whose shoulders the cares of the day lay heavily, for he is constantly obsessed with prices of sheeting and yarn, cost of labor and laundry, plus various other overheads which will help to run up the ultimate cost of his brain-child, the finished spread." Andre described the earlier candlewick designs as created by amateurs who translated wallpapers into "lovely but impractical patterns for spreads." Newer designs, he said, were submitted by large New York studios, "who, because of ignorance of production costs, continue to deliver under contract very, very pretty pictures, which are very, very unsuitable for the modern-day chenille design," even though those designs might have worked on candlewick spreads, "on which the labor cost was practically negligible." He described how labor and material costs forced modern chenille designs to be conservative and said that the modern chenille designer had "to be not only a drawer of patterns" but someone who understood production and sales issues. Though Andre referred specifically to spreads, his sentiments seem applicable to tufted garments as well.

Dalton's Jewish Community

One notable change in Dalton during the 1930s was the growth of the Jewish community, largely due to families moving to the area to work with the tufted textile industry. Ivan Millender shared his recollections of growing up in Dalton's Jewish community for a Whitfield-Murray Historical Society publication in 2002, noting that the number of Jewish families increased from six in 1930 to over fifty by the 1950s.[34] Some of the first Jewish families involved in the industry were the Hurowitzes, who started Blue Ridge Spread Company; the family of Phil Phillips, who opened Everwear Candlewick Corporation; the Lorberbaums, who founded Lawtex; and the Rosens, who started LaRose Bedspread. As the chenille industry boomed in the late 1930s, more Jewish families moved to Dalton, including

the Sauls, who later started Queen Chenille;
the Nicholases, who later opened Duchess
Chenilles; and the Richmans, who later established Art-Rich. By 1942 the community was
large enough that planning and fund-raising
for a synagogue began, with the building
completed in 1947.[35]

An important resource for information
on the tufted textile industry is the *Southern
Israelite*, a publication started as a temple bulletin in Augusta, Georgia, in 1925 and devel-

Two couples wearing
each other's clothes,
one man wearing
chenille robe, ca. 1942,
found photograph,
private collection

oped into a monthly magazine and short weekly newspaper based in Atlanta
in 1934. Many chenille businesses, both Jewish and non-Jewish, advertised
in the publication, and in 1948 the *Southern Israelite* featured an article by
Adolph Rosenberg discussing the contributions of Jewish families to the
development of Dalton's tufted textile industry. Rosenberg's article is significant because it records important early stories, especially about leaders in the
garment industry, not documented elsewhere.[36]

Robes during World War II

Wartime Changes in Chenille Production

Chenille production in Northwest Georgia continued smoothly
through the end of 1941. A few weeks after the bombing of
Pearl Harbor, the *Dalton News* still reported optimism among
plant managers and no shortage of materials, although that
prospect loomed, as demands for the national defense program
were increasing daily.[37] A month later, in January 1942, the
paper reported that the industry faced decreased availability of
supplies; a diminished labor force as workers joined the army
and the navy and went to work for defense industries; and tire
rationing, which limited the travel for employees.[38] Businesses
reacted to the challenges in a variety of ways.

According to the *Washington Post* in 1947, many small producers continued making chenille products during the war.[39]
Mrs. J. H. Bennett in Resaca, Georgia, got enough sheeting
and yarn from a supplier named Clarence Thomason for her

Woman wearing a chenille robe over a
swimsuit, ca. 1942, found photograph,
private collection. Handwritten on
back: "Here I'm wearing the blue
bathing suit + the robe you gave me
before you left for the Army. Note hair
on my face it was kind of windy."

Duchess Chenilles

Aaron Harry Nicholas (1881–?), who was born in Dvinsk, Russia, and immigrated to the United States around 1895, arrived in Dalton in 1939 to be the designer and production manager for G. H. Rauschenberg's robe department.[a] The *Dalton Citizen* in 1941 described him as "a pioneer in the chenille ready-to-wear industry, contributing largely to the development of the business," and credited him with introducing "ideas which are now being used by many manufacturers in the robe, beachwear and sportswear designs." Before moving to Dalton, Nicholas ran his own "model studio" in New York, "making designs and styles for many chenille and sportswear manufacturers."[b]

In April 1945, probably with little work to do because of wartime restrictions, Nicholas left Dalton for a position in Gaffney, South Carolina, as the general manager of an industrial plant.[c] He returned in September, though, and established Duchess Chenilles, which became one of the leading producers of chenille robes.[d] His wife, Rae (née Smith or Schmidt, 1894–1977, born in Russia as well and whom he married in Greenwich, Connecticut, in 1937), also participated in the company.[e] The details of the history of Duchess are unclear, but Dalton city directories indicate that by 1951 the Nicholases owned Duchess Laundry, a chenille products laundry, in addition to Duchess Chenilles, and that by 1953 they owned a chenille products laundry business called National Robe and Spread Company. In 1953 and 1954 the TTMA directories list "National Robes" as the robe trade name for National Robe and Spread. The related businesses of Duchess Chenilles and National Robe and Spread Company last appear in the Dalton city directories in 1957, and by 1958 the Nicholases had moved to Miami Beach, where city directories record them from 1958 to at least 1960.

a Harry Nicholas became a naturalized citizen in Boston in 1901. Rae Smith Nicholas, United States of America Petition for Naturalization, no. 3562, June 30, 1943, District Court of the United States of America, Atlanta, Georgia, Atlanta Naturalization Petitions 10/42–5/43 (Box 5). The 1940 Dalton city directory lists him as "Harry Nichlous," a designer for G. H. Rauschenberg.

b "Designer and Production Manager," *Dalton Citizen*, September 2, 1941.

c "A. H. Nicholas Resigns to Accept Gaffney Job," *Dalton News*, April 24, 1945.

d The *Dalton News* reported that Nicholas established an unnamed chenille business with John McCarty in September 1945, and Duchess Chenille was in existence by November 1946. It seems reasonable to assume that Duchess was started in September 1945. "Harry Nicholas Returns," *Dalton News*, September 20, 1945; "Duchess Chenille Workers Reject Union in Vote," *Dalton News*, November 19, 1946.

e Rae Smith Nicholas, United States of America Petition for Naturalization, no. 3562, June 30, 1943, District Court of the United States of America, Atlanta, Georgia, Atlanta Naturalization Petitions 10/42–5/43 (Box 5).

Art-Rich Manufacturing Company

Arthur "Artie" Richman (1904–65) was born in Poland in 1905 and immigrated to the United States in 1912, becoming a naturalized citizen in New York in 1920. The 1925 New York State Census lists him living with his parents, Aaron and Sarah, with Arthur working as a salesman and Aaron as a tailor. Arthur married Rose Wasserman (1906–98) in 1928. From 1936 (if not earlier) to 1938, they lived in Waterford, Connecticut, and Richman worked as a designer and plant manager for the Lombardy Dress Company in nearby New London, along with his friend Mannie Ringel, who was the company's manager. Ringel later operated a chenille robe business in New York, Crowntuft.[a] Richman's son Martin "Marty" (1929–2007) married Ringel's daughter Ellen.

Richman next worked in New York as a garment designer and then arrived in Dalton in 1939 to work as the production manager and stylist of the Robe and Sportswear Department at Blue Ridge Spread Company, successfully building that department until he left to open his own company, Ann-Lee Chenilles, sometime prior to January 1945.[b] This company advertised in the *Southern Israelite* in June 1945 as "Styled by Ann Lee," and advertised again in 1946.[c] By 1947, Richman established Art-Rich Manufacturing Company, a large, long-lived company that focused on the design and production of chenille robes.[d] The lines included Art-Rich robes for women and Roslyn Products robes for children. Art-Rich advertised in the 1952 TTMA directory: "Your Acceptance of the ART-RICH line has made it America's Top Chenille Line!"[e]

For many years Art-Rich used the same basic pattern to produce traditional wraparound robes. Fannie L. Hooker, who worked in the tufting department for Art-Rich on and off for about fifteen years, recalled the production process: they tufted yardage, cut out pieces and serged them together, hemmed the robes and added pockets, and then added tufted flowers and edge rows, sometimes using four-needle machines.[f] Art-Rich developed a particular style of chenille used in some of its robes that it called Richwale (a trademarked name), which looked similar to corduroy.[g] The company typically added "Art-Rich" labels to its robes.

Richman served as the TTMA president in 1961–62. Martin Richman assumed leadership of Art-Rich shortly before his father died in 1965.[h] According

to Arthur Richman's granddaughter (Martin's daughter, Joy Richman), chenille was Art-Rich's main product until about 1966. Art-Rich then diversified from chenille, and Joy recalls that they made a lot of beachwear out of terrycloth as well as lacy beach coverups and loungewear. She also remembers that they had a huge business making floor-length robes out of towels (terrycloth towels from Cannon Mills), with empire waists and three-quarter sleeves. The company's three largest customers were Montgomery Ward, J. C. Penney, and Sears, Roebuck, at least during 1960–75. By the late 1970s, however, low-cost imported robes began to reduce Art-Rich's profits. Joy Richman recalls Martin's frustration when they were shopping together and he checked labels and saw that items were produced overseas.[i] Art-Rich appears in the Dalton city directories through 1983.

a Joy Richman, interview by author, March 28, 2012, Bethlehem, Georgia; Victor Ringel (Mannie Ringel's son), e-mail to author, November 5, 2013.

b Ann-Lee Chenilles began with a factory in Tunnel Hill, then Richman added a larger plant in Dalton by January 1945. "Ann-Lee Chenilles Opens New Plant," *Dalton News*, January 9, 1945.

c Advertisement, Ann Lee Chenilles, *Southern Israelite*, June 22, 1945; list of advertisers, *Southern Israelite*, June 28, 1946.

d Art-Rich page, Centennial Edition, *Dalton Citizen*, October 16, 1947.

e Advertisement, Art-Rich, *Tufted Textile Manufacturers Association Directory and Yearbook, 1952* (Dalton, Ga.: Tufted Textile Manufacturers Association, 1952), 59.

f Cheryl Wykoff, "Fannie L. Hooker," based on Wykoff's interview of Hooker, April 5, 1988, Wykoff's chenille bedspread oral history notebook, Crown Gardens & Archives.

g See, for example, advertisement, Art-Rich, *Tufted Textile Manufacturers Association Directory*, 1952 (Dalton, Ga.: Tufted Textile Manufacturers Association, 1952), 59.

h "Art Richman Textile Leader Dies in Dalton," *Southern Israelite*, June 4, 1965.

i Joy Richman interview.

Woman wearing a
chenille robe, ca. 1942,
found photograph,
private collection

one-woman operation, while Mrs. Fred Caldwell acquired remnant sheeting from a sympathetic salesman at Bibb Manufacturing Company in Macon.[40] Caldwell recalled, "I kept on working. I could use the scraps for making small size coats and housecoats and different things." She added, "There's no telling . . . how much money I made off of those scraps that that company gave me."[41]

Amid this uncertainty, newspaper editor (and former secretary of Dalton's chamber of commerce) Henry Nevin wrote an article highlighting chenille robes and their "oomph appeal." He noted that in just three years chenille garments had become a major factor in the chenille industry and that the industry was on track to sell three million robes in 1942. He listed the leaders of chenille garment production as G. H. Rauschenberg, Blue Ridge Spread Company, Lawtex Corporation, LaRose Bedspread Company, Gordo Bedspreads, Novelty Mills, and Looper's. He stated: "Chenille robes today are superbly form-fitting and seriously constructed to slenderize and enhance the beauty of the wearer. Colors are richer and more flattering. Not only does a woman look more appealing in a chenille robe, but she KNOWS that she does, and thus attains a confidence in her beauty justified by the confidence she has in the robe she wears."[42]

During the war, in February 1943, Rauschenberg announced that it was focusing its production exclusively on chenille garments, forgoing the manufacture of bedspreads, which during the previous two years had already become a smaller part of its output. The *Dalton News* framed the decision in patriotic terms, explaining, "Due to government restrictions on the temperature of buildings and the shortage of fuel oil, the demand for chenille garments is far exceeding production facilities, as the chenille robe is unquestionably the outstanding practical robe on today's market for warmth and serviceability." The newspaper added, "Mr. Rauschenberg feels that under such conditions the company will be contributing more toward the war effort by devoting the entire production of the plant to the manufacture of these essential garments," though he hoped to make spreads again after the war.[43]

In 1943 Arthur Richman demonstrated Blue Ridge Spread's continued interest early in the war in robe production by patenting a group of four chenille robe designs for the company. On each, a playing card suit motif (clubs, diamonds, spades, or hearts) is repeated in a row along the bottom, centered on the back, and used as a pocket. The chenille rows form inverted chevrons

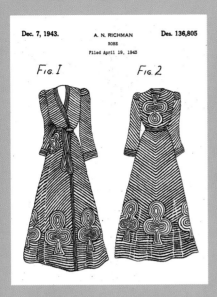

Chenille robe, U.S. patent design by A. N. (Arthur) Richman, filed April 19, 1943, granted December 7, 1943, des. 136,805

Chenille robe, U.S. patent design by A. N. (Arthur) Richman, filed April 19, 1943, granted December 7, 1943, des. 136,806

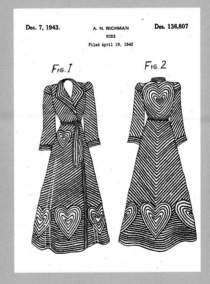

Chenille robe, U.S. patent design by A. N. (Arthur) Richman, filed April 19, 1943, granted December 7, 1943, des. 136,807

Chenille robe, U.S. patent design by A. N. (Arthur) Richman, filed April 19, 1943, granted December 7, 1943, des. 136,808

Four Queens
CHENILLE ROBES

for that PIN-UP GIRL glamour!

You'll always be his queen when you have that *youthful,* tailored look
that a beautifully washable FOUR QUEENS robe gives you. We are
still trying to make shipments of FOUR QUEENS to at least one store
in each city so that you may have *yours.* All of the popular colors are
still manufactured. Every clever pre-war stitch still goes into each FOUR
QUEENS style to assure continued fine quality! Each
of the four styles is PATENTED for your full protection against imitations . . . Moderately priced . . .
Sizes 12 through 20.

BLUE RIDGE MFG. CO.
DALTON, GEORGIA

Advertisement for Blue Ridge Manufacturing,
November 1944, *Glamour*

down in the back, with a wide border of horizontal rows along the bottom. The motifs were worked into the overall chenille pattern (not overlaid). Richman filed for patents in April 1943, and was granted them in December, after "a considerable portion of [Blue Ridge's] manufacturing facilities" was turned over to war production.[44]

Blue Ridge featured the heart-motif robe in an ad that appeared in *Glamour* magazine: "Four Queens Chenille Robes for that Pin-Up Girl glamour!" At the top of the ad, a seated woman wearing the heart-motif robe looks back over her shoulder, surrounded by an ornate picture frame. From the bottom of the ad, a soldier gazes up at her. The text between the images conveys stylishness: "You'll always be his queen when you have that *youthful,* tailored look that a beautifully washable FOUR QUEENS robe gives you." It also addresses the realities of the market: "We are still trying to make shipments of FOUR QUEENS to at least one store in each city so that you may have *yours.* All of the popular colors are still manufactured. Every clever pre-war stitch still goes into each FOUR QUEENS style to assure continued fine quality!"[45] Blue Ridge's heart-motif robe also appeared in ads in the *Atlanta Constitution* in 1943, when it was presented as an ideal "heating system," and in late 1945, when it was promoted as "made in Georgia."[46]

The ad in *Glamour* highlighted the fact that the design was patented: "Each of the four styles is PATENTED for your full protection against imitations." The patent did not prevent other companies from manufacturing similar heart-themed robes, however, and several variations of the design predate and postdate the patent. For example, the Adrian Evans line included a nearly identical robe in June 1944, promoted as having been advertised in *Mademoiselle*.[47]

Many of the large chenille plants eventually converted at least partly to war production. The *Dalton News* reported that the first chenille company to receive a defense contract was Superior Textiles in North Vernon, Indiana, which switched from exclusively producing chenille bath sets to dividing its production evenly between the bath sets and various canvas items for the military.[48] Blue Ridge began making fragmentation bomb parachutes, insect bars (mosquito nets), and mattress covers around September 1943 and by 1945 the company was making sleeping bag covers and WAC (Women's Army Corps) uniforms as well.[49] Other companies that manufactured robes also took on war contracts. Lawtex made army uniforms, clothing for Lend-Lease (a federal program initiated to share goods with other Allied countries), and textiles used by the navy for mattress covers and pillow covers. LaRose made insect bars, head nets, barrack bags, and "half tents" shelters, while G. H. Rauschenberg manufactured olive drab handkerchiefs for the army.[50]

B. J. Bandy's company in Cartersville continued producing chenille into 1944 but was forced to turn away buyers "almost every day" because of the limited availability of materials and workers.[51] By the beginning of 1945 it had become increasingly difficult for plants to continue even limited chenille production, as war restrictions tightened. Specifically, the War Production Board (WPB) prohibited the use of tufting yarn for chenille, stating that the yarn was needed for the production of cotton duck and duck substitutes.[52] The ban lasted from mid-January through late March, when the WPB allowed a forty-five-day window in which companies could use the inventory of yarn they had on hand, though some companies had no yarn, others had no employees, and paperwork requirements provided additional obstacles. When the yarn was completely released from restrictions later in the year, the industry still faced the lack of ready supplies of sheeting.

Demand for chenille robes did not cease during the war years, though, and in 1944 an unnamed manufacturer of children's wear from New York advertised in the *Dalton News* that it wanted to contact a local manufacturer of chenille housecoats, stating, "Can use all or part of your production for entire year."[53] Also, surprisingly, in the fall of 1944, as the industry struggled with war restrictions, S. J. Williams opened his Chenille Shop (also called Williams Chenille Company) at the corner of North Highland and Ponce

Pacific Chenille Craft and SuperTex of Australia

Chenille production was not limited to Georgia, or even to the United States. Wyche reported that by 1948 the industry had spread to Canada, England, Australia, New Zealand, Africa, India, and South America.[a] Australia, in particular, had a thriving chenille industry, and the leading manufacturer was Pacific Chenille Craft, later renamed SuperTex of Australia (there are numerous permutations of the names).

Australian newspapers mention candlewick bedspreads by the late 1920s, with one article even giving detailed instructions on how to make them.[b] By the late 1930s, chenille garments imported from the United States were popular. The *Adelaide Advertiser* reported in 1939, "Beach coats have a distinctive new note in their American design, showing candlewick stripes, some of which are diagonal, worked to a diamond design on the back, and others with circular bands." It also described a "coat-frock" with a flared skirt and short-sleeved bodice by Polly Prentiss.[c] As late as 1950 Australian ads continued to connect chenille to Georgia, and one states that Pacific Super-Tex Chenille "originated in Georgia some 130 years ago," likely referring to the early-nineteenth-century candlewick spreads that inspired the birth of the chenille industry.[d]

The *Goulburn Evening Post* reported that two Americans brought Pacific Chenille Craft to Australia in 1940, but it did not provide details.[e] Telephone and city directories for Los Angeles indicate that Pacific Chenille Craft existed there by 1939, was owned by M. L. Hopkinson and Owen W. Schaeffer, and manufactured chenille robes, sportswear, spreads, rugs, and drapes.[f] The 1940 U.S. Census lists Owen's wife Frances Schaeffer (who patented a robe design) as a chenille designer.

The *Dalton Citizen* reported in 1947 that Pacific Chenille Craft used the trade name "SuperTex of Australia," and advertisements support the idea that SuperTex was a product line name for Pacific Chenille Craft at least early in its history.[g] Pacific Chenille Craft formally changed its name to SuperTex Industries Ltd. in 1954, though the name SuperTex appears in ads prior to that change, as early as 1941, in connection with chenille, and the names appear together on some ads in the late 1940s.[h] The name SuperTex may have predated the expansion of Pacific Chenille Craft to Australia, as one early jacket has a label with both "Pacific Chenille-Craft" and "SuperTex of California."

Pacific Chenille Craft (SuperTex) operated factories in numerous cities, including Sydney, Goulburn, Newcastle, and Yass, and it was especially successful in the 1950s, slightly later than the pinnacle of chenille's popularity in the United States. Another company, Jeldi, which manufactured robes and spreads and was acquired by SuperTex in the late 1980s, advertised itself in 1951 as the first company to manufacture chenille in Australia.[i]

Pacific Chenille Craft (SuperTex) manufactured spreads and garments with designs that appear to have been created on single-needle machines as well as overlay designs on tufted yardage. By 1947 the company even hosted a chenille week for a "world premiere of its 1948 fashions in dressing gowns, beach coats and bedspreads."[j] The company promoted itself as high-fashion, advertising in 1950, "There is only one Christian Dior in Paris . . . and only one name in chenille, Pacific Super-Tex of Australia."[k] The flexibility of the terms "candlewick" and "chenille" persisted across the globe, and an ad for Pacific Chenille-Craft/SuperTex from 1947 for chenille robes or dressing gowns notes that they came in both "candlewick chenille" and "the new light-weight *Baby* Chenille," though by 1947 they almost certainly were all made by machine.[l]

In the 1940s and 1950s Australia produced a wide variety of chenille garments, including ice-skating costumes, jerkins, and fitted jackets with zippers, in addition to regular jackets, capes, and robes.[m] Ads in *Australian Women's Weekly* suggest that Pacific Chenille Craft was more daring in its robe designs than its counterparts in Northwest Georgia, employing more all-over patterns and large geometrics in addition to the typical, restrained florals and scrolls. Also, wraparound style robes with side ties appear more often in Australian ads than in ones for chenille robes made in the United States.

When marketing garments, Pacific Chenille Craft/SuperTex repeatedly drew upon the allure of Hollywood by advertising that their garments

were "designed in Hollywood," and some ads list Hollywood as one of the company's locations. One has the words "Fashioned on the film sets of Hollywood," while another claims, "There's a jauntiness . . . a gay holiday air about these smart new Pacific SUPERTEX Chenille Beach Coats that is typically Californian . . . and because they are made up in genuine American Candlewick Chenille they are as practical as they are beautiful."[n]

Leo P. Keating, chairman of the directors (or managing director) of Pacific Chenille Craft in Australia visited Dalton several times. The *Dalton Citizen* reported on a visit by Keating in 1947 to study chenille manufacturing operations and to

Advertisement, Pacific Super-Tex of Australia, *Australian Women's Weekly*, October 21, 1953, courtesy of *Australian Women's Weekly*/Bauer Media Limited

Advertisement, SuperTex of Australia, *Australian Women's Weekly*, March 29, 1941, courtesy of *Australian Women's Weekly*/Bauer Media Limited

Chenille feature, *Australian Women's Weekly*,
July 26, 1941, courtesy of *Australian Women's Weekly*/Bauer
Media Limited

Advertisement, Pacific Super-Tex of Australia, *Australian
Women's Weekly*, March 18, 1950, courtesy of *Australian
Women's Weekly*/Bauer Media Limited

purchase skip-stitch machines.° The newspaper
noted that he had been buying machines from
the Crook Brothers in Dalton for the past six
years, and that prior to his current visit to Dalton
he had traveled to the West Coast, Chicago, and
New York to evaluate demand for chenille in large
department stores. The newspaper observed that
while chenille manufacturers in the United States
faced limited supplies of yarn and sheeting during
the war, Australian factories had faced "less serious
hardships."ᴾ The Goulburn newspaper reported on
a later trip by Keating to visit chenille factories in
America in 1953. q

Leonard Lorberbaum recalled a visit to Lawtex by
someone from a company in Australia, who "asked

to go through the plant and see what he could
see." Lorberbaum explained, "I figured he was no
competition being in Australia, and I didn't envision
our being competition to him, and I showed him
around."ʳ Betti Brooker Denson, whose family was
involved in the chenille industry in Dalton, also
recalled a chenille company in Australia: "They had
some beautiful designs. . . . Two of the men from
Australia, they alternated, Hugh James and I forget
the other man's name . . . would come by here, one
of 'em one year and one of 'em next year . . . they
went around the world checking textile designs,
machinery, and everything."ˢ

a   Murray E. Wyche, "The Tufted Textile Industry in the South," 1948, 2, Bedspread Industry box, Articles on History, Companies, and Machinery folder, Crown Gardens & Archives.

b   "Fluffy Tufts," *Brisbane (Australia) Queenslander*, October 17, 1929.

c   Betty Ann, "Play Suits—in Gay Colors," *Adelaide (Australia) Advertiser*, October 13, 1939.

d   Advertisement, Pacific Super-Tex Chenille, "How Lovely She'll Look in Chenille," *Geraldton (Australia) Guardian*, August 12, 1950.

e   "Minister on Housing, Its Importance in Relation to Decentralisation," *Goulburn (Australia) Evening Post*, July 20, 1948.

f   Los Angeles telephone directory, 1939; Los Angeles city directory, 1942; advertisement for workers, *California Eagle* (Los Angeles), May 6, 1943.

g   "Dalton Attracts Many Interested in Chenille Plants," *Dalton Citizen*, October 16, 1947.

h   The names appear in a variety of formats, including "Pacific Chenille-Craft," "Super-tex," "Supertex," "SuperTex," and "Pacific Super-Tex of Australia."

i   See, for example, advertisement, Jeldi, *West Australian* (Perth), October 8, 1951. Sydney's Powerhouse Museum's website states that SuperTex at one point exported eighty thousand chenille bathrobes per year to the United States, where they were sold in major department stores including Saks, Bergdorf Goodman, and Neiman Marcus. Object 98/130/1 Bathrobe, women's, Jeldi Manufacturing, Sydney, Australia, Powerhouse Museum Collection, http://www.powerhousemuseum.com /collection/database/?irn=161178.

j   "Chenille Week in Goulburn," *Goulburn (Australia) Evening Post*, November 18, 1947.

k   Advertisement, Pacific Super-Tex of Australia, *Australian Women's Weekly*, March 18, 1950, 14.

l   Advertisement, Pacific Chenille-Craft/Super-Tex, "Flashed by Cable from Hollywood," *Australian Women's Weekly*, April 19, 1947, 14.

m   "Chenille . . . in Brand-New Styles for the Smartest Occasions," *Australian Women's Weekly*, July 26, 1941.

n   Advertisement, Pacific Chenille-Craft/Super-Tex, "Fashioned on the Film Sets of Hollywood," *Australian Women's Weekly*, February 28, 1948, 27; advertisement, Pacific Chenille-Craft/Super-Tex, "California's Most Colorful Beach Coats," *Australian Women's Weekly*, October 8, 1947, 8.

o   Leslie Bellamy, from Surrey, England, paid a similar visit to Dalton in 1946, observing factories and purchasing machines. "England Learns about Chenille from Dalton," *Atlanta Journal*, reprinted in "Chenille Business Is One of Georgia's Newest and Best Sources of Revenue," *Georgia Progress* 3, no. 4 (October 1, 1946).

p   "Dalton Attracts Many Interested in Chenille Plants," *Dalton Citizen*, October 16, 1947.

q   "Mr. Leo Keating in America," *Goulburn (Australia) Evening Post*, July 22, 1953.

r   Cheryl Wykoff, "Lawtex Corporation," based on Wykoff's interview of Leonard Lorberbaum, April 18, 1988, Wykoff's chenille bedspread oral history notebook, Crown Gardens & Archives.

s   Cheryl Wykoff, "Brooker Spread Company," based on Wykoff's interview of Joe Billy Denson and Betti Brooker Denson, February 6, 1989, Wykoff's chenille bedspread oral history notebook, Crown Gardens & Archives.

J. W. Bray Company

By 1930 James Wellborn Bray Sr. (1904–85) was the proprietor in Dalton of a shoe repair shop, a business he operated for over a decade. He was a creative tinkerer, and his son, James Wellborn Bray Jr., bragged that his father could "take the right shoe and make a left shoe out of it."[a] James Wellborn Bray Sr. also was involved with the local government, serving as tax commissioner from 1940 to at least 1951. Bray worked as a shoe repairman while the chenille business was flourishing and found a way to combine his specific skills with the popular—and readily available—textile. He first incorporated chenille into footwear in his basement, where he used discarded two-by-fours and a handsaw to make wooden clogs to which he added chenille tops using tacks from his shoe shop. Initially he gathered chenille scraps from the trash or got castoffs from the mills, and he gave his early experiments as gifts to friends and family.[b] As his business grew, he moved to his garage, then to a dedicated building. In 1945, Bray founded the J. W. Bray Company as a manufacturer of chenille "scuffies" or "scuffs" (both period terms for "slippers"). Like other chenille garments, the scuffies first appeared at spreadlines on the highway. Bray's son recalled that as owners of the small shops on

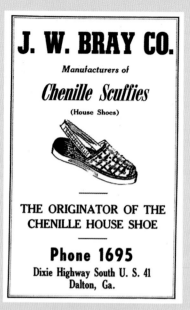

Advertisement for J. W. Bray Company, *Polk's Dalton City Directory*, 1953

Chenille scuffy, J. W. Bray Co., 1940s, unidentified photographer (possibly Ward's Photo Service, Dalton, Georgia), courtesy of Betty Talley

Bedspread Boulevard heard about the scuffies, more and more "began asking for them."[c]

Early in the company's history, to make scuffies Bray cut the parts by hand and glued the layers of the soles together by running them through rollers on old-fashioned washing machines. His grandson, James Wellborn Bray III, recalls hearing stories about how Bray would wake up at "two or three in the morning to cut out materials so that the ladies would have materials to sew during the day."[d] By the late 1960s, the company used die presses instead of scissors to cut out parts and glued them together with a laminating machine. The business grew in the 1950s and 1960s, and even into the 1970s, and Bray's scuffies were sold from spreadlines, department stores, and catalogs, including J. C. Penney, Montgomery Ward, and Sears, Roebuck.

Sears was supportive and worked closely with the company, and it presented J. W. Bray with a "Symbol of Excellence" award in 1973. One of the company's first large accounts and best customers was the James Company of Hickory, North Carolina.[c] By the 1960s the J. W. Bray Company had three hundred employees, produced up to one thousand pairs of slippers a day, and proclaimed, "We try softer" (the company's motto). James Wellborn Bray Sr.'s son, a skilled salesman, joined him in the early 1950s, and his grandson Jim joined the company in 1979.

According to Jim Bray, the J. W. Bray Company started with the approach of high volume and low margin, meaning that it sold large quantities of slippers but only made a small profit from each unit, a model the company followed for many years. The company worked with numerous chenille manufacturers to offer coordinated items (at least by the mid-1950s). Other companies would send or sell

Children's chenille scuffies by J. W. Bray Co. for the James Company, ca. 1950, private collection, photograph by Michael McKelvey

it tufted yardage that Bray would use to make scuffies that matched each company's robes. Bray revived this practice in the 1990s when it worked with the California-based Damze Company and its Canyon Group line of robes.[f]

Jim Bray explains that while chenille got his grandfather into the business, the company had to diversify. As the tufted textile industry shifted its focus from chenille to carpet, Bray adjusted his products as well, even producing some slippers with soles made of carpet. The company mostly stopped making chenille scuffies by about 1980, but it continued making slippers of other materials. As more imported slippers entered the U.S. market in the 1980s, the company shifted to a low-volume, high-margin approach, making higher-end luxury slippers, such as mink slippers that it sold to Neiman Marcus, and other specialty slippers, including ones printed with a design by noted Northwest Georgia folk artist Howard Finster, whom J. W. Bray Jr. had befriended through his work as a journalist. The family took pride in offering products that were made in the United States. Eventually unable to compete with low-cost imports, the J. W. Bray Company closed around 2000.[g]

a Nina Diamond, "People Have a Way of Walking All over Town," *Chattanooga Times*, October 26, 1975.
b Information page from J. W. Bray Company, Inc., in Wykoff's chenille bedspread oral history notebook, Crown Gardens & Archives; Pam Jenkins, "J. W. Bray Co. a Leader in Footwear," *Dalton Daily Citizen-News*, February 28, 1983.
c Diamond, "People Have a Way of Walking."
d James Wellborn Bray III, interview by author, December 23, 2012, Dalton, Georgia.
e James Wellborn Bray III, e-mail to author, January 28, 2013.
f After the J. W. Bray Company closed, Damze reluctantly had slippers made in China. Don Chapman, e-mail to author, January 24, 2013.
g James Wellborn Bray III interview.

de Leon Avenues in Atlanta. He carried bedspreads, robes, mats, and toys such as stuffed animals, both hand tufted and machine made.[54] His business lasted until at least 1946.[55] Prices for robes during the war ranged from about $3 to $8, or about $40–$110 in 2014.

During the war years and the years leading up to the war, several thrifty entrepreneurs found novel uses for the leftovers produced by the chenille industry, developing successful companies around the manufacture of chenille slippers (which had appeared on the market by at least the late 1930s, as chenille robes became popular) and dolls. Multiple individuals and companies made these items, but the main manufacturer of slippers was J. W. Bray in Dalton, and one of the leading producers of dolls was the Mary-Anne Novelty Company in Cartersville. While manufacturers that included garments and rugs in their production often advertised "chenille products," as opposed to just "chenille spreads," manufacturers and retailers that ventured into even less-expected items, like slippers and dolls, typically advertised "chenille novelties."

Postwar Robes

Challenges and Growth

As the chenille garment industry matured after the war, manufacturers of robes faced new obstacles from the Office of Price Administration (OPA), a short-lived government agency intended to regulate unstable prices during the war years. The TTMA challenged the OPA's claim that chenille robes fell under the agency's Maximum Price Regulation No. 570.[56] In an article in February 1946 critical of the OPA's pricing methods, the *Christian Science Monitor*'s Harold Fleming wrote, "Most of the chenille robe makers are in Georgia and for a while they didn't know they were subject to MAP [Maximum Average Price regulations]. Then OPA told them they were. But their average MAP price is $2.25, and the lowest at which they can break even is $3.25. So they are all changing over to bedspreads, which are not subject to MAP. But meantime, 12,000 chenille robes are now available at $7.00— in the black market."[57] Following a meeting between the TTMA and OPA in Atlanta in April 1946, Arthur Richman explained, "The chenille industry . . . is unique in that it has more labor costs than any other textile industry. Thirty-one different operations . . . go into making a chenille robe, which requires more handling than any other garment manufactured." He also cited the indirect costs of "maintenance of 'homemade' machines, laundry

Woman wearing
a chenille robe,
ca. 1950, found
photograph, private
collection

Woman wearing a chenille robe in the snow,
ca. 1950, found photograph, private collection

and dyeing and the bulk of the garment itself, which requires more floor
space as well as increased packing and shipping costs."[58] The MAP program
ended in 1946 and the OPA was abolished in May 1947.

The industry also experienced difficulties in the immediate postwar years
as large numbers of inexperienced operators manufactured inferior chenille
products, flooding the market with cheap, undesirable goods. The challenges of fluctuating orders resulting from the addition of low-quality robes
to the market were compounded by inconsistent availability of materials
during these years.[59] The *Wall Street Journal* reported that by the fall of 1947,
though, the "'fly-by-night' operators [were] rapidly going out of business."[60]

Despite these challenges, the robe industry grew. Wyche reported that
robes accounted for 22 million dollars "of the 122 million dollar volume
done by the [chenille] industry" in 1946, and he said that robe production
increased over 412 percent from 1940 to 1946.[61] According to the TTMA,
the output of robes and housecoats in 1949 was 5,440,000, which was

Sparks, Inc.

One large postwar company to produce chenille robes was Sparks, Inc. William "Bill" Hansel Sparks (1908–79) was born in Georgia and grew up in Cañon City, Colorado, where he ran a movie theater. After it burned, he returned with his young family to Hill City (a Georgia community between Calhoun and Dalton), where his in-laws owned a farm. He worked on the farm for a while, then worked for Redwine and Strain (a chenille business in Hill City) as a designer and for Hy-Way Arts (a chenille business in Calhoun) as a designer and manager. Sparks moved with his family to Dalton in 1941 and began working with G. H. Rauschenberg as a sales manager. Together with Carter Pittman, a local attorney and president of the TTMA from 1945–47, by 1945 he established Sparks-Pittman Company, which manufactured garments, rugs, spreads, and novelties. They set aside a space in the factory for Charlie Gish to make chenille toys, and Gish soon formally joined the company.[a] Sparks bought out his partners and established Sparks, Inc., in 1947, making robes and bedspreads.[b]

An ad in the 1951 Dalton city directory states the company's motto ("Quality, Service, Dependability"), presents its trademark ("It's a Spar-kay Chenille"), and lists offices in New York, Chicago, and Los Angeles.[c] Sparks, like many of the other leaders in the chenille industry, was friendly with his peers, loaning materials if another company ran short, and, as his daughter Alice Young recalls, engaging with every employee when he entered his building each morning.

In the early 1950s Sparks bought a chenille company in Calhoun called Mayfair Chenilles, selling enough equipment from it to cover the cost of the building and still having plenty of machines remaining. In 1953–55 Sparks and Mayfair advertised jointly, listing Sparks in Dalton and Mayfair Chenilles in Calhoun.[d] Sparks served as president of the TTMA from 1957–58.

Jewell Ponder, a secretary at Sparks, Inc., modeling a chenille robe next to racks of robes, early 1950s, collection of Alice Sparks Young

Sparks's son Wilbur Hugh Sparks (1928–83), also known as Bill, became president of Sparks, Inc., in 1958. By 1963 the company made chenille robes and terrycloth robes as well as beach jackets and small rugs. It also made scuffies, which it sold paired with children's robes.[e] Sparks's biggest customers included Sears and Montgomery Ward, and the company typically added labels for large customers (with the customer's name) to the robes, using just size labels for smaller clients. At a later date, probably in the late 1960s, Buck Creek Industries of Birmingham, Alabama, bought Sparks, Inc.

Women modeling chenille robes at Sparks, Inc., early 1950s, collection of Alice Sparks Young

In May 1955 Collins and Aikman of New York purchased Mayfair Chenilles and moved a portion of its operations to a new plant in Dalton, with the rest moving in February 1958. Collins and Aikman's Mayfair Division produced tufted automotive fabrics, scatter rugs, and apparel fabrics.[f] Bill Sparks Sr. became a vice president of Collins and Aikman in 1959, retiring in 1967.[g]

a Vivian Sparks (daughter-in-law of William Hansel Sparks), telephone conversation with author, September 24, 2013; "Industrialist Sparks Dies," *Dalton Daily Citizen*, May 2, 1979.

b Advertisement, Sparks-Pittman Company, *Southern Israelite*, June 22, 1945; advertisement, Sparks, Inc., Progress Edition, *Dalton Citizen-News*, March 30, 1963; "Industrialist Sparks Dies," *Dalton Daily Citizen*, May 2, 1979. An ad from October 1947 still lists Sparks-Pittman, so the change must have occurred late that year. Advertisement, Sparks-Pittman Company, Centennial Edition, *Dalton Citizen*, October 16, 1947. An ad from 1958 describes Sparks, Inc., as "creators of robe fashions for over 17 years," placing the starting date in 1941, the year Sparks moved to Dalton. Advertisement, Sparks, Inc., "Wise Buyers Know," *Tufted Textile Manufacturers Association Directory, 1958* (Dalton, Ga.: Tufted Textile Manufacturers Association, 1958), 126.

c Advertisement, Sparks, Inc., *Polk's Dalton City Directory* (Richmond, Va.: R. L. Polk, 1951), 101.

d Advertisement, Sparks, Inc., and Mayfair Chenilles, Inc., *Polk's Dalton City Directory* (Richmond, Va.: R. L. Polk, 1953), 116; advertisement, Sparks-Mayfair, *Tufted Textile Manufacturers Association Directory, 1954* (Dalton, Ga.: Tufted Textile Manufacturers Association, 1954), 81; advertisement, Sparks-Mayfair, *Tufted Textile Manufacturers Association Directory, 1955* (Dalton, Ga.: Tufted Textile Manufacturers Association, 1955), 110.

e Advertisement, Sparks, Inc., Progress Edition, *Dalton Citizen-News*, March 30, 1963; Alice Young, e-mail to author, September 29, 2013.

f "Togetherness Applies to Dalton and C&A, Says Bill Sparks," Progress Edition, *Dalton Daily Citizen-News*, March 30, 1963.

g Vivian Sparks (daughter-in-law of William Hansel Sparks), interview by author, July 25, 2013, Dalton, Georgia; Alice Young (daughter of William Hansel Sparks), telephone conversation with author, September 24, 2013; Alice Young, e-mail to author, September 29, 2013; William H. Sparks Retirement Dinner invitation, November 28, 1967, collection of Alice Young; "Sparks Named Collins-Aikman Vice President," *Southern Textile News*, March 21, 1959.

"slightly more than a six percent gain over 1946."[62] In its 1950 directory, the TTMA ran a selection of chenille robe ads along with a letter from the Adam, Meldrum and Anderson Company (AM&A) department store in Buffalo, New York, that reported to Blue Ridge Spread Company on its spectacular sales. AM&A said it had sold two thousand units in two days and that the Federal Reserve had called the store to check the increase in its profits since "it was so phenomenal."[63]

Manufacturing Chenille Robes

A key development in the growth of the chenille robe industry was the invention of yardage machines prior to the war and their extensive employment after the war. With multi-needle yardage machines, companies could quickly tuft lengths of sheeting that they then cut into pieces to be assembled into robes. In 1948 Wyche said that yardage machines had been "the greatest development in the robe industry," and he cited their chief use as in the robe factories.[64] He explained, "In the beginning, the narrow sheeting used was first sewn with a single-needle machine, an operation that consumed much time and labor." He credited Harry Nicholas of Duchess Chenilles with conceiving the idea of the multi-needle yardage machines, adding, "Now, with the yardage machine one operator can do the work of dozens with the old single-needle machine, sewing seams straighter and at considerable lower operating costs."[65]

When using chenille yardage, manufacturers often added overlay designs. Generally this would involve stamping a pattern onto the back of tufted yardage (either flat or partially assembled into a robe), then using a single-needle (or sometimes a small multi-needle) machine to embroider the additional design. The overlay designs could be executed in the same color as the rest of the robe (or added before the robe was dyed) or in one or more contrasting colors. The industry also developed special machines that automatically executed particular patterns, such as scrolls or flowers. Overlay likely originated along with the yardage machines, but it became popular after World War II, and the technique is mentioned in ads by 1949. Most overlay designs for women's robes were scrolls, flowers, or bows. Children's robes, especially after the war, featured a variety of animals and characters including Mickey Mouse, Puss in Boots, Jack and Jill, and Rudolph the Red-Nosed Reindeer. Even large companies with access to yardage machines, though, still produced some robes into the 1950s in the older style of decoration

Model wearing a
chenille robe with
an overlay design,
ca. 1953, courtesy
of Bandy Heritage
Center for Northwest
Georgia, Carpet
and Rug Institute
Photograph Collection.
Handwritten on back:
"Max Levine, Coll.
Hotel, 7. W. 35th St."

Child wearing a chenille robe with Puss in Boots motif, December 1954, found photograph, private collection

using single-needle machines, with the design worked into the chenille pattern rather than added as overlay.

In 1947, WSB radio in Atlanta covered Dalton's chenille industry, including interviews with employees in an unidentified factory, in its *Forward Georgia* series. A worker explained to the reporter:

"We take a roll of sheeting and run it back and forth on this long table until we have more than a hundred thicknesses. Then we trace patterns on the top sheet. After that, the patterns are cut through all the sheets at the same time by an electric knife. . . . Incidentally, tufts have already been put in this sheeting in parallel rows by a machine that tufts 72 rows at a time. When the different parts of the robe have been cut out, they're sent on to girls at sewing machines who assemble them." The reporter then went to one of the seamstresses, who described her role: "My job is to take the different parts of the robe from the cutting table and sew them together into the complete garment. . . . After that, the robe is usually sent to the marking table for an additional pattern for tufting and then on to the tufting machines. . . . After the robes and spreads have been inspected, they're ready for the laundry." At the laundry the products were dyed, bleached, or just laundered. They were washed to remove markings, spun in machines to remove most of the water, dried in special dryers that fluffed the tufts, then trimmed of any loose threads. The same basic process persisted for the duration of chenille robes' popularity, with ongoing improvements in the size and quality of the machines.[66]

Businesses in Dalton sometimes improvised when it came to fitting and modeling robes. Fred Rosen shared a story about an employee of LaRose who announced to the front office that a truck had arrived with "a bunch of artificial women" and asked what the company was going to do with them. It turned out that they were mannequins, according to Rosen, "one size 14 and . . . a size 40." Rosen explained, "When we finished the robe, the designer was able to put it on the model and see if it fit properly."[67] Some companies used live models. When interviewed in 1996, Patsy Cooper said that when her father worked at Lawtex and her family lived adjacent to the factory, she was asked sometimes to model children's housecoats when buyers from New York arrived.[68] Family and friends also sometimes modeled for promotional photographs. These included young Linda Saul, who modeled a child's robe for her parents' company, Queen Chenille; Laurice Looper (Swann), who as

Model wearing chenille robe with an overlay design, ca. 1960, courtesy of Bandy Heritage Center for Northwest Georgia, Carpet and Rug Institute Photograph Collection

Child's chenille robe with Donald Duck design, ca. late 1940s, cotton, 39½ inches long, collection of Peter and Sandy Loose-Schrantz, photograph by Michael McKelvey. Label: "Pacific / Chenille Craft Co., / ©Walt Disney Productions." In this early robe, the design is worked into the chenille pattern rather than added as an overlay.

Detail, advertisement, Montgomery Ward, November 26, 1950, *Sunday Press* (Binghamton, N.Y.)

R. P. Bailey Chenille Company

R. P. Bailey Chenille, a small business, focused on robes. Before starting his company, Robert Paul Bailey (1900–1980) worked for the Westcott Hosiery Mills in Dalton. Then, during the Depression, he tried unsuccessfully to run a farm, while his wife hand tufted for one of the candlewick companies, possibly the B. J. Bandy Company. After the war started Bailey moved to Cincinnati to work in a defense plant, finally saving enough money to return and start his business.[a] The company existed from 1945 until 1958, based in a building behind his house on U.S. 41. He employed approximately ten people. He used sheeting that was fairly thin and not of especially high quality, and machines that had about six needles. The operators ran the fabric back and forth to produce tufted yardage (white on white), then stacked sheets on a large table, placed the pattern on top (a tissue pattern, like the ones made by Butterick, that Bailey bought at the store), cut out the pieces with an electric saw, sewed them together, and had them dyed. When the robes returned from being dyed, workers stamped the designs for the overlay tufting and added the flowers or swirls with single-needle machines. Often he had home tufters sew the overlay patterns. The company included peacock spreads and robes in its inventory.

Bailey sold his robes and small rugs primarily through three roadside gift shops in Horse Cave, Cave City, and Elizabethtown, Kentucky, all on the Dixie Highway, although he sometimes filled orders from a few other small stores. He packed them in his station wagon, along with other gift items he selected in Atlanta, and delivered them to the people who ran the shops for him. Bailey also made a wool jacket, in red, green, or white, with chenille decorations of Mexicana themes—one of which was sold to actor Cesar Romero for his wife.[b] Bailey discontinued his business in 1958.

a Vivian Sparks, daughter of R.P. Bailey, interview by author, July 25, 2013, Dalton, Georgia.
b The wool jackets sold by Bailey were similar to the ones that survive today with labels reading "La Muchacha / Shepherd Bros. Mfg. Co. / Calhoun, Ga. / 100% Wool / Dry Clean Only."

Queen Chenille

Queen Chenille, one of the major chenille companies established after World War II, stands out for its initial focus on children's robes. Harry Saul (1908–94), its founder, was born in Hartwell, Georgia, then lived in Atlanta and Miami before arriving in Dalton in 1939. He and his wife Helen (1908–84) operated Saul's Department Store in downtown Dalton, which carried clothing and shoes as well as Boy Scout uniforms and merit badges. They lost their lease after the war, though, when the owner's son, named Paul, returned home and took over the space, changing the "S" in the "Saul's" sign to "P." They moved to a new location, but in 1947 their new landlord's son returned home wanting to open a business at an established location, and they lost their lease again. The Sauls then decided to expand what they had started as a part-time chenille robe business into a full-time venture, and they established Queen Chenille.[a] They had purchased a small chenille operation in Dalton from C. T. Pratt the previous year for $1,750, which included three eight-needle machines, seven single-needle machines, a serger, and a few other pieces of equipment.[b]

When interviewed in 1988, Harry Saul explained that he started with children's robes because he discerned an opening in the market for them, and "that's where I felt like I had more experience."[c] In an article on a leading British robe manufacturer, Pasolds, social anthropologist Kaori O'Connor discusses the importance of children's robes after the war as coveted symbols of idyllic childhood and as a market response to the postwar baby boom. This indicates that the consumer interest Saul sensed was not limited to the United States and was a result of cultural changes after World War II.[d] To make robes, both children's and women's, Queen Chenille's employees used the eight-needle machines to run yardage that they cut, sewed, and dyed. Queen's robes usually featured pretty floral or scroll overlay designs, as well as peacocks.

Queen began with eight employees and the slogan "Fit for a Queen." It focused first on making robes, selling to department stores and mail-order businesses (including Macy's, Gimbels, May, Sears, Montgomery Ward, Rich's, and Davison's) as well as to spreadlines, then expanded production to include bedspreads and bathroom sets and later scatter rugs and Glo-Coater pads for Johnson's Floor Wax.[e]

Queen Chenille became Queen Carpet by 1969 at the urging of the Sauls' son Julian, who joined the company in 1963, and Queen Carpet merged with Shaw Industries in 1998.[f]

a Randall L. Patton, *Shaw Industries: A History* (Athens: University of Georgia Press, 2002), 163–64.
b Receipt/Inventory, C. T. Pratt Chenille Company, Dalton, Georgia, May, 15, 1946, collection of Julian Saul.
c Cheryl Wykoff, "Harry Saul, Queen Chenille," based on Wykoff's interview of Saul, June 16, 1988, Wykoff's chenille bedspread oral history notebook, Crown Gardens & Archives.
d Kaori O'Connor, "The Ladybird, the Dressing Gown and Pasolds: Cultural Icons of the 'Golden Age' of British Childhood," *Textile History* 42, no. 1 (May 2011): 28, 30.
e "The Beginning," Queen Carpet, 1946–96, fiftieth anniversary brochure, Queen folder, Carpet and Rug Institute Records, box 1 of 8, 2011.2, MSS 006, Bandy Heritage Center for Northwest Georgia.
f Julian Saul, interview by author, June 6, 2013, Dalton, Georgia; Karen Diamond, text for Queen Carpet from the exhibition *Main, Market and Beyond: Yesterday's Local Jewish Merchants*, Jewish Cultural Center, Chattanooga, Tennessee, 2013.

Woman wearing a "shorty" chenille robe, ca. 1945, found photograph, private collection

a teenager modeled a robe used in a 1941 Looper's ad by her uncle, Glenn Looper; and Vivian Sparks, who modeled a robe by her father-in-law's company, Sparks, in 1957.[69]

After the war, most of the robes reflected the cinched waist and full skirt look popular at the time, with less pronounced shoulders. Wyche acknowledged that "in styling they have kept pace with fashion's new look."[70] Though the majority of robes were still full-length wraparounds, usually with belt ties and wide lapel collars, there was some variety. "Shorty" (knee-length) robes were introduced and promoted as "ideal for at-home, travel, or beachwear."[71] Lawtex made a beach robe in 1948 of its "Candlewick Washenille," a thigh-length jacket-like garment with "cute frontier-type fringed yoke and cuffs."[72] Also, for many years after the war, robes came in a rainbow of colors. In 1951 the TTMA highlighted the advertising benefits of this variety, which encouraged prominent displays in department stores and eye-catching color ads in Sunday newspapers.[73] In 1952 the TTMA described robes as "likely items for impulse buying" and stressed the importance of attractive displays.[74] Prices for chenille robes between the end of the war and about 1953 ranged from $3 to $8, or about $30–$80 in 2014.

Seasonal Business

An ongoing issue with the chenille robe industry, especially after the war when robes primarily were promoted for use in the home, was that business was seasonal. Fred Rosen explained that it "was strictly a 6 months business [that] started in the summer, June, and ended in November. The next six months it employed a skeleton crew. People that worked in the industry only worked six months of the year. The skeleton crew would be preparing the styling and designs they planned to produce for the following year. And there was no way we could make that into a 12 month business; it was impossible."[75] Norman Reints also recalled how the robes were a seasonal item: "At one time one of our mechanics said it remind[ed] him of a flood. The little stores begin to buy robes in the middle of the summer, the bigger ones, the bigger ones and by Christmas they were a big . . . item.

Christmas 1941

Maxine

Girl wearing a chenille robe and playing an accordion by a Christmas tree, 1941, found photograph, private collection

Girl wearing a chenille robe and playing a toy piano by a Christmas tree, ca. 1950, found photograph, private collection

Will

Girl in a chenille robe in front of a Christmas tree with her brother, 1942, found photograph, private collection

Woman wearing a chenille robe and sitting by a Christmas tree, ca. 1945, found photograph, private collection

They couldn't get enough. [The manufacturers would] run day and night, and Sundays trying to furnish all these stores with robes. Then it was over by January because it was strictly a Christmas item."[76] Victor Ringel, whose father, Mannie Ringel, ran Crowntuft, recalled the company spending half of the year building inventory and the other half disposing of it, a situation that left his father "in fear of a fire, which would have killed the business."[77]

Some businesses tried to balance the winter holiday boom by producing lighter-weight robes that would sell at other times of the year.[78] Henry Ball stated in 1950, "Many [merchants] have promoted lightweight robes in the summer with considerable success, and with new colors, designs, collars and sleeves."[79] The TTMA, though promoting the year-round sales efforts, still embraced the holiday boom: "The multiple tiny tufts of cotton and soft, fluffy appearance of the robes give them a natural winter-holiday appeal. This is emphasized by using the tufted robes as a center of attention in gift windows where they aid in creating the desired holiday atmosphere. Children's departments, especially, find it profitable to give tufted designs a prominent part in holiday displays. They constitute an important gift item from the apparel section during this season."[80]

Wyche noted the move toward lighter fabrics as well and explained that even before the war "the chenille robe industry was switching from 9- and 10-ply yarn"—referring to the thickness of the yarns used to make the tufts—"to 4-ply, which was given the name of 'baby chenille,'" a term that appears in period advertisements.[81] As part of the move to make robes appealing year-round, by 1948 the industry was using an even lighter weight 2-ply yarn, which Wyche said "should make these robes light enough for even the hottest summer weather."[82]

Flammability

Another challenge for the chenille robe industry, especially as it grew larger and subject to increasing regulations, was the issue of flammability. By 1948 the industry was working, with difficulty, to flameproof chenille garments because by then Congress was considering a bill—for the fifth time—that would outlaw the interstate transportation of highly flammable apparel fabrics.[83] Mason Chenille quit making robes when they determined that they could not meet the government's requirements. Reints recalled that it was hard to keep the flame retardant materials in the fabric.[84] When interviewed in 1989, George Hanson, who owned a small chenille business in the 1940s, explained:

Just before the war ended several [women] had gotten burned up wearing chenille robes. There wasn't so many homes with central heat and air condition. They had open fires. People wearing robes would back up to the fire and [a] spark [would] hit it and burn them up before they could get the robe off. Or the heater would get too hot and [start] a flash fire on the bedspread and burn a lot of homes. You couldn't fireproof the yarn, which you had to do, so the government outlawed it. That killed Dalton. . . . None of the mills were running. . . . People were out of work. They had nothing to eat. The plants were down. They closed La Rose Bedspread. They closed down Blue Ridge, Kenner, and Rauschenberg. They were all just about closed up. Only thing they were doing was making a few spreads.[85]

In 1953 the government passed the Flammable Fabrics Act to regulate the manufacture and sale of highly flammable clothing, and flammability continued to be a concern with chenille robes for decades.[86]

Two girls wearing chenille robes, ca. 1950, found photograph, private collection. The girl in front wears an older-style robe, possibly a hand-me-down.

Decline and New Styles

Chenille robes began to decline in popularity around 1953, as fashions changed and as the tufted textile industry's focus shifted to carpet. In 1946 the industry was divided into 57 percent bedspreads, 18 percent robes, and 25 percent carpets and rugs. By 1953 it was 30 percent bedspreads, 6 percent robes, and 64 percent carpets and rugs.[87]

The decline in popularity is reflected in the emergence in popular culture of the old, worn chenille robe as symbol of unfashionableness. Ruth M. Clow, writing in 1953 of Shirley Booth's Oscar-winning appearance in *Come Back, Little Sheba* described her portrayal of modern American womanhood through "uncombed hair and unwashed face, wearing run-down, heel-less slippers and a rumpled chenille robe." Clow exclaimed, "Frankly, it wouldn't amaze me if that picture ruined the sale of chenille robes for the next few years. I'll sell mine at a loss."[88] In 1964, Phyllis Diller used a chenille robe in one of her jokes to help convey a housewife's inactivity: "Mrs. Smith is sitting at her kitchen table drinking coffee, reading the paper, wearing an old chenille robe, curlers in her hair and bedroom slippers, and the kitchen is a mess of dirty dishes. Her husband arrives at the back door with his briefcase after a hard day's work, and she looks up in surprise and says: 'Are you home already?'"[89] And in the mid-1960s, storyteller Jean Shepherd

Woman wearing a chenille robe, ca. 1955, found photograph, private collection

Children in costumes, one wearing a chenille cape, ca. 1940, found photograph, private collection

described his mother's "rump-sprung Chinese-red chenille bathrobe with tiny flecks of petrified egg on the lapels," an image memorably depicted in the movie version of his childhood tales, *A Christmas Story* (1983).[90] Similarly, in an Oscar-winning performance in *The Last Picture Show* (1971) Cloris Leachman wore a chenille robe that helped identify her character as unsexy and desperate.

The tufted textile industry remained optimistic and continued actively promoting chenille robes throughout the 1950s, and manufacturers sought to retain and gain markets by offering an increased variety of robe styles. In 1953, Margot Herzog, fashion director for the National Cotton Council of America, reported in the TTMA directory that designers "gave [robes] smart new lines, interesting neck treatment, new push-up sleeves," that some robes now featured contrasting piping, and that belts seldom circled the waist, instead tying in front to leave the back uncluttered.[91] In 1954 she reported that "very fine, corduroy-like fabrics with close, 'pinwale' tufting have virtually supplanted the traditional tufted types in which the lines of tufting are spaced farther apart," and she said that many robes now had contrasting colors inside, providing nice accents when sleeves were rolled up.[92] Herzog commented in the 1955 TTMA directory that "fine-gauge, $\frac{3}{16}$th-inch tufting continues the dominant texture."[93]

A major stylistic development for chenille robes was the introduction of the duster (typically three-quarter-length robes) in 1951.[94] In 1953 Herzog called dusters "the designers' darling," and she said that "their shorter length makes them more adaptable to new treatment." She listed the variety of duster styles, claiming that individuality was the order of the day, likely a reflection of the tufted garment industry's efforts to appeal to the emerging youth market. She wrote, "Some are fitted in dressmaker fashion; others feature the straight-as-a-reed cut of the short coat. Some fall directly from the shoulder into a wide flare; others feature yokes from which stem a soft fullness. Some bell out front and back; others are severely straight and belted in front, and gaily flaring in back."[95] In the 1954 TTMA directory, Herzog promoted the "three-way" duster, which could be worn "with the belt loose, with the belt drawn tight in back and left loose in front, or with the belt drawn tight in front and loose in back."[96] Duster sales surpassed the sales of

Model wearing a duster-style chenille robe, ca. 1960, courtesy of Bandy Heritage Center for Northwest Georgia, Carpet and Rug Institute Photograph Collection

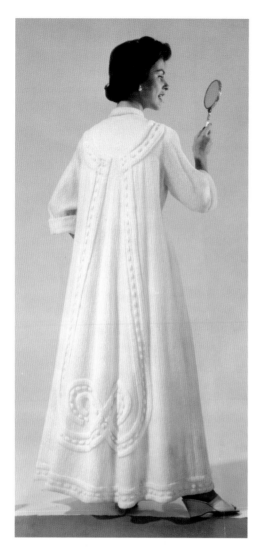

Model wearing a
chenille robe by
Art-Rich, ca. 1962,
courtesy of Bandy
Heritage Center for
Northwest Georgia,
Carpet and Rug
Institute Photograph
Collection

traditional wraparound robes by 1955, and by 1958 they outsold the traditional robes by about three to one.[97] The 1959 TTMA directory reported that sales of dusters far exceeded those of traditional robes, adding that "the full-length robe retains a loyal following among those who prefer the flowing classic lines," obliquely acknowledging that the traditional robes no longer were considered modern.[98]

Arthur Richman wrote an article for the 1954 TTMA directory on chenille robes, addressing how the production of robes had shifted from employing single-needle machines and one pattern that was used for years "with just some variations in overlay design" to an industry with "constantly changing" styles requiring "new patterns . . . to keep pace with the trend." He explained: "Chenille robes and dusters are being styled the same as rayon, nylon and cotton negligees and robes. . . . The peignoir type robe is just as important today in chenilles as it is in satins or quilts." He also pointed out the small changes that required additional materials and labor, including the buttons and buttonholes and various trimmings that were required for dusters.[99] Sada Nell Williams, publicity director for the TTMA, writing for the 1958 directory, echoed Richman's observation of the increased complexity of producing chenille robes, stating, "Overlay designs, in many cases, have given ground to buttons, braids, and other types of trims." Williams said that new metallic yarns (in keeping with the use of innovative materials and space-age themes popular in other areas of design at the time) gave added richness to the robes.[100]

While the details became more complex in the late 1950s, the colors became more limited, and in an effort to efficiently meet market demands, companies only produced robes in the most popular hues.[101] An article in the *Dalton Citizen* in 1958 explained that rather than offer a wide range of "spectacular, but unnecessary" colors, manufacturers now focused on just a few, including pink and aqua as well as other blues and greens, with white decreasing to just 10 percent of production. The newspaper noted a change in materials as well, with "synthetic fibers, fairly new in robe production . . . now appearing in between 10 and 20 percent of overall volume."[102] By 1958 Lawtex offered cotton and rayon robes, and Gotsch offered cotton, rayon, and nylon ones.[103] In 1960 Martin Richman, Arthur Richman's son, praised the new rayon viscose yarns (man-made but not synthetic) used over the prior few years in tufted robes, saying they had a "different 'feel' and look" and gave off less lint, a perpetual problem with chenille.[104] By 1963, manufacturers used nylon as well to make tufted robes.[105]

By the late 1950s and early 1960s, the remaining manufacturers further diversified their robe offerings. For example, by 1959 Art-Rich began selling terrycloth robes, and Sparks made robes of terrycloth, denim, and seersucker during the off-season.[106] The TTMA even promoted terrycloth robes

Chenille robe, back and front, ca. 1965, courtesy of Bandy Heritage Center for Northwest Georgia, Carpet and Rug Institute Photograph Collection

Unidentified chenille robe factory, early 1960s, photograph by Gabriel Benzur, Atlanta, courtesy of Bandy Heritage Center for Northwest Georgia, Carpet and Rug Institute Photograph Collection

as a form of tufted robes in its April 1962 *News for Women* newsletter, recommending them for women, men, and children, in a variety of colors for use at home or at poolside, even though terrycloth is a woven textile with a looped pile rather than an embroidered textile like chenille.[107]

While praising the variety of robes available for 1961, the TTMA directory acknowledged a decrease in tufted robe production over the previous decade, attributing the slide to the market and to the "production shift to tufted floorcoverings."[108] Figures from 1951 through the beginning of 1964 show steadily decreasing sales: from $10,956,000 worth of robe shipments in 1951, to $8,303,000 in 1954, $5,407,000 in 1957, and $4,181,000 in 1963.[109] By 1965 "a relatively limited number of companies" produced robes, but the TTMA claimed that those companies, which now offered robes for the whole family, maintained steady and healthy volumes.[110] By 1967 the TTMA suggested that a new trend was to buy matching robes for the whole family, and that tufted robes were "still looming large on the apparel scene," a hopeful but inaccurate assessment.[111]

New Tufted Apparel Fabrics

As robe manufacturers expanded into alternative materials like terrycloth, other companies investigated the possibilities of new tufted apparel fabrics. The 1965 TTMA directory proclaimed that "a lot of manufacturers have drawn a line straight from the floor covering side of the tufted industry to the world of fashion."[112] Of particular note is the "Sherpa" material developed by Collins and Aikman with the Fibers Division of the American Cyanimid Company around 1960. This acrylic fabric with a pile resembling animal fur proved popular for coat linings. Collins and Aikman promoted Sherpa as the "warmest, cuddliest curly pile fabric man ever made" and as their "most famous apparel success."[113] The 1963 TTMA directory even called the new tufted fabrics like Sherpa the "heir apparent" to tufted apparel. The directory explained that the fabrics were made by a "fine gauge needle tufting machine which turns out many brushed fabrics that look as though they came straight off some precious animal's back." The directory described how the new tufted fabrics came in many forms, from curly (like Sherpa) to "smooth and cashmere-like." These new fabrics appeared as coats, raincoat linings, and men's sports coat linings.[114] The directory also observed that the fabrics were priced "so that a woman whose bank book won't tolerate *the real thing* can walk serenely into the club in the next best thing—marvelous tufted fakes."[115] The new acrylic fur also offered the practical benefit of being machine washable.[116] The 1965 TTMA directory noted that Sherpa's popularity had gone up and down but that it was especially popular then for use in skiwear.[117] Later the TTMA highlighted Sherpa as a good fit with the new "western-look" in fashion.[118]

Miss Georgia 1959, Kayanne Shoffner, wearing a tufted (faux fur) coat, with Bill Sparks, Mayfair, Dalton, Georgia, 1959, collection of Alice Sparks Young

Handsome and rugged, this Robert Lewis design of smart suede is lined with "Sherpa", luxurious man-made fur by Collins & Aikman.

Suede coat by Robert Lewis with Sherpa lining by Collins and Aikman, illustrated in the TTMA *News for Women* newsletter, November 1962, courtesy of Bandy Heritage Center for Northwest Georgia, Carpet and Rug Institute Collection

The TTMA continued to promote tufted pile fabrics, in 1967 highlighting the development of "fake fur" coats and praising the fabrics as being easy to wash, offering "so much warmth with so little weight," and looking expensive while being affordable. The TTMA cited major coat designers including North Bay Coats, Modelia, and Doby Girl Coat Company as using the new tufted pile fabrics to attractive effect.[119]

Carpet Fashion

Just as innovators used chenille scraps to develop new businesses, individuals did the same with carpet. In particular, several companies used carpet remnants to create fashionable handbags. Even before that, though, carpet appeared as fashion during part of a publicity stunt by Lees Carpets in Glasgow, Virginia. In 1963, Anne Mason, a home decorator for Lees, appeared on the television program *Profile*, on Roanoke, Virginia, station WSLS, wearing a long evening skirt and coat by noted fashion designer Hannah Troy. Both skirt and coat were made of carpet, from a special line of area rugs (Lees Lively Arts Collection) by New York designer William Pahlman. Sally Victor, a New York milliner, constructed two hats from the same rug collection.[120] One hat was bright blue, cut pile, with a peaked cap, folded brim, and an ochre button, and the other was a Kelly green pillbox hat to match the Hannah Troy coat.

Tufted handbags, made from carpet, appeared in the mid-1960s, and the 1965 TTMA directory described them as one of the industry's "latest innovations." They came in tufted and looped piles and in solid and variegated colors, and often the burlap carpet backing served as the interior of the handbags. The directory reported that they first had been introduced in Atlanta and "are now being stocked by retailers in some 18 states." The handbags the directory described came in two sizes, a large all-purpose handbag and a smaller one for dress occasions, and in a wide range of colors, and they could be vacuumed and washed just like carpet on the floor. The directory notes: "The carpetbags—Southern-style—are just another example of the ingenuity of people in the tufted textile field and . . . another in a long line of highly successful 'tufted' novelty items."[121]

The directory does not mention the name of the company that manufactured the carpet handbags, but it probably was referring to Carpet Bag, Inc., founded by Lloyd C. Yeargin (1918–76), a medical doctor in Dalton.[122] Carpet

Bag was a family business, with Lloyd as president, his son Randy as vice president, and his wife Ruby as secretary and treasurer. Early labels read: "From Floor to Fashion / by / Carpet Bag, Inc./ 30720 [Dalton's zip Code]," while later ones, red on yellow, read: "THE CARPET BAG / Made from a continuous line of quality carpet / produced by a leading manufacturer. / Manufactured By: / CARPET BAG, INC.," followed by the company's address and telephone number. The company last appears in the Dalton city directory in 1974–75 and went out of business sometime before Dr. Yeargin died in May 1976.

Handbags by Carpet Bag, Inc., Dalton, Georgia, ca. 1965-75, private collection, photograph by Michael McKelvey

Detail of Carpet Bag, Inc., label from the smallest bag shown above, ca. 1965, photograph by author

THE MOST PUBLICIZED MAN AND PRODUCT IN THE ENTIRE HISTORY OF THE HANDBAG INDUSTRY WILL BE FEATURED IN . . .

- 122 National & Local Television Shows
- 27 National Magazines
- 186 Radio Stations
- 164 Metropolitan & Local Newspapers

DON'T MISS OUT!

Display and Advertise The Original Jerry Terrence Carpet Bag. It is the "NAME BRAND" your customers will be definitely asking for!

JERRY TERRENCE OF CALIFORNIA
MAIN OFFICE 7105 PACIFIC BLVD.
HUNTINGTON PARK, CALIFORNIA
(AREA 213) 583-5243

NEW YORK Showroom
STEVE LEOPOLD
172 Madison Ave.
N.Y. 16, New York
MU 3-5888

MIDWEST Showroom
WES CARLSON & ASSOCIATES
36 S. State Street
Chicago, Illinois
ST 2-9347

SOUTH Showroom
EDDIE CLASZ Company
Room 2648, Apparel Mart
2300 Stemmons Freeway
Dallas, Texas 75207

MIDWEST
JERRY STEIN
Res. 1255 E. 91st St.
Indianapolis 40, Indiana

SOUTHEAST Showroom
EDDIE CLASZ CO.
405-B Merchandise
Mart
Atlanta, Georgia

LOS ANGELES Showroom
HARVEY KRASNER
607 So. Hill
Los Angeles, California
MA 2-4285

Promotional material for Jerry Terrence Carpet Bag of California, 1964, courtesy of Jerry Terrence

Jerry Terrence of California founded a carpet handbag company in 1964, a year earlier than Carpet Bag, Inc. His father established Al Terrence Carpet Company in the Los Angeles area in 1945, but Jerry felt that he was not, as he said, "a carpet guy." Of the popularity of his handbags, he recalls, "The bags were so popular we had to have three shifts working every day. I ran out of remnants. I had to buy new carpet."[123] He offered a wide variety of styles and colors (forty-seven in 1966) and developed a special sewing machine to assemble his product.[124] In 1965 the *Yonkers (N.Y.) Herald Statesman* called carpet handbags "pure Americana" and Terrence the "singularly iconoclastic son of a California carpet manufacturer."[125]

While the Carpet Bag, Inc., handbags were referred to as "Southern-style," Terrence was known as the "California Carpetbagger." Jerry Terrence Carpet Bags enjoyed great popularity for several years, with extensive press coverage and fanfare, and the company stopped doing business in 1967.[126] Its labels, in red and black on yellow, read: "The Original / Jerry Terrence / Carpet / Bag / Huntington Park / California." Terrence revived his carpet handbag business in 2006, replacing the brass hardware with silver, and he introduced another new line in 2013.[127]

Carpet handbags had a roadside presence as well. Willene Morgan, who ran a chenille business with her husband on U.S. 41 in Tunnel Hill for forty years, made carpet handbags by hand in multiple sizes, including a large bag and a clutch, as well as a small bag for children. When asked about other manufacturers of carpetbags, she confidently responded, "Well, they followed my lead is all."[128]

Chapter Six

Revival and Nostalgia

⇀ ⇀ ⇀ BEGINNING BY THE EARLY 1970S, crafters and designers began cutting up old tufted bedspreads to make new products, including garments. Many were motivated by nostalgia for the early textiles as well as an interest in recycling encouraged by the growing environmental movement. Tufted spreads have been (and continue to be) repurposed to make a variety of garments including jackets, robes, dresses, bloomers, aprons, bibs, and pullover blouses. To find materials, designers started searching antique shops, flea markets, thrift stores, and estate sales, which were brimming with chenille in the 1980s and 1990s, and in the 2010s "cutter" spreads are abundant in online marketplaces.[1] Julia Szabo, writing for *Martha Stewart Living* in 1995, described chenille bedspreads as a "uniquely cheerful bit of Americana . . . the textile equivalent of comfort food." She allowed an antiques dealer in Ossining, New York, Nancy Lockwood, to sum up the typical reactions to chenille at that time: "1. Oh, wow! Remember these? We had these on our bed years ago, and I always loved them! 2. Ugh—I always hated chenille. 3. Oh, I had one of those on my bed as a kid, and I used to sit and pull all the little things [tufts] out."[2] Like comfort food, chenille inspires a mix of reverence and revulsion.

The new garments of recycled chenille stand apart from their predecessors because of their more playful patterning. Instead of having designs confined to borders or corners, the new garments generally feature allover patterns, often with a patchwork appearance. The contrasting patterns, bright and pastel colors, and nostalgia for the 1950s reflected in the chenille revival all fit well within the postmodern design trends of the 1980s and early 1990s.

OPPOSITE: Chenille robe, Canyon Group by Damze, ca. 1995, collection of Peter and Sandy Loose-Schrantz, photograph by Michael McKelvey

⇀ ⇀ ⇀ 153

The revival of interest in tufted textiles in Northwest Georgia is reflected by the informal renaming of Bedspread Boulevard to Peacock Alley, in honor of the plethora of tufted peacocks found along the roadside for many decades. Though Peacock Alley is the primary name by which the route is known today, it likely dates toward the end of chenille's roadside presence, possibly as late as the mid-1980s.[3] Following a period during which many local residents held the route in disregard, by the late 1980s they warmly embraced Peacock Alley and celebrated it as a key part of Dalton's identity.

Early Chenille Recyclers

One of the earliest companies to repurpose chenille was the Ruff n' Ready Underware Company of New York, a design house run by Carol and Jack Bradin, which incorporated recycled chenille into its ready-to-wear line for high-end department stores by 1970.[4] The Bradins were motivated both by nostalgia for the textiles (remembering their own childhoods) and an interest in recycling and environmental issues.[5] Their initial design, a vintage denim jacket with chenille sleeves, sold so successfully that they could not find enough old spreads—they had been acquiring bales of spreads that were destined to be cut into rags—and had new chenille yardage made by Edgewood Chenille, a company that was still tufting in Tunnel Hill, Georgia.[6] According to Jack Bradin, Ruff n' Ready's stylish garments had similar fits to clothing by designer Betsey Johnson, a business friend of Carol Bradin's. Incidentally, Johnson also was an early adopter of recycled chenille fashion, appearing in a photograph in the *Oregonian* in 1972 wearing a colorful skirt made from a peacock spread.[7] Ruff n' Ready existed from about 1969–76, though Jack Bradin sold his interest in 1975. One concern he noted with using chenille in garments, both recycled and new, is that the textile is highly flammable, and he explained that Ruff n' Ready double-washed both the vintage spreads and the new yardage it used in a flame retardant called Pyrovatex.[8]

Subsequent designers working with vintage chenille included Frank Ballotta of Laguna Beach, California, who used chenille and other old fabrics by the late 1980s to create garments under the label Kokonuts.[9] Ballotta enjoyed making clothes that were different from what he viewed as the homogeneous merchandise available in department stores, and he appreciated the character of the vintage textiles, explaining, "I'm a fabric junkie . . . I love the way the fabric feels, the way it moves, the patterns."[10]

Toronto's *Globe and Mail* in 1992 reported on the fad for reusing old chenille spreads to make new items: "Mostly . . . these mementos are being cut up and turned into clothing." The newspaper described a chenille collector and antiques dealer from Florida, Louise Pinson, as being "delighted at the number of chenille-clad collectors at New York's Triple Pier Antique Show," and comparing their outfits to "frosting on a birthday cake."[11] Pinson began buying chenille in the mid-1970s, when old spreads had minimal monetary value, and sold her collection in the early 2000s.[12] Pinson also recalls a designer, Elaine Rush, who frequented the Brimfield Antique Show in Massachusetts in the 1980s and 1990s wearing chenille garments of her own creation.[13] The material continues to intrigue well into the twenty-first century, with offbeat filmmaker John Waters seen sporting a pink candlewick jacket, with ball fringe, in late 2013.[14]

Some of the designers acquired old tufting machines as well. For example, Wayne H. Caron of Westerly, Rhode Island, started a company called Totally Tufted, creating new tufted items, mostly pillows and upholstery, with machines that he collected in the South. According to the *New York Times*, he decided to make his own chenille "because the supply of vintage fabric was fast being depleted."[15]

CoCo:Chenille

One of the leading fashion designers to repurpose chenille spreads was Christina Lynn Whited of High Bridge, New Jersey, whose business was called CoCo:Chenille. She grew up interested in fabrics and sewing and studied at the Fashion Institute of Technology in New York. An avid thrifter and frequenter of yard sales, she became fascinated with chenille in the summer of 1990 and amassed three carloads of it to start her business. She collected some Martha Washington fabric, jacquard, and 1940s barkcloth, as well, but was captivated most by chenille because of its variety of color, pattern, and texture.[16]

Around 1991 she began creating jackets, then made vests and pants to go with them, adding dresses and home goods (including stuffed animals) a couple of years later. She sometimes altered the chenille, dyeing it or strategically moving tufts from seams or other places where they were not visible to places where she desired them. Whited acquired three chenille machines and did some machine tufting of her own, but she found the machines difficult to maintain without the help of Northwest Georgia's specially trained mechanics.[17]

Christina Lynn Whited with some of her recycled chenille creations, courtesy of the artist.

Whited considered recycling to be an important aspect of her work and called herself "the Martha Stewart of recycling."[18] She even labeled her garments "CoCo:Chenille / Comfort with a Conscience." In 1996 she received an award from the governor of New Jersey for her contributions to the local economy, an honor she attributes to her efforts to make CoCo:Chenille a green company.[19]

Though initially drawn to chenille by her interest in recycling, Whited soon came to appreciate the nostalgia and history associated with it as well.[20] She credited chenille's late twentieth-century popularity revival to a national desire for comfort, explaining, "The fact that it's so tactile and comforting is increasingly important in our mechanized society. When people come in and touch the chenille, they say it reminds them of their grandmother's house, a time when they were safer, not as threatened. Even my adult customers tell me they sleep with the teddy bears. One woman said she gets more hugs on the days she wears her chenille blouse than any others."[21] When asked about her customers, she stated, "The nostalgia touched everyone," adding that her customers ranged in age from thirty to sixty and remembered chenille from their grandmothers' homes or their childhoods.[22]

Whited considers chenille an "American classic" and worked to preserve what she saw as an important part of American women's history. She told the *New York Times* that up to the 1970s "a lot of vintage chenille was being shredded and used for packing gas pipes . . . or just tossed out. It was simply being lost."[23] She recognized some of the tufted textiles she found as especially important, and she set aside select items as a collection that she presented in Chenille Heaven, a museum space she opened next door to her shop. She even traveled to Dalton several times to learn more about the history of the fabric.[24] Personally, she was attracted by "the fact that [the chenille industry] was started and nurtured by women" and believes that the industry thrived because women knew what women needed.[25]

When Shelly Phillips wrote in 1999 about recycling chenille, she described how Whited and another designer, Marilyn Wolf of Marilyn Wolf Designs, were secretive about their sources, explaining, "They can't divulge them, because when all the old bedspreads have been plucked from thrift shops and rummage sales, flea markets and rag merchants, that's it—the supply will be gone."[26] CoCo:Chenille hibernated for a period, and now that it is revived Whited works with a wider variety of materials. She feels that she has investigated the range of chenille's possibilities, and the supply of vintage spreads is too limited now.[27] Also, Whited believes that popular views of chenille have changed since the 1990s and that while consumers still associate it with comfort and appeal, they are too far removed from its heyday to appreciate its nostalgic quality.[28]

Marilyn Wolf Designs

Marilyn Wolf, another chenille recycler, established her small manufacturing business in Narberth, Pennsylvania, around 1970. She designed a variety of products including soft luggage and handbags, often with monograms, and accessories such as belts, jewelry, and scarves, as well as terry-cloth robes. Her business exists now primarily as a monogram company.[29]

For about a decade starting in the mid-1990s, Wolf focused on using vintage chenille to make garments and a few accessories, including teddy bears and baby blankets. Initially she worked with a limited batch of chenille yardage that she purchased from a closeout sale, but the robes she made from that sold quickly, and she did not have the fabric to make more. She mentioned this brief success to an acquaintance, who happened to own a rag factory (a business that collected leftover fabrics from thrift stores and other sources). The acquaintance offered her access to a "never-ending" supply of vintage chenille bedspreads, allowing her and her helpers to roam the three-square-block rag factory with its nine-hundred-pound bales of fabric to find

"Jackets fashioned from vintage chenille," flyer, ca. 1997, Marilyn Wolf Designs, Narberth, Pennsylvania, collection of the artist

Children's recycled chenille bathrobes, Marilyn Wolf Designs, postcard, 1997, Michael Scott Studio, New York City, collection of the artist

chenille. She eventually gained admittance to several other rag factories as well, and with this new source of material she developed a line of garments in which she mixed pieces from many different spreads to create one-of-a-kind, patchwork robes and jackets with bright colors and bold patterns.

As supplies of chenille dwindled and the material became more precious, and as the market for high-end art clothing for children increased, she turned her attention to children's clothing, as it required smaller pieces of fabric. She made children's robes, rompers, and jackets and often combined the chenille with other fabrics, vintage buttons, and marabou. Her designs sold in exclusive stores, including Nordstrom and Bloomingdale's, and children's boutiques across the country, especially in Texas, New York, and Las Vegas.[30] One of her robes appeared in the movie *It Takes Two* (1995), starring Mary-Kate and Ashley Olsen. At the height of her work with chenille, Wolf employed about seventeen people in-house and about ten home workers.

Like Whited, Wolf was interested in the recycling aspect of her work, but she was motivated more by the creative process of combining the fabrics in interesting ways. Though she sometimes paused before cutting up a particularly "gorgeous" spread, she derived little satisfaction from seeing a single spread on a bed but great pleasure from giving a design like a peacock new life by incorporating it into a "big, swooping design" for a garment. When she could no longer find adequate supplies of quality chenille, she worked with other materials.

A few manufacturers of chenille robes survived into the 1990s and 2000s. One of the most prominent manufacturers associated with these later robes is Crowntuft, which trademarked the names "Tuftees" in the late 1970s and "Herbcraft" in the early 1990s. Kellwood Company of St. Louis purchased Crowntuft in 1989 and eventually closed its factory in the United States.[31] A leading designer for Crowntuft was Stan Herman, who started designing chenille robes in the 1970s. He established his own company, and his robes were especially popular on QVC, the home shopping network, from the early 1990s into the 2000s.[32]

Edgewood Chenille and Soft Goods

Retha Quinton (1909–94) founded Edgewood Chenille and ran it with her husband Paul in Tunnel Hill, Georgia.[33] She first made spreads in her home in Dalton, starting in 1945, then moved into the woodshed behind her house and named the business Edgewood Chenille. She worked with single-needle machines initially, then added multi-needle machines (up to twelve needles) around 1948, eventually acquiring a skip-stitch machine and scroll and flower machines.[34] She moved to U.S. 41 in Tunnel Hill in 1948 in order to display her goods where tourists driving to Florida could see them.[35] She also traveled as far as Colorado, Texas, and Florida during the summers selling chenille.[36] The Quintons' daughter Sue (1928–2011) joined the company in 1951, and Sue's husband Harry Gordon began working there in 1959. Edgewood grew from a twelve-by-twenty-four-foot building to one with about fourteen thousand square feet by 1970. By the 1970s, Edgewood produced spreads, bath mats, scatter rugs, and robes. The latter became quite popular and appeared on television shows, including *Laverne and Shirley* and *In the Heat of the Night*. Flammability of chenille robes continued to be a problem, though, and following a lawsuit, a recall of their cotton garments, and skyrocketing insurance rates, the Quintons decided to retire. They sold the business to the Gordons in 1981, at which time the name changed to Soft Goods, Inc.

Frances Bonner modeling a Soft Goods, Inc., jacket and Beth Ogle modeling a Soft Goods, Inc., shirt, 1980s, photograph by Harry E. Gordon

Soft Goods, Inc., Chenille jacket, n.d., cotton, collection of Harry E. Gordon, photograph by Michael McKelvey

Soft Goods, Inc., chenille jacket labeled "Sadie Grey," 1980s, polyester and cotton, collection of Harry E. Gordon, photograph by Michael McKelvey

The Gordons switched from cotton to a less-flammable cotton-polyester blend and continued making chenille garments and spreads. They developed a chenille jacket that sold in leading department stores and also sold spreads to DMZ (and then Damze Company) of California, which made its own chenille jackets. The *Dalton Citizen-News* reported in 1991 that most of the company's "flower basket and peacock spreads are shipped to Santa Barbara, Calif., with the express purpose of being turned into jackets."[37] An undated promotional flyer from Soft Goods explains that even though machines were used to make its chenille products, "the hand guiding of single needle tufting machines by our experienced operators gives each bedspread or robe some individuality," bestowing them with an "artisanal" appeal.[38] Soft Goods also had some television success: Tracey Ullman wore one of its chenille robes at the end of each episode of *The Tracey Ullman Show*.[39] By the late 1980s Soft Goods filled orders for chenille spreads and sportswear still using many of Retha Quinton's original patterns as well as designs by Sue Gordon.[40]

In 1991 Jody and Don Chapman, who owned Damze and were based in Tustin, California, in Orange County, purchased Soft Goods, Inc., and formed Soft Goods Industries.[41] The Chapmans found it difficult to run a business split between Georgia and California, so they eventually moved all of the single-needle, multineedle, scroll, and flower machines to Santa Ana, California, bringing Soft Goods to an end. They continued to have tufted yardage manufactured in Georgia, shifting that production from Tunnel Hill to Dalton, maintaining a connection with their product's regional birthplace.

Beth Ogle and Frances Bonner modeling Soft Goods, Inc., chenille robes, 1980s, photograph by Harry E. Gordon

Damze Company

Debra Maria Zomparelli began making jackets out of vintage chenille spreads and old tablecloths and curtains around 1980 through her business Debbie's Rainbow in California. The vintage materials sometimes proved too fragile, though, so she and her father, Rocco Zomparelli (1926–2013), began purchasing new chenille spreads from Soft Goods and established DMZ, the name comprising Debbie's initials, in San Diego. The Zomparellis worked with Sue Gordon to design a special spread with two baskets that was ideal for cutting up to make jackets of Debbie's design, with minimal wasted material. The company successfully sold jackets and shorts through Nordstrom and the Neiman-Marcus holiday catalog, as well as through boutiques in Hawaii (some owned by the Chapman family) and other beach resorts.[42]

In 1989 the Zomparellis sold DMZ to Jody and Don Chapman, who renamed it Damze (pronounced "Dames"). After graduating from the University of Southern California (USC), Don Chapman had worked with his family's business, Chapman's Men's Wear, which had retail stores in California, Arizona, Nevada, and Hawaii. Shortly before his family sold its business, he acquired Damze and continued making jackets and selling them to boutiques, mostly in Hawaii.

Initially the Chapmans worked with the specially designed spreads from Soft Goods with the double basket pattern. At their factory in California they stacked the spreads fifteen at a time on a spread-sized table and cut them into pieces, with each spread yielding four jackets. Then workers sewed the pieces together and shipped jackets to clients. Don Chapman explained: "These jackets were sold all over the country, but the majority . . . were sold in Waikiki and later Guam." He noted, "They were extremely popular with Japanese tourists." These zippered jackets (style 1010) "provided the foundation for [the company's] growth in the early years," and the most popular colorways were a "Multi" and "Pastel."[43]

The first department store to work with Damze on a large scale was Henri Bendel, an upscale women's specialty store. Henri Bendel's success with Damze's robes (and enthusiasm for them) helped bring their product to the attention of other department stores, and the company grew quickly. They sold in Nordstrom specialty stores, Victoria's Secret catalogs, Macy's, and Neiman Marcus, with most robes just carrying the stores' labels (not Damze's). Many of their custom designs for department stores use or reference traditional chenille spread designs but are cut at angles, crafted into short robes, or otherwise modernized.

When the Chapmans purchased Soft Goods, they gained new flexibility and were able to play with designs and build their business in new ways. Don Chapman recalls being aware of people using old spreads to make garments and toys, but he saw them as having a limited supply, whereas he could make as much fabric as he wanted. The Chapmans met in Tunnel Hill with sales representatives from New York and Los Angeles to discuss

Damze chenille jacket and shorts, ca. early 1990s, private collection,
photograph by Michael McKelvey

the company's future. They decided to make "fun, whimsical robes," which became their Canyon Group line, and started with a moon-and-stars design, which they modified slightly over time.[44] Jody Chapman, also a USC graduate, became their designer. She had worked with Nordstrom before her children were born, stayed at home with them when they were young, then began working part-time at Damze as they grew. The designs came to include numerous cheerful patterns with cute names, such as "Coffee Talk" (with coffee cups), "Rise and Shine" (featuring breakfast food), and "Falling Daisies."

Don Chapman explained that having access to the rare, vintage machines allowed Damze to create a unique product, as the specialized machinery made it prohibitively expensive for other companies to start doing from scratch what they were doing. Their only strong competition was Crowntuft, which had the Stan Herman line, and which, according to Chapman, was influenced stylistically by Damze's lighthearted creations.[45] Damze had the tufting and dyeing done in Georgia, then trucked the fabric to California for the cutting, sewing, and overlay. Initially they used tufting machines from

Canyon Group by Damze child's chenille robe, ca. 1990s, collection of Sydney Brown, photograph by Michael McKelvey

Canyon Group
billboard, Interstate
405 near Los Angeles,
date unknown, courtesy
of Don Chapman

the 1940s (Retha Quinton's old machines), but when Bob Shaw, a leader in Dalton's carpet industry, offered to trade them newer machines (converted from carpet production back to chenille), the Chapmans accepted, and Shaw added the antique machines to his collection.

Canyon Group robes received significant exposure through appearances on television shows, including *Melrose Place, Northern Exposure, Friends, The Nanny, Frasier, Ellen, One Life to Live, Baywatch, NYPD Blue, General Hospital, Murphy Brown,* and *Beverly Hills, 90210.* By 1996 the list included over twenty television shows and several movies.[46] Chapman explained that designers for television shows saw the company's Canyon Group robes in department stores and bought them for their wardrobe departments, and that soon the designers started contacting the Chapmans directly. Also, when Don Chapman read an article about the costume designer for *Northern Exposure* wishing to know more about the robes she had selected for the character Shelly to wear, he wrote to her explaining the history of chenille and his company. The designer wanted more robes and they ended up in a wardrobe department shared by many shows.

Don Chapman, when interviewed by *Women's Wear Daily* in 1995, cited a 20 percent increase in sales due to the television exposure, especially *Melrose Place,* which prompted his company to expand production capacity significantly. *WWD* noted that the popular television shows focused on affordable, youthful fashions, a clear description of how Damze's robes were viewed.[47] Costume designer Kirsten Everberg told the *Orange County Register* that her "phones rang for days" after actress Courtney Thorne-Smith first wore a blue chenille robe with a yellow moon on *Melrose Place*.[48] A later costume designer for *Melrose Place*, Denise Wingate, reported to *Entertainment Weekly* that she received "calls from as far away as Australia asking where to find it."[49] Damze's West Coast sales representative, Trevor Riewer, told *Entertainment Weekly* that during audience warm-ups for *The Nanny*, the second most-asked question (after "Is that Fran Drescher's real voice?") was "Where do you get those robes?" Brenda Cooper, costume designer for *The Nanny*, used a robe in almost every episode, adding shoulder pads "for a heightened sense of glamour."[50]

One particularly notable big screen appearance of a Canyon Group robe was in *Fight Club* in 1999. The production department called the Chapmans and requested a robe for actor Brad Pitt. After Don Chapman reminded them that his company made *women's* robes, he agreed to make a lavender robe with a coffee cup motif, designed to Pitt's measurements, which became an iconic costume from the movie.

Damze even worked with QVC, as well, at one point having six hour-long programs a year, with Jody as the spokeswoman. They hired two other designers and added home goods such as bedspreads and shower curtains to their production. As Damze got larger, the company signed licensing agreements with a few universities and with Dr. Seuss Enterprises. In 1996 Damze robes sold for $100–$130. Department stores, however, kept asking Damze to lower its prices, and some even started adding decorative patches to terrycloth robes to mimic Damze products, although, according to Chapman, these did not sell well. The Chapmans were proud to offer a product made in the United States and resisted moving production to China. As competition from low-cost imports increased, however, the Chapmans decided in 2006 to sell the company. The robes continue to be manufactured in the United States by the company's new owners.[51] The Chapmans enjoyed being part of the chenille tradition and resurrecting it with updated designs.[52]

Conclusion

The birth, decline, and revival of Northwest Georgia's tufted textile industry is a great story of American ingenuity, fashion, and culture. It plays out generational shifts in taste, with the first generation finding tufted garments glamorous, the next generation growing to view them as outdated, and a third generation developing a new appreciation for them. It also provides an interesting arc from handcraft through industrialization and then back to handcraft. The range of tufted textile manufacturers, from large companies with designers trained in New York in the ready-to-wear trade to a single woman working in a log cabin, attests to the pervasiveness of this industry in Northwest Georgia. The widespread appearance of chenille robes in popular culture demonstrates their status as iconic American apparel, which swung from glamour symbol (with lead actresses wearing chenille robes in Hollywood films) to shorthand for unfashionableness (as portrayed by the mother in Jean Shepherd's stories). They appear in countless anonymous snapshots that have entered the vast world of vintage found photographs, and they were widespread in 1990s television. As we move further away from chenille's heyday, appreciation for these tufted garments is shifting from a nostalgic view to one reflecting interest in new understandings of their roles in the history of American craft and industry. Chenille robes are part of this country's material culture and a rare example of a southern Appalachian fashion product that reached a national audience.

Appendix
Tufted Garment Manufacturers

Below are brief biographies of individuals and histories of companies associated with the production or in some cases marketing of tufted fashion. The list is not exhaustive, as likely hundreds of businesses and families made tufted garments at least briefly. Many entries provide incomplete accounts due to the scarcity of extant business records.

Acme Chenille, *Dalton, Georgia*

Acme Chenille belonged to J. Roy Whitener (Catherine Evans Whitener's brother-in-law) and initially (at least in the late 1920s, when Wanamaker's in Philadelphia was a customer) existed under his name. As Acme it made housecoats. Harry Saul later bought the Acme building, and it became the home of Queen Chenille.[1]

Ann-Lee Chenilles, *Tunnel Hill and Dalton, Georgia*

Arthur Richman (1904–65), see "Art-Rich Manufacturing," started Ann-Lee Chenilles sometime prior to January 1945. He began with a factory in Tunnel Hill, then added a larger plant in Dalton by January 1945. This survived through at least June 1946, probably until Richman established Art-Rich Manufacturing.[2]

Art-Rich Manufacturing Company, *Dalton, Georgia*

Arthur "Artie" Richman was born in Poland in 1904 and immigrated to the United States in 1912, becoming a naturalized citizen in New York in 1920. He married Rose Wasserman (1906–98) in 1928. They lived from at least 1936–38 in Waterford, Connecticut, when Richman worked as a designer and plant manager for the Lombardy Dress Company in nearby New London.[3] Richman then worked in New York City as a garment designer.

Richman arrived in Dalton in 1939 to work as the production manager and stylist of the Robe and Sportswear Department at Blue Ridge Spread Company, successfully building that department until he left to open his own company, Ann-Lee Chenilles. By 1947, Richman established Art-Rich Manufacturing, a large, long-lived company that focused on chenille robes.[4] The lines included Art-Rich robes for women and Roslyn Products robes for children.

Martin Richman (1929–2007), Artie's son, assumed leadership of Art-Rich shortly before his father died in 1965.[5] Art-Rich diversified its offerings, but by the late 1970s low-cost imported robes began to reduce Art-Rich's profits.[6] Art-Rich appears in the Dalton city directories through 1983.

R. P. Bailey Chenille Company, *Dalton, Georgia*

Robert Paul Bailey (1900–80) operated the R. P. Bailey Chenille Company, a small chenille business focused on the production of robes, from 1945 until 1958, in a building behind his house on U.S. 41. Bailey sold robes and small rugs primarily through three roadside gift shops, in Horse Cave, Cave City, and Elizabethtown, in Kentucky, all on the Dixie Highway, although he sometimes filled orders from other small stores.[7]

Frank Ballotta, *Laguna Beach, California*

Designer Frank Ballotta used chenille and other vintage fabrics by the late 1980s to create garments under the label Kokonuts.[8]

B. J. Bandy Company, *Dalton and Cartersville, Georgia*

Burl Judson "B. J." Bandy (1888–1948), a "pioneer in the development of the chenille bedspread and garment industry in northwest Georgia," and his wife Dicksie Bradley Bandy (1890–1971) were instrumental in the growth of the tufted textile industry. Before World War I, they owned several small country stores around Calhoun and Sugar Valley, and B. J. worked as a telegrapher for the railroad. After World War I, the couple faced significant debts as an economic recession meant that many farmers were unable to pay their bills to the stores.

Catherine Evans Whitener helped the Bandy couple enter the candlewick business by sharing bedspread designs with them. They started the candlewick spread company Bandy and Muse with J. Marvin Muse around 1920 in Sugar Valley, working with haulers and home tufters, and later established a highly successful spread business in Dalton, B. J. Bandy and Company, around 1929. B. J. encouraged Dicksie to travel to northeastern department stores using his railway pass. She made such

successful sales on her first trip that she returned home with enough orders to keep the company busy for a month or two, and she had continuing success on many subsequent trips. Bandy helped lead the transition to machine production through the purchase in 1934 from Erskine E. Boyce of Boysell Manufacturing Company of Gastonia, North Carolina, which had numerous tufting machines and patents. B. J. and Dicksie Bandy also established Southern Craft in Rome, J and C Bedspread Company in Ellijay (named after their son-in-law Joe McCutchen and daughter Christine), and Bartow Textiles in Cartersville. They made numerous chenille products, including robes and jackets, until 1953.[9]

Beckler's Chenille, *Dalton, Georgia*

Claudell and Burch Beckler (1907–75) owned a series of spreadlines between Cartersville and Tunnel Hill, including Beckler's Chenille. They started a small business in Dalton after World War II, then went into business with R. C. "Clarence" Thomason around 1944–45. Thomason and Beckler Chenille lasted until 1949–50, when the Becklers went into business on their own, opening Beckler's Chenille in either late 1950 or early 1951. They manufactured chenille briefly but soon switched to retailing a variety of chenille goods from other manufacturers. In 1964 the business's name changed from Beckler's Chenille to Beckler's Carpet, which it remains today.[10]

Bell Textile Company, Inc., *New York City*
Dixie Belle Mills, *Calhoun, Georgia*
Belcraft Chenilles, *Dalton, Georgia*

Israel Belsky founded Bell Textile Company, a textile jobbing business, in New York City around 1910. Bell Textile sold quantities of sheeting to Dalton companies in the 1930s, and Belsky decided to enter the tufting business in 1937. Bell Textile purchased Dixie Spread Company of Calhoun in 1939, which was the beginning of Dixie Belle Mills. Ben Winkler, Irving Funk, and Nathan Snow had founded the Dixie Spread Company in 1937.[11] Bell Textiles in 1945 organized Belcraft Chenilles, which purchased several other companies, including Ken-Rau and Redwine and Strain in 1950, and the Walter M. Gotsch Company, which manufactured the Adrian Evans line of tufted robes, in the early 1950s. By 1953 Bell Textiles advertised the Adrian Evans, Belcraft, and Dixie Belle brands, promoting the Dixie Belle line as the "best of the popular priced chenilles" and the Belcraft line as the "best of the better chenilles."[12] In 1954 Bell Textiles offered Hopalong Cassidy and Tom Corbett, Space Cadet, chenille bedroom ensembles, adding Davy Crockett by 1956. In the 1960 Dalton city directory, the company advertised that it manufactured bedspreads, robes, bath mats, rugs, and carpeting. By 1963 the company's executives in Dalton were Ben Winkler, David Winkler, and Irving Funk, and the Belsky family remained involved.[13] Fulton Industries bought the Dixie Belle mills in Calhoun in 1963.[14]

Mrs. J. H. Bennett, *Resaca and Dalton, Georgia*

Mrs. J. H. Bennett (née Emily Mealer or Mealor, 1904–97), ran a one-woman tufted textile business on U.S. 41 from the 1930s to the 1960s. She initially lived in the country and sold hand-tufted goods through a friend with a spreadline, while her husband farmed. The family moved to U.S. 41 in the 1930s and she operated her own spreadline just south of the Gordon County and Whitfield County lines. Her first building was a log cabin that her husband built especially for her tufting work. Later, probably in the late 1930s, the Bennetts moved, and she got a new little spreadline house on U.S. 41. As a hand tufter, Bennett made spreads, aprons, and pillows, and she began making robes after she bought a single-needle machine. Bennett continued her business, which came to be called Bennett's Chenille Products, until I-75 opened and drew away all of the tourist traffic.[15]

Blue Ridge Spread (or Manufacturing) Company, *Dalton, Georgia*

Samuel B. Hurowitz (ca. 1897–1968) founded Blue Ridge in 1933, and it grew to be one of the leading candlewick and then chenille bedspread manufacturers. He added a garment department by 1939, hiring Arthur Richman, an experienced robe designer from New York (see "Art-Rich Manufacturing"), to serve as production manager and stylist. The company last appears in the annual TTMA directory as a manufacturer of robes in 1956 and in the

Blue Ridge Manufacturing Company advertising matchbook cover, ca. 1945, private collection

Dalton city directory around 1961 (with A. B. Tenenbaum as president).[16]

Boyd Purse Company, *Athens, Tennessee*

Boyd Purse Company, founded by L. R. Boyd (1929–2012), produced carpet handbags probably in the late 1960s and 1970s. Boyd pursued numerous careers, working as a railroad detective in Bakersfield, California; a car lot owner in Dalton, Georgia; and a service station operator in Tennessee.[17] The labels on his carpet handbags read, in red on yellow: "Go Everywhere / The All Occasion / 'Carpet Bags' / Made from 100% undetermined fibers / Manufactured and Sold by / Boyd Purse Company," with the business's address and telephone number underneath.

Boysell, *Cartersville, Georgia*

Boysell, possibly part of B. J. Bandy's business, advertised tufted spreads, robes, bath sets, and rugs in 1950.[18]

J. W. Bray Company, *Dalton, Georgia*

In 1945 James Wellborn Bray Sr. (1904–85), a shoe repairman, founded a company that produced chenille scuffies (slippers). His business started with him tinkering in his basement with chenille scraps, then grew into a successful producer of a variety of types of slippers. Bray's son, James

Wellborn Bray Jr., joined him in the early 1950s, and a grandson, James Wellborn Bray III, joined the company in 1979. The family took pride in offering products that were made in the United States and used the motto "We try softer." Unable to compete with low-cost imports, J. W. Bray Company closed around 2000.[19]

Brooker Spread Company, *Dalton, Georgia*

Maude Brooker and William Westbrook established a business in a small shop next to Brooker's house in 1932. By 1937 the business was known as Brooker Spread Company. One of their early products was beach capes (made on single-needle machines), and then they added housecoats and bedspreads. By 1945 Brooker focused on the production of spreads, housecoats, and rugs. The company went out of business in 1983.[20]

Daphne and Fred Caldwell, *Resaca, Georgia*

Daphne Cleo Sloan Caldwell (1903–79) of Resaca, Georgia, worked with tufted textiles in the 1930s and 1940s.[21] Starting in 1936 she worked as a hauler for the B. J. Bandy Company. Then, in 1938, the Caldwells moved from the country to the highway, to a former filling station with an adjacent house, and started their own spreadline, with Daphne hand tufting. She operated the spreadline for three or four years, and unlike most spreadline owners she offered garments. Daphne worked for about six months around 1940 for H. F. "Super" Jones at Hy-Way Arts, which is where she learned to operate a chenille machine. Then she bought her first single-needle machine and made housecoats and crib spreads. Her husband, Fred Greenberry Caldwell (1901–75), helped maintain the tufting machines and cut the fabric for robes. The Caldwells operated their chenille business in the former gas station during and just after the war. Their business grew to have fifteen machines and about thirty-five to thirty-eight employees. The Caldwells' chenille business ended shortly after World War II.

California Chenille Crafters, *Los Angeles, California*

A jacket, ca. 1940, survives with a label reading "California / Chenille / Crafters / Los Angeles."

Carpet Bag, Inc., label, ca. 1970, photograph by author

Carpet Bag, Inc., *Dalton, Georgia*

Lloyd C. Yeargin (1918–76), a medical doctor, founded Carpet Bag, Inc., around 1965.[22] Carpet Bag was a family business, with Lloyd as president, his son Randy as vice president, and his wife Ruby as secretary and treasurer. Early labels read "From Floor to Fashion / by / Carpet Bag, Inc. / 30720 [Dalton's ZIP Code]," while later ones, in red on yellow, read, "THE CARPET BAG / Made from a continuous line of quality carpet / produced by a leading manufacturer. / Manufactured By: / CARPET BAG, INC.," with the company's address and telephone number underneath. The company last appears in the Dalton city directory in 1974–75. It went out of business sometime before Dr. Yeargin died in May 1976.

Chenille Craft, *Dalton, Georgia*

Chenille Craft existed by 1951, when it advertised for salesmen for its bedspreads.[23] The 1953 and 1954 TTMA directories list "Chenille Craft" and "Darling" as robe trade names for the company, which was owned by Benjamin Levitt (1905–82).[24] The company appears in Dalton city directories at least through 1961 as a manufacturer of robes and spreads, and by 1963 it is listed simply as the manufacturer of Velvetuft chenille bedspreads.

Chenille Manufacturing Company, Inc., *Sand Springs, Oklahoma*

The 1953 and 1954 TTMA directories list "Suzanna" as a robe trade name for Chenille Manufacturing Company, which produced robes and bedspreads and was owned by Eva Gavril (1899–1963) and Samuel Gavril (1895–1992), both born in Russia. They established their company in Sand Springs, Oklahoma, around 1941.[25]

Thurmon Chitwood, *Resaca, Georgia*

Thurman Chitwood (1911–94) and his wife, Martha, opened a spreadline at their home on U.S. 41 in 1935, stamping the spreads themselves and hiring women in the community to hand tuft them.[26] In 1938 Chitwood purchased two single-needle machines, which he used to make chenille robes. The Chitwoods began making bath mat sets in 1939 and then made scatter rugs.[27] Chitwood temporarily closed his business while he served in World War II. In 1946 he advertised bath sets, rugs, spreads, and robes, but he soon came to focus on rugs.[28]

CoCo:Chenille, *High Bridge, New Jersey*

Christina Lynn Whited founded CoCo:Chenille in the early 1990s. She grew up interested in fabrics and sewing and studied at the Fashion Institute of Technology in New York. An avid thrifter and yard saler, she became fascinated with chenille in the summer of 1990 and amassed three carloads of it to start her business.[29] Around 1991 she began creating jackets from the vintage spreads, then made vests and pants to go with them, adding dresses and home goods (including stuffed animals) a couple of years later. Whited considered recycling to be an important aspect of her work and even labeled her garments "CoCo:Chenille / Comfort with a Conscience."

CoCo:Chenille hibernated for a period, and now that it is revived Whited works with a wider variety of materials, as the current supply of vintage spreads is too limited.[30]

College Chenille Craft, *Keene, Texas*

In the fall of 1940 Southwestern Junior College (now Southwestern Adventist University) in Keene, Texas, established chenille production as part of its industrial training, in an effort to find work specifically for young women. It produced both robes and spreads, often designed by the students.[31] R. L. Carr served as the superintendent of the factory.[32] The business survived at least until 1954, when the TTMA directory listed the robe trade name "College Craft" for College Chenille Craft.

Colonial Craft, *Tunnel Hill, Georgia*

Georgia Lee Putnam (1925–2011) and Robert "Elbert" Putnam (1919–81) opened the roadside chenille business Colonial Craft on U.S. 41 in Tunnel Hill in 1950. They sold housecoats, pillows, bath sets, spreads, children's robes, scuffies, dolls, and short jackets, both wholesale and retail. They closed Colonial Craft probably in the mid-1960s and opened Dalton Carpet Jobbers.

Diana Cowpe (Erie) Ltd., *Dún Laoghaire, Ireland*

The Diana Cowpe company is listed in the 1956 and 1957 TTMA directories as a manufacturer of tufted robes. The company, which was founded by Eric Cowpe and named after his daughter Diana, began making chenille bedspreads in 1949. It still exists, although it has been purchased by a series of larger companies.[33]

Craftex, Inc., *Dalton, Georgia*

In January 1939 the *Dalton Citizen* reported on the organization by Lester T. Burrows, Harlan D. Broadrick, and William M. Sapp of Craftex, Inc., to make spreads, draperies, mats, wearing apparel, novelties, and other textile products.[34]

Crown Chenille Manufacturing Company, *Chatsworth, Georgia*

Sidney L. Quitman of Philadelphia, Sidney Milan of New York, and Glenn Boyd of Dalton founded Crown Chenille in the spring of 1941. The company first made bath mat sets and scatter rugs, then added chenille robes. Irving Ostow bought the company in the late 1960s or early 1970s. Phil Bernstein bought the company in the late 1970s, and Mohawk Industries acquired it in the 1990s.[35]

Crowntuft Chenille Manufacturing Company, Inc., *Fall River, Massachusetts; Heflin, Alabama; and New York City*

Mannie Ringel (1899–1985) and Irving Mace (1904–81), with Louis Barer and Irving Wallach, established the chenille robe company Crowntuft in Fall River, Massachusetts, with offices in New York, around 1945. Mace oversaw manufacturing, and Ringel was responsible for the styling, selling, and marketing. Ringel previously worked for the Gordon brothers, who ran a chenille spread and robe company in New York, possibly Gordo, which may have later moved to Dalton.[36] Crowntuft moved to Heflin, Alabama, around 1952. Customers for Crowntuft included Montgomery Ward, J. C. Penney, Spiegel, Aldens, Lerner Shops, Darling Shops, National Bellas Hess, Lane Bryant, and other catalog sales and chain stores. An early label reads "Crowntuft / Chenille Products" and includes an image of a crown with the slogans "Fit for a Queen" and "Tops Them All." A slightly later duster-style robe, probably from around 1960, has a paper tag with the "Fit for a Queen" slogan and "Crown-tuft / Chenille / Products."

Ringel sold the business around 1974 to Gabe Hakim and another man. Later robes have labels with the company's name in bubble letters. Crowntuft trademarked the names "Tuftees" in the late 1970s and "Herbcraft" in the early 1990s. Tuftees labels have the same style bubble letters. The Herbcraft products feature a variety of labels, including "Stan Herman / for / Herbcraft." Kellwood Company of St. Louis purchased Crowntuft in 1989 and eventually closed its factory in the United States.[37]

Damze Company, Inc., *Tustin, California*
In 1989 Jody and Don Chapman bought the company DMZ from Debra Maria Zomparelli and her father Rocco Zomparelli and renamed it Damze (pronounced "dames"). As DMZ had done, the Chapmans continued making jackets with chenille they acquired from Soft Goods in Georgia, and selling them to boutiques, mostly in Hawaii.[38] They purchased Soft Goods in 1991, gaining the ability to control the chenille production, and decided to make "fun, whimsical robes," which became their popular Canyon Group line.[39] Damze had the tufting and dyeing done in Georgia, then trucked the fabric to California for the cutting, sewing, and overlay. Early on, Damze worked with numerous department stores and catalogs, including Henri Bendel, Nordstrom, Victoria's Secret, Macy's, and Neiman Marcus, with most robes just carrying the stores' labels (not Damze's). Damze's Canyon Group robes received significant exposure through appearances on television shows, with the list including over twenty shows and several movies by 1996.

The Chapmans sold the company in 2006, and the robes continue to be manufactured in the United States by the company's new owners.[40]

Dellinger Spread Company, Inc., *Rome, Georgia*
Walter Edwin Dellinger (1885–1964) founded Dellinger Spread Company in 1934 in Rome, Georgia. Dellinger manufactured robes from at least 1947 to 1950. Labels surviving on spreads read, "Dellinger Spread Company / Dixie-Dell / Candlewicks and Chenilles / Rome, GA." The company's name changed to Dellinger, Inc., in 1952.[41] By 1955, the Rome city directory lists Dellinger as a manufacturer of spreads and rugs, and the company eventually focused on carpet.[42]

Devens and Son, Inc., *New York City and Dalton, Georgia*
In May 1941 the *Dalton News* reported that Devens and Son of New York had leased an old bedspread plant in Dalton and planned to manufacture coats and garments there.[43]

DMZ, *San Diego, California*
Debra Maria Zomparelli began making jackets out of vintage chenille spreads and old tablecloths and curtains around 1980 through her business Debbie's Rainbow. The vintage materials sometimes proved too fragile, though, so she and her father, Rocco Zomparelli (1926–2013), began purchasing new chenille spreads from Soft Goods, in Tunnel Hill, Georgia, and formed DMZ, the name incorporating Debbie's initials, in San Diego. The company successfully sold jackets and shorts through Nordstrom and the Neiman-Marcus holiday catalog, as well as through boutiques in Hawaii (some owned by the Chapman family) and other beach resorts.[44] In 1989 the Zomparellis sold DMZ to Jody and Don Chapman, who renamed it Damze.

Duchess Chenilles, *Dalton, Georgia*
Aaron Harry Nicholas (1881–?) established Duchess Chenilles, one of the leading producers of chenille robes, in September 1945.[45] Before moving to Dalton Nicholas ran his own "model studio" in New York, "making

designs and styles for many chenille and sportswear manufacturers."[46] Harry and his wife Rae (née Smith or Schmidt, 1894–1977) moved to Dalton around 1939 for him to be the designer and production manager for the G. H. Rauschenberg Company's robe department.[47] The details of the history of Duchess are unclear, but Dalton city directories indicate that by 1951 the Nicholases owned Duchess Laundry, a chenille products laundry, in addition to Duchess Chenilles, and that by 1953 they owned a chenille products laundry business called National Robe and Spread Company. In 1953 and 1954 the TTMA directories listed "National Robes" as the robe trade name for National Robe and Spread. The related businesses of Duchess Chenilles and National Robe and Spread last appear in the Dalton city directories in 1957, and by 1958 the Nicholases had moved to Miami Beach, where city directories record them from 1958 to at least 1960.

Edgewood Chenille, *Tunnel Hill, Georgia*

Retha Quinton (1909–94) founded Edgewood Chenille and ran it with her husband Paul.[48] She first made spreads in her home, starting in 1945, and then moved into the woodshed behind her house and named the business Edgewood Chenille. She moved to U.S. 41 in 1948 in order to display her goods where tourists traveling to Florida could see them. The Quintons' daughter Sue (1928–2011) joined the company in 1951, and Sue's husband Harry Gordon began working there in 1959. Edgewood grew from a twelve-by-twenty-four-foot building to one with about fourteen thousand square feet by 1970. By the 1970s, Edgewood produced spreads, bath mats, scatter rugs, and housecoats. The housecoats became quite popular and appeared on television shows including *Laverne and Shirley* and *In the Heat of the Night.* When the Quintons retired in 1981, they sold the business to the Gordons, at which time the name changed to Soft Goods, Inc.

Everwear Candlewick Corporation, *Dalton, Georgia, and New York City*

Everwear Candlewick Corporation established a plant in Dalton in 1934, managed by Phil Phillips (ca. 1885–1947). Listing an address on Madison Avenue, Everwear advertised candlewick pajama ensembles, bathrobes, and playsuits in 1935.[49] Luckey's Basement in Poughkeepsie, New York, advertised Everwear's candlewick Hooverettes (Depression-era dress-like aprons) in 1937, with colored tufts in an allover design on a natural ground.[50] The company transitioned from candlewick to chenille and grew from twenty employees in one building to occupying five buildings by 1940.[51] The name appeared in several variants, with the *Dalton News* listing it as Everwear Spread Company in 1939 and an ad in the *Southern Israelite* in 1945 listing Everwear Candlewick Company.[52] The 1945 ad indicated that Everwear's chenille products were available through the sales offices and showrooms of Shapiro and Son in New York and Chicago. In 1946 the *Dalton News* cited Jerry Shapiro as the president of the company, and Phillips's obituary (October 1947) states that he was survived by his brother Charles Shapiro.[53] Ads in 1947 and 1948 also listed Jerry Shapiro as manager of the Dalton plant and indicated that other plants existed in New York City and Easton, Pennsylvania.[54] The company ceases to appear in the Dalton city directories by 1951, though Shapiro and Son Curtain Corporation continued to produce bedspreads under the Everwear name for at least a few years, and the 1953 and 1954 TTMA directories list "Everwear" as a robe trade name for Shapiro and Son.[55] Labels for Everwear chenille garments typically featured an old-fashioned candlestick with a lighted candle on the left and "Everwear" in script, sometimes "Everwear / styled" and other times "Everwear / Chenille / Product." A business card for Basil Glass, director of Everwear Candlewick Ltd. in London, features a similar logo with "Everwear / Candlewick" and shows that the company manufactured bedspreads, rugs, and dressing gowns.[56] Vantona Textiles absorbed the English branch of the company.

F. and H. Chenille, *Dalton, Georgia*

F. and H. Chenille advertised in the 1951 Dalton city directory as a manufacturer of chenille spreads, robes, and rugs, owned by Homer W. Hackney (1902–71). In the 1953 and 1955 directories the company advertised bath mats, spreads, and rugs, adding that it specialized in the manufacture of "novelty chenille products." It moved from downtown Dalton to U.S. 41 in the late 1950s and advertised "promotional chenille products" instead of novelty products. In 1964 the company added dust mops to its offerings. It last appears in Dalton city directories in 1971.

Famous Chenille Corporation, *New York City*

A business card for Famous Chenille Corporation survives in Catherine Evans Whitener's papers. It indicates that the company dealt in women's, children's, and infant's chenille robes, and it lists the address 648 Broadway and the name Arnold Savitt, crossed out and replaced by Daniel P. Savitt.[57] This company existed from 1942 (if not earlier) to at least 1949.

Fireside Handcrafts Company, *Dalton, Georgia*

Mrs. Anne Brown (ca. 1891–?) founded Fireside Handcrafts Company, which focused on the production of tufted garments, in 1935. She created the designs and began with candlewick, then worked with chenille. In 1939 she formed a partnership with her son, William B. Patey, who had extensive experience with sewing machines and patented several tufting machine designs. By 1940 Fireside produced evening wraps, coats, sports jackets, boleros, robes, housecoats, bed jackets, and beach coats. Brown trademarked the name "Fluffy-Anne" for some of her garments. The company closed in the early 1940s.[58]

Fort Mountain Chenille Company, *Dalton, Georgia*

Ila Ford White (1898–1985) and her husband, Alvin White (1898–1961), owned Fort Mountain Chenille, located south of Dalton on U.S. 41. Ila began making candlewick spreads around 1920, before she married, working with a few employees and selling her wares in Dallas, Texas. She continued her business "in a small way" after she married, and then when the couple moved to a house on the highway around 1930, they established a small plant. In 1937 the company transitioned from candlewick to chenille, starting with ten machines. By 1940 the company was operating seventy. At that time, Fort Mountain Chenille made spreads, housecoats, beachwear, bath mat sets, drapes, and rugs. The Whites also operated a gas station and tourist camp.[59] The three buildings composing the plant burned in April 1941.[60]

Fulton Chenille Robe Company, *Alpharetta, Georgia*

Fulton Chenille Robe appears in the 1950, 1951, and 1952 TTMA directories as a tufted robe manufacturer, with Q. A. Wills listed as the contact. According to the Atlanta city directory, in 1945 Wills was associated with the Berry-Wills Bedspread Company.

Gordo Bedspreads, Inc., *Dalton, Georgia*

Gordo Bedspreads, Inc., began as a manufacturer of bedspreads in 1936, adding chenille garments for a period at least by 1941.[61] Mrs. Margaret Wrench (1901–58) managed the company for several years before leaving to work with Cabin Crafts in March 1941. Then David Stein served as manager.[62] Susie Wilson began working at Gordo as a tufter, was promoted to office work, and bought the company by 1951.[63] Under Wilson's leadership the company continued as a manufacturer of spreads, last appearing in the Dalton city directories in 1972.

Walter M. Gotsch Company, *Chicago, Illinois, and Dalton, Georgia*

Walter Martin Gotsch (1891–1988) is listed in the 1940 U.S. Census in Chicago as manager of a chenille bedspread business. His World War II draft registration card lists his place of employment as Walter M. Gotsch Company. Gotsch produced the high-end Adrian Evans line of chenille robes, often promoted as "Hollywood styled" and labeled Adrian Evans / Hollywood Style / original."[64] By 1950 Gotsch and his family lived in Dalton, where he was listed as president of the company, his wife as vice president, and his son as secretary. In the

1953 Dalton city directory, Gotsch advertised jointly with Belcraft Chenilles, Inc., which purchased the company in the early 1950s.

Gravley Spread Company, *Dalton, Georgia*
Pearl T. Gravely (Mrs. Jesse Floyd Gravley, 1892–1977) and her daughter-in-law Pearl R. Gravley (Mrs. Jesse Wauline Gravley, 1917–81) started a chenille business informally in 1941, when they moved to a home on U.S. 41 south of Dalton. In 1943 they purchased a single-needle machine and started making bath sets and then spreads, later adding bathrobes, including peacock robes. They acquired three- and eight-needle machines and also had home workers tuft for them. They sold both to tourists and to stores in Chicago. The company closed in 1958.[65]

Mr. and Mrs. Carl Hall, *Kennesaw, Georgia*
Homer Lee Hall (née McClure, 1918–86) and her husband Carl William Hall (1906–85) operated a chenille business on U.S. 41 in Kennesaw, toward the southern end of Northwest Georgia's roadside chenille phenomenon. They sold tufted wares from about 1936 to the early 1950s, beginning with hand-tufted spreads and garments. Their daughter Joanne Hall Garner recalls learning to use a chenille machine around 1944. Together with one employee, the couple made all of the goods. They sold them roadside and for several years shipped spreads to a business in Waco, Texas, as well. They included peacocks among their designs, and Homer Lee developed some of her own patterns as well.[66]

Hamlin's Chenille Shop, *Dania, Florida*
Gladys and Milton Hamlin owned a roadside shop on the South Federal Highway from 1947 (if not earlier) through about 1957. The 1947 Hollywood, Florida, city directory advertises that they sold chenille spreads, robes, and coats, as well as antiques. They later sold produce.

Hanson Chenille Company, *Dalton, Georgia*
George Hanson worked a variety of textile mill jobs and was an expert mechanic. In 1940 he moved to Dalton and went into business with Mose Painter, though they soon dissolved the partnership, with Painter keeping a welding business (Dalton Welding and Machine Company) and Hanson owning the tufting business, Hanson and Painter Rug Company. By the end of World War II Hanson made small rugs, bath sets, spreads, and robes, though he soon focused on larger rugs and carpet.[67] Hanson sold Hanson Chenille Company to Said Shaheen in 1945.[68]

Carl and Homer Lee Hall at their chenille business on U.S. 41 in Kennesaw (now Marietta), Georgia, ca. 1945, collection of Joanne Hall Garner

Herbcraft Textiles, Inc., *Calhoun, Georgia*

Herbcraft Textiles, established in 1948, manufactured housecoats and duster-style robes. Max Cohn served as president, Herbert Cohn as secretary and treasurer, and John D. Shelton Jr. as manager.[69] Shelton became a partner in the business, which sold in 1985.[70] This company may have been connected with Crowntuft in New York City, which used the name "Herbcraft" with its chenille robes and loungewear in the 1960s–80s.

Stan Herman, *New York City*

Stan Herman started designing chenille robes in the 1970s. By the early 1990s and into the 2000s his robes had become especially popular on QVC, the home shopping network.[71]

High Grade Candlewicks and Chenilles, *unidentified location*

A hooded chenille cape with a label reading "High Grade / Candlewicks / And / Chenilles" survives, dating from around 1940. High Grade also made bedspreads.

Hy-Way Arts, Inc., *Calhoun, Georgia*

An ad from 1941 states that the Hy-Way Arts plant was established in 1921 by Henry Franklin "Super" Jones (1884–1954). Jones previously served as superintendent and then president at Echota Cotton Mills.[72] William Hansel Sparks worked as a designer and manager for Hy-Way Arts briefly around 1940. By 1941 Hy-Way Arts made spreads, robes, and bath mat sets and worked with the selling agents M. E. Schwarz Corporation in New York.[73] By 1945 the company used selling agents Milton Sklarz Company in New York.[74] The TTMA directories list the company as a manufacturer of robes from 1950–54, with H. T. Jones (probably the founder's son Henry Thomas Jones, 1923–64) and Paul Shoffner (1908–74) as contacts.

Jay's Chenille Shop, *Dalton, Georgia*

The 1965 and 1967 Dalton city directories include ads for Jay's Chenille Shop on U.S. 41, owned by Ruth Sales (1917–2004) and offering bath sets, spreads, chenille pillows and robes, toys, and specialties.

Hy-Way Arts, Calhoun, Georgia, with William Hansel Sparks (*fourth from left*), ca. 1940, collection of Alice Sparks Young

Jeldi, *Australia*

Jeldi manufactured robes and spreads beginning in the 1940s and was acquired by SuperTex in the late 1980s. It advertised in 1951 as the first company to manufacture chenille in Australia.[75]

Jerry Terrence Carpet Bag, *Huntington Park, California*

Jerry Terrence operated a carpet handbag company from 1964 to 1967, reviving it in 2006.[76] Of the popularity of his handbags, he recalls, "The bags were so popular we had to have three shifts working every day. I ran out of remnants. I had to buy new carpet."[77] He offered a wide variety of styles and colors (forty-seven in 1966) and developed a special sewing machine to assemble his handbags.[78] His labels, in red and black on yellow, read "The Original / Jerry Terrence / Carpet / Bag / Huntington Park / California."

H. T. Jones and Company, *Calhoun, Georgia*

H. T. Jones and Company advertised in the *Southern Israelite* in 1945 as a manufacturer of infants' chenille products.[79] It probably was owned by Henry Thomas Jones (1923–64), son of H. F. Jones, who owned Hy-Way Arts.

J. A. Keller, *Dalton, Georgia, and Wisconsin Dells, Wisconsin*

Postcards survive advertising spreads, rugs, robes, and mats by J. A. Keller on Route 1 in Dalton. Several have handwritten prices added to the cards, and some are stamped "J. A. Keller Chenille Co. / Box 163, Wisconsin Dells, Wis."

LaRose Bedspread Company (LaRose Textiles), *Dalton, Georgia*

Louis Rosen (1882–1960), a textiles importer in New York, founded LaRose Bedspread Company in 1935 in Dalton with his sons Frederick (1917–2003) and Ira (1909–60). The company first worked with home candlewick tufters, then added machines in 1937, maintaining their candlewick business concurrently for a while. LaRose began making garments by 1939, and Fred

explained, "We had to bring people in that understood the ready-to-wear business."[80] The last year the TTMA directories list LaRose as a robe manufacturer is 1951, and the company switched to making carpet around 1954.[81]

Lawtex Corporation, *Dalton, Georgia*

Lawtex Corporation grew out of a business first called the Newport Trading Company, founded in 1898 and renamed Laurel Textile Company in 1912, owned by the Lorberbaum family in New York.[82] The Lorberbaums bought and sold candlewick spreads from Dalton by 1930. Seymour Lorberbaum (1912–83) moved to Dalton in 1935 and started Lawtex Corporation ("Lawtex" from "Laurel" and "Textile"). The company transitioned from candlewick to chenille in 1937. Lorberbaum's brother-in-law, Morris William "Bill" Wiesen (1916–2008), moved to Dalton in 1938 and ran the housecoat division.[83] Lawtex used the name "Candlewick Washenille" to promote some of its garments, drawing attention to the material's easy care. The company also used the name "Karabeth" with its robes.[84] Lawtex hired a piece goods maker from New York to design robes.[85] By at least the early 1950s Lawtex operated mills in Dalton and Ellijay in Georgia and Piedmont, Alabama. Lawtex stopped making chenille bedspreads around 1963 and quit making robes by 1968 (1967 is the last year the company is listed as a robe manufacturer in the TTMA directories). After experimenting with carpet, the company focused on room-size rugs.[86] Spring Mills acquired Lawtex in 1979.[87]

Lawtex employees, ca. 1947, Ward's Photo Service, Dalton, Georgia, courtesy of the estate of Leonard Lorberbaum

Ledford Chenilles, *Dalton, Georgia*

Ledford Chenilles, owned by Ethel T. Ledford (1918–2004) and Albert A. Ledford (1913–2000), appears in the Dalton city directories from 1953 through 1970. Through 1957 the company advertised spreads and rugs, and by 1958–59 the company added bath sets and women's robes, specifying that they made single-needle peacocks.

Looper's, Inc., *Dalton, Georgia*

Glenn Looper (1899–1970), better known for his foundry and often credited as the inventor of the first tufting machine, established Looper's in the late 1930s. By 1940 the company manufactured chenille spreads, capes, coats, robes, wraps, and beachwear.[88] It advertised in 1941 that it "specialized in high quality Ladies', Misses', and Children's Robes, as well as Chenille Spreads."[89] Looper married Frances Kenner, daughter of Walter Kenner of Kenner and Rauschenberg.[90] Harry Looper served as the company's vice president and treasurer.

Marilyn Wolf Designs, *Narberth, Pennsylvania*

Marilyn Wolf established a small manufacturing business in Narberth, Pennsylvania, around 1970. From the mid-1990s through the early 2000s she used vintage chenille, primarily procured from rag factories, to make one-of-a-kind patchwork garments, first for women, then for children as supplies of chenille dwindled and material became more precious. She made robes, jackets, rompers, and slippers that sold in high-end stores and children's boutiques across the country. At the height of her work with chenille, she employed about seventeen people in-house and about ten home workers. The labels were screenprinted on a variety of fabrics, with the words "Marilyn / Wolf / Designs / Narberth, Pennsylvania / Use in good health" and a Gibson Girl image. When she could no longer find adequate supplies of quality chenille, she worked with other materials. The business exists now primarily as a monogram company.[91]

Mary-Anne Novelty Company, *Cartersville, Georgia*

Mrs. Mary P. Galt (ca. 1906–62) and Miss Anne Walton (possibly 1915–88) established the Mary-Anne Novelty Company in the fall of 1941 in Cartersville, Georgia, making stuffed animals and dolls.[92] The company began with just the two women and a small sewing room, and in less than two years it grew to occupy a modern ten-thousand-square-foot plant with over 150 employees. They started with chenille scraps from a local bedspread factory and took twelve dozen "Dutch dolls" to Miami Beach, where they "sold like hotcakes" and generated more orders. Many chenille dolls, and probably those made by Mary-Anne Novelty, had plastic faces and were filled with lint, often swept from the chenille factory floors. During the war, and after a trip to New York in which their Dutch dolls were not warmly received (the Netherlands was occupied by Germany during the war), Mary-Anne Novelty began making soldier, sailor, nurse, and WAC and WAVE dolls instead.[93]

During World War II the company proudly provided jobs for women "over the age considered employable

Chenille dolls, ca. 1950, collection of Peter and Sandy Loose-Schrantz, photograph by Michael McKelvey

in war work," allowing them to contribute to the war effort by buying bonds, and offering the women, many of whom had sons in the war, "new incentive and new interests to occupy their thoughts."[94] Around 1943 the company had sales offices in New York, San Francisco, and Chicago.[95] In late 1944 the company offered Flopsy Rabbit, Bunny Babe, and Peter Rabbit for upcoming Easter sales.[96] As the end of the war neared, they developed a line of peace dolls in nine styles and introduced a new product, outsized (or plus-size) robes, as well.[97] By 1954, the company made dolls and animals representing characters from folklore and fiction, varying its offerings annually.[98]

Mason Chenille Company, *Dalton, Georgia*

J. Mason Treadwell (1903–96) and Norman Reints (1911–94) established Mason Chenille as a bedspread plant in 1938. The company also made women's and children's wear, especially in the early 1940s. They made children's robes in sizes 1, 2, and 3, cutting everything to a size 2 and sewing the robes larger or smaller to make the other sizes, and then often adding designs from nursery rhymes. They often added floral or geometric designs to women's robes.[99] The company advertised in 1952 that it specialized in children's robes and crib spreads.[100] Mason Chenille stopped making robes when it could not comply with new flameproofing requirements for garments. It began making scatter rugs after the war and closed around 1956.[101]

Mayfair Chenilles, Inc., *Calhoun, Georgia*

Mayfair Chenilles advertised chenille robes by the late 1940s.[102] William "Bill" Hansel Sparks (1908–79) of Sparks, Inc., purchased Mayfair in the early 1950s. During 1953–55 Sparks and Mayfair advertised chenille robes jointly, listing Sparks, Inc., in Dalton and Mayfair Chenilles in Calhoun.[103] The 1954 and 1955 TTMA directories list J. O. Thomas as the contact for Mayfair. In May 1955 Collins and Aikman of New York purchased Mayfair Chenilles and moved a portion of its operations to a new plant in Dalton, with the rest moving in February 1958. Collins and Aikman's Mayfair Division produced tufted automotive fabrics, scatter rugs, and apparel fabrics.[104]

Monarch Textile Corporation, *Fall River, Massachusetts*

Monarch Textile Corporation was established in the late 1930s.[105] Murray M. Taradash (1903–61) served as its president, with Mendel A. Taradash serving as vice president, secretary, and treasurer.[106] In 1939 the company manufactured bedspreads, rugs, bath mats, toilet covers, housecoats, and shopping bags.[107] The 1953 and 1954 TTMA directories list the following robe trade names for the company: "Duster," "Gracious Lady" (which appears in ads by 1947), "Lady Beautiful" (which appears in ads by 1948), "Peignoir," "Polo-Coat," "Princess Elizabeth," "Princess Margaret," "Princess Royal," "Study Coat," "3-Way Robe," and "Year Rounder." Taradash last appears in the Fall River city directories as president of Monarch in 1955.

Morgan Manufacturing Company, *Tunnel Hill, Georgia*

Willene and Jack Morgan operated Morgan Manufacturing on U.S. 41 in Tunnel Hill from 1952 to 1992. They made their own goods and sold products manufactured by other companies, catering primarily to the tourist market.

National Chenille Products Company, *Dalton, Georgia*

National Chenille Products advertised in the *Southern Israelite* in 1948, offering "Everything in Chenilles," with an office in New York and factories in Tullahoma, Tennessee; Paterson, New Jersey; and Dalton.[108] The 1950 TTMA directory lists the company as a manufacturer of tufted garments, with Mrs. Margaret Wrench as the contact in Dalton and Philip Bernstein as the contact at the home office in New York. In 1956 the Bates Manufacturing Company of Maine took over the operation of the National Chenille Products plants in Dalton and Tullahoma.[109]

National Robe and Spread Company, *Dalton, Georgia*

National Robe and Spread Company was connected to Rae and Harry Nicholas and their company Duchess Chenilles. The 1953 and 1955 Dalton city directories indicate that the Nicholases owned National Robe and Spread, which is described as a chenille products laundry business. In 1953 and 1954 the TTMA directories list "National Robes" as the robe trade name for National Robe and Spread. The related businesses of Duchess Chenilles and National Robe and Spread last appear in the Dalton city directories in 1957, and by 1958 the Nicholases had moved to Miami Beach.

Norville Chenille Company, *Watkinsville, Georgia*

Hallie McRee Norville (1903–90) operated Norville Chenille Company from 1945 to 1949, primarily making spreads but also robes and some aprons.[110] Although her son, Zack Norville, maintained machines for her while he was in school at the nearby University of Georgia, the distance from the dye houses, experienced labor, and yarn sources made the business unsustainable. The company's customers included department stores in St. Louis, Chicago, and Minneapolis. Hallie did her own designing, and Zack believed that she came up with designs by shopping in Atlanta or by responding to requests from customers. Most of her robes had floral designs, although she also made single and double peacocks. Zack recalled that robes were made from either single-needle or multi-needle machines, usually with a 5/8th gauge.

Novelty Mills, Inc., *Dalton, Georgia*

Novelty Mills was established 1938.[111] In 1941 the *Dalton Citizen* lists S. Sitt in New York as president, S. J. Laniado in New York as secretary, and Marco Ancona (1894–1967) in Dalton as treasurer and general manager of the chenille bedspread company.[112] By 1942 the company made garments as well.[113] The company existed in Dalton under Ancona's direction at least until 1951. By 1953 Ancona is listed in the Dalton city directory as supervisor at Empire Tufting, although Novelty Mills is still listed in the New York city directory that year.

O'Jay Mills and Ostow and Jacobs, *Dalton, Georgia; Calhoun, Georgia; and New York City*

David Ostow (1903–89) and Mr. Jacobs founded two companies in 1937: O'Jay Mills in Georgia and Ostow and Jacobs in New York. The companies initially made candlewick spreads, then worked with chenille. Ostow's obituary credits O'Jay's with making "some of the first chenille robes."[114] O'Jay's closed in 1991.[115]

Pacific Chenille Craft, *Los Angeles, California, and Australia*

Pacific Chenille Craft existed in Los Angeles by 1939, was owned by M. L. Hopkinson and Owen W. Schaeffer, and manufactured chenille robes, sportswear, spreads, rugs, and drapes.[116] The company expanded to Australia in 1940.[117] Australia developed a thriving chenille industry, and the leading manufacturer was Pacific Chenille Craft, later renamed SuperTex of Australia (though there are numerous permutations of the names).

The *Dalton Citizen* reported in 1947 that Pacific Chenille Craft used the trade name "SuperTex of Australia," and advertisements support the idea that SuperTex was a product line name for Pacific Chenille Craft, although it may predate the expansion of Pacific Chenille Craft to Australia.[118] In Australia, Pacific Chenille Craft formally changed its name to SuperTex Industries Ltd. in 1954, although the name "SuperTex" appears in ads prior to that change, as early as 1941, in connection with chenille, and the names appear together on some advertisements in the late 1940s.[119] Pacific Chenille Craft (SuperTex) operated factories in numerous cities in Australia, including Sydney, Goulburn, Newcastle, and Yass, and was especially successful in the 1950s, slightly later than the chenille heyday in the United States.

Painted Pony Clothing, *San Antonio, Texas*

Kathy Hoermann started Painted Pony in 1991 and used a variety of textiles, including vintage chenille bedspreads, to make new jackets.[120]

Piedmont Spread Company, *Cartersville, Georgia*

The Piedmont Spread Company was founded by the late 1930s and focused on the production of chenille robes during the World War II era. Abe Benton Tenenbaum and Irving Delancy (1915–60) were the company's executives.[121]

Polly Prentiss, *Sumter, South Carolina*

Mr. and Mrs. O. C. Moore (Otis Corcoran Moore, 1893–1939, and Annie Norine West, 1896–1995) founded one of the leading manufacturers of chenille garments, Polly Prentiss, Inc., in 1933.[122] In the mid-1930s the company regularly sent young women, known as the "Polly Prentiss Cabin Girls," to department stores to conduct "advertising demonstrations" in which they sang traditional songs and gave tufting demonstrations.

By 1938 O. C. Moore had established Asbury-Prentiss, Inc., "a pioneer company in the use of chenille process for making wearing apparel," in connection with Asbury Mills in New York.[123] Asbury Mills manufactured beachwear from the 1910s through the 1940s, and one of its two owners, Leonard C. Asch (1885–1959), was a noted bathing suit designer.[124] Asbury-Prentiss is listed at the same addresses as Asbury Mills and Asch in the New York city directories from 1940 (if not earlier) to 1946—1410 Broadway and then 1350 Broadway—and is not listed by 1949. By 1939 Polly Prentiss advertised robes, beach coats, jackets, and beach bags and sometimes added "Polly Prentiss" labels to the garments.[125]

In 1941 M. G. Scher, John F. Fitzgerald, and Harry Berger of New York joined Mrs. Moore in the management of the company. By 1950 Polly Prentiss beach and house robes were advertised as part of M. G. Scher and Associates.[126] The company closed sometime before the early 1970s.[127]

Proffitt Textile Company, *Dalton, Georgia*

In 1947 Proffitt Textile Company advertised itself as having been "back in Dalton for two years" and as the manufacturer of Asbury Chenille Robes, with offices at Asbury Mills in New York, the same company associated with Polly Prentiss.[128] In the 1951 Dalton city directory the company advertised spreads, chenille specialties, "Aristocraft" rugs, and "Leisurelux" robes for infants, children, and women. It added dusting and polishing mitts by 1953. The company is listed as a tufted garment manufacturer in the 1952–54 TTMA directories, with John R. Proffitt (1897–1991) as the contact, and in 1953 and 1954 with the robe trade name "Leisurelux." By 1958 the company had quit listing robes among its offerings.

Put's Chenille Center, *Tunnel Hill, Georgia*

Georgia Lee Putnam (1925–2011) and Robert "Elbert" Putnam (1919–81) started their first chenille business, Put's Chenille Center, around 1943–45 on U.S. 41.[129] Initially they made their own tufted textiles, and then they retailed spreads and garments manufactured by others. In 1950 the Putnams opened Colonial Craft.

Ben Putnam, *Resaca, Georgia*

Benjamin Revis Putnam (1913–76) is listed in the 1940 U.S. Census as a chenille operator at home, living on the Dixie Highway. He supplied chenille goods, including robes, to businesses including Colonial Craft and Beckler's Chenille. He married Malvia Lucinda Chitwood. His mother, Lillie Maude Young Putnam, tufted and sold candlewick spreads and is listed in the 1930 U.S. Census as having a "spread yard" at home.[130]

Malvia Putnam Chenilles, *Resaca, Georgia*

Malvia Lucinda Chitwood Putnam (later Poole, 1913–86), wife of Ben Putman, is mentioned in the *St. Petersburg (Fla.) Evening Independent* as a maker of peacock robes in 1970.[131]

Queen Chenille Company, *Dalton, Georgia*

Harry Saul (1908–94) and his wife Helen (1908–84) moved to Dalton in 1939 and operated Saul's Department Store for several years. Then, in 1946, they expanded what they had started as a part-time chenille robe business into a full-time venture, Queen Chenille.

Saul started with children's robes, explaining : "That's where I felt like I had more experience . . . and there was an opening [for the product]." Queen began with eight employees and the slogan "Fit for a Queen." The Sauls focused on making robes at first, selling to department stores and mail-order companies as well as to spreadlines, then expanded to bedspreads and bathroom sets and later to scatter rugs and Glo-Coater pads for Johnson's Floor Wax.[132] The company advertised itself in 1956 as a manufacturer of spreads, crib spreads, and robes.[133]

Queen Chenille became Queen Carpet by 1969 at the urging of the Sauls' son Julian, who joined the company in 1963, and Queen Carpet merged with Shaw Industries in 1998.[134]

G. H. Rauschenberg Company, *Dalton, Georgia*
Mrs. G. H. Rauschenberg (née Beulah E. Swick, 1888–1972) and her sister Mrs. W. T. Kenner (née Mary Jane Swick, 1872–1953) started hand tufting bedspreads probably in the late 1910s.[135] Encouraged by their success and by the increasing numbers of packages he observed leaving Dalton while he worked with the railroad, Gerhardt Henry Rauschenberg (1890–1957) joined with his brother-in-law Walter Tibbs Kenner (1868–1953) around 1920 to form Kenner and Rauschenberg, which became one of the largest candlewick companies.[136] Following a fire in the Kenner and Rauschenberg plant in 1937, the two men established separate businesses. Kenner started Ken-Rau, and Rauschenberg started G. H. Rauschenberg Company, one of the first companies to manufacture chenille robes on a large scale.[137]

The G. H. Rauschenberg Company began making chenille robes in addition to spreads in June 1939 by transferring two machines from bedspread to robe production.[138] Rauschenberg hired A. H. Nicholas, a designer in New York, to run the new robe department. The company's main robe line was "Lady Beth," with "Miss Beth" and "Baby Beth" for children and infants.[139]

The company focused on robe production and military contracts during the war. After that the company resumed full production, and by 1947 it had sales offices in New York, Chicago, Boston, Dallas, Denver, and Los Angeles.[140] In the early 1950s, the company began producing carpet as well. James Calhoun, plant manager, stated that they quit making spreads by 1953 and only made rugs and robes.[141] The last year they are listed in the TTMA directories as manufacturers of robes is 1955. Rauschenberg's son-in-law, Arthur Linton Zachry Jr. (1915–85), took over the company in 1957 and continued its move toward carpet.[142] Columbus Fiber Mills bought the company around 1960.[143]

Ruff n' Ready Underware Company, *New York City*
Carol and Jack Bradin ran the design house Ruff n' Ready Underware Company, incorporating recycled materials including chenille into its ready-to-wear line for high-end department stores, from around 1969–76.[144] They were motivated both by nostalgia for the textiles of their youth and an interest in recycling and environmental issues.[145] Their initial design, a vintage denim jacket with chenille sleeves, sold so successfully that they could not find enough old spreads to keep up. They had been acquiring bales of spreads destined to be cut into rags but began to have new chenille yardage made by Edgewood Chenille in Tunnel Hill, Georgia.[146] Ruff n' Ready added clothing labels featuring silver text stitched on a blue background.

San-Rog Spreads, Inc., *Dalton, Georgia*
San-Rog began in October 1938 with John Sansom (1892–1954) as president and J. Herbert Rogers (1907–2003) as secretary and treasurer. The company manufactured bedspreads, robes, bath mats, and novelties, and it expanded its production capabilities within a year.[147] By 1941 San-Rog promoted its Princess line of spreads.[148] The company survived until the early 1950s.[149]

Shapiro and Son, *New York City*
The 1953 and 1954 TTMA directories indicate that Shapiro and Son manufactured chenille robes under the name Everwear, likely reflecting a connection with the Everwear Candlewick Corporation.

Shenandoah Spread Manufacturing Company, *North Georgia*

The Shenandoah Spread Manufacturing Company signed a contract with the International Ladies' Garment Workers' Union in 1939, suggesting that it made garments.[150]

Shahzad Apparels Ltd., *Karachi, Pakistan*

Shahzad Apparels in Pakistan is a contemporary joint venture of the United States–based Kellwood Company and manufactures chenille yardage and apparel.[151]

Shepherd Brothers Manufacturing Company, *Calhoun, Georgia*

Shepherd Brothers manufactured wool jackets with Mexicana chenille ornamentation. The labels read: "La Muchacha / Shepherd Bros. Mfg. Co. / Calhoun, GA. / 100% wool / Dry Clean Only."

Silhouette, Inc., *Montreal, Canada*

A bed jacket with a label reading "Chenilles / By / Silhouette / Inc." indicates that this company existed around 1940. The 1950 and 1951 TTMA directories list Silhouette as a manufacturer of tufted garments, with Godfrey E. Fochs as the contact.

Soft Goods, Inc., *Tunnel Hill, Georgia*

When Sue and Harry Gordon purchased Edgewood Chenille from Sue's parents, Retha and Paul Quinton, in 1981, they renamed it Soft Goods, Inc., and continued making chenille garments. They developed a chenille jacket that sold in leading department stores, and they also sold yardage and spreads to DMZ (later Damze Company) of California, which made chenille jackets. In 1991 Jody and Don Chapman, who owned Damze and were based in California, purchased Soft Goods, Inc., and formed Soft Goods Industries. Soft Goods Industries ended a few years later when the Chapmans moved much of the production from Georgia to California.[152]

Southern Chenille, *Cartersville, Georgia*

Hallie Norville (1903–90) and her sister Mavis Slaughter (1905–83) established Southern Chenille in 1943, selling it to relatives a few years later. Norville did the designing for the company, which made housecoats and baby blankets.[153]

Sparks, Inc., *Dalton, Georgia*

William "Bill" Hansel Sparks (1908–79) bought out his partners in the Sparks-Pittman Company and established Sparks, Inc., in 1947, making robes and spreads.[154] An ad in the 1951 Dalton city directory states the company's motto ("Quality, Service, Dependability") and presents its trademark: "It's a Spar-kay Chenille."[155] In the early 1950s Sparks bought a chenille company in Calhoun called Mayfair Chenilles, and in 1953–55 Sparks and Mayfair advertised jointly, listing Sparks in Dalton and Mayfair Chenilles in Calhoun.[156]

Sparks's son Wilbur Hugh Sparks (1928–83), also known as Bill, became president of Sparks, Inc., in 1958. By 1963 the company made chenille robes and terry-cloth robes as well as beach jackets and small rugs. It also made scuffies, which it sold paired with children's robes.[157] The company's biggest customers included Sears and Montgomery Ward. At a later date, probably in the late 1960s, Buck Creek Industries of Birmingham, Alabama, bought Sparks, Inc.[158]

Sparks-Pittman Company, *Dalton, Georgia*

William Hansel Sparks, together with Carter Pittman, a local attorney and president of the TTMA from 1945 to 1947, established Sparks-Pittman Company by 1945. The business manufactured garments, rugs, spreads, and novelties. The owners set aside a space in the factory for Charlie Gish to make chenille toys, and Gish soon formally joined the company.[159] Sparks bought out his partners and established Sparks, Inc., in 1947.[160]

SuperTex of Australia

The *Dalton Citizen* reported in 1947 that Pacific Chenille Craft in Australia used the trade name "SuperTex of

Australia."[161] Ads support the idea that SuperTex began as a product line name for Pacific Chenille Craft, and it may have had, like Pacific Chenille Craft, roots in California. In Australia, Pacific Chenille Craft formally changed its name to SuperTex Industries Ltd. in 1954, though the name "SuperTex" appears in ads prior to that change, as early as 1941, in connection with chenille spreads and garments, and the names appear together on some ads in the late 1940s.[162]

Tennoga Hooked Rugs (or Tennoga Handcrafts), *Cleveland, Tennessee, and Dalton, Georgia*

Mary McBryde Sims (1878–1942) briefly included hand-tufted kimonos in the inventory of her company Tennoga Hooked Rugs ("Tennoga" comes from "Tennessee and North Georgia"). An undated brochure, probably from the early to mid-1920s, includes illustrations of candle-wick bedspreads and hooked rugs and descriptions of the colors and designs available, with a brief listing for "Kimonas (hand-tufted)." Tennoga sold products through women's organizations and to gift shops, camp craft shops, and individuals.[163] After Sims died, Mrs. H. L. Jarvis (née Eugenia Bitting, 1877–1966) continued with her workers. Mary Gene Dykes, granddaughter of both women, ran Tennoga for a while beginning in 1959 until she no longer had enough workers to continue.

Underwood Chenille Company, *Dalton, Georgia*

Underwood Chenille Company advertised in 1949 for mail order and door-to-door salesmen for its chenille spreads, housecoats, and rugs.[164]

Catherine Evans Whitener, *Dalton, Georgia*

Catherine Evans Whitener (1880–1964) is considered the founding mother of the tufted textile industry in Northwest Georgia. In addition to candlewick bed-spreads, she made kimonos and aprons.

Mrs. C. B. Wood, *Dalton and Rocky Face, Georgia*

Mrs. C. B. Wood (Kate Deck Wood, 1869–1945) estab-lished one of the earliest candlewick bedspread compa-nies, C. B. Wood and Company, in 1921.[165] Her company also made chenille garments, including capes, slacks, and coats, in the late 1930s and early 1940s.[166] A designer from New York came to Georgia to make the patterns. Wood's daughter closed the business shortly after her mother died.

Acknowledgments

I deeply appreciate the generosity of the foundations and businesses that have supported *Southern Tufts*: the Center for Craft, Creativity and Design; Shaw Industries; the Harry and Helen Saul Foundation; the Brown-Whitworth Foundation; and Norville Industries. Thank you!

Thanks too are due to all the staff at the University of Georgia Press, and to Mark Callahan for all of his thoughtful feedback and for directing me to Jean Shepherd's writing and Cloris Leachman's performance in *The Last Picture Show*; Nunally Benzing for bringing Katharine Hepburn's chenille robe in *Holiday* to my attention; Patrick Allen for bringing Carole Lombard's chenille robes to my attention; Megan Searing Young for her assistance locating and assessing the records of the Women's Bureau, Department of Labor at the National Archives; Betty Alice Fowler for noticing John Waters's pink candlewick jacket; and Joy Richman for sharing Zack Norville's autobiography with me.

Many thanks also to these individuals for their assistance and support:

Gary Albert
Patrick Allen, University of Georgia Press
Philis Alvic
Jack Bandy
Sidney Baxter
Claudell Beckler
Randy Beckler
Carolyn Benesh, *Ornament Magazine*
Nunally Benzing
Linda Blackman

José Blanco and Raúl Vázquez
David Bowman, Shaw Industries Group, Inc.
Jack Bradin
Mr. and Mrs. James Wellborn Bray III
Alys and Trevor Brown
Jeannette Brown
Priscilla and Mike Brown
David Cady
Mr. and Mrs. Calvin Caldwell
Arrow Callahan

Copper Callahan
Mark Callahan
Don Chapman
Colter Chitwood
Sheila Cohen
Carolyn Cook
Mike Cook
Dale Couch
Thomas M. Deaton
Jennifer Detweiler, Whitfield-Murray
    Historical Society
Carol Dolson
Mary Gene Dykes
David Edelman
Gerald Embry
Clarissa Esguerra, Los Angeles County
    Museum of Art
Joseph R. Evans
Anna Fariello
Betty Alice Fowler
John Derrick Fowler, Bandy Heritage Center
    for Northwest Georgia
Sean Garrett
Harry Gordon
Paula Swann Hall
Brian Hilliard, Bandy Heritage Center for
    Northwest Georgia
Regan Huff
Patricia Hunt-Hurst
Helen and Paul Johnson
Jamie Jones, *Dalton Daily Citizen*
Nolan Kenner
Christine King
Jewel King
Leanne Lawson, Creative Arts Guild
Local History Staff, Chattanooga Public Library
Sandy and Peter Loose-Schrantz
Deb Lorberbaum
Leonard J. Lorberbaum
Jean Lowrey
Debbie Lynch
Janet McKinney
Sandy Moore, Bartow History Museum

Willene Morgan
Rita and Zack Norville
Abbie Tucker Parks
Jane Pate
Louise Pinson
Bradley Putnam
Uzair Rauf, Shahzad Apparels
Joy Richman
Julian Saul
Madelyn Shaw
Paul Shoffner and Kayanne Shoffner Massey
Pete Sigmon, Shaw Industries Group, Inc.
Sandra Sims
Ty Snyder, Heritage Center Museum, Historic
    Western and Atlantic Railroad Tunnel
Sabra Sparks
Vivian Sparks
Mary Spector
Dixie Chitwood Stanley
Jeffrey Stegall
Pat Taft
Jerry Terrence
Ellen Thompson
Terry Tomasello, Creative Arts Guild
Jane Powers Weldon
Marcelle White
Christina Lynn Whited
Frances Stiles Whitener
Marsha Franklin Whitener
Lynn Whitworth
Marilyn Wolf
Alice Young
Megan Searing Young
Gerhardt H. Zachry
Debra Marie Zomparelli

This research was supported by a
Craft Research Fund grant from the Center
for Craft, Creativity and Design.

Notes

Foreword

1 See, for example, Michael D. Schulman and Jeffrey Leiter, "Southern Textiles: Contested Puzzles and Continuing Paradoxes," in Jeffrey Leiter, Michael D. Schulman, and Rhonda Zingraff, eds., *Hanging by a Thread: Social Change in Southern Textiles* (Ithaca, N.Y.: ILR Press, 1991), 6–13.

2 The interplay between Paris and American fashion in the first half of the twentieth century was the focus of an exhibition and accompanying catalogue: Susan Anderson Hay, ed., *From Paris to Providence: Fashion, Art, and the Tirocchi Dressmakers' Shop, 1915–1947* (Providence: Rhode Island School of Design Museum of Art, 2001).

3 Traphagen was an important figure in American fashion, teaching in several design schools in New York before opening her own fashion design school. She and her students were very involved in the "Made in America" campaign and the associated contests. A recent master's thesis, Cassidy Zachary, *Ethel Traphagen: American Fashion Pioneer*, Fashion Institute of Technology, State University of New York, 2013, is available at http://www.academia.edu/6704244/Ethel_Traphagen_paper.

4 Fashion Group, *The Fashion Group Presents New York's Fashion Futures* (New York: Advertising Composition, 1940), 10.

CHAPTER 1. *The History of Candlewick Bedspreads in Northwest Georgia*

1 "The Hand-Tufted Spread Industry," *Dalton Citizen*, September 17, 1925.

2 For more on Catherine Evans Whitener and the women involved in the tufted textile industry, see Randall L. Patton, "Catherine Evans Whitener (1881–1964): The Creation of North Georgia's Tufted Textile Industry," in Ann Short Chirhart and Kathleen Ann Clark, ed., *Georgia Women: Their Lives and Times*, vol. 2 (Athens: University of Georgia Press, 2014), 86–113.

3 Sybil Reed Tate, "A Short History of Dogwood Valley, 1830–1950: History, Photographs and Memories," booklet, 1994, Whitfield-Murray Historical Society; "Mrs. Will Whitener, Founder of a Georgia Textile Trade," *New York Times*, June 3, 1964.

4 Stiles Martin, "Daltonite Who Began Tufted Industry Tells Newsletter of First Bedspread," *Georgia Department of Commerce Newsletter*, August 10, 1953 (reprinted in the *Dalton Citizen* sometime in 1953 in an article titled, "Founding of Tufted Textile Industry Is Recalled in Commerce Publication"); Mrs. William (Catherine Evans) Whitener, "The Tufted Bed Spread Industry: A History" (unpublished typed manuscript with handwritten edits, ca. 1938), Catherine Evans Whitener Scrapbook, gift

of the Evans family, Whitfield-Murray Historical Society, Crown Gardens & Archives, Dalton, Georgia. Whitener's story, more or less as it appears in the typed manuscript, is recounted in "Mrs. Whitener Tells Students at North Dalton about Start of Bedspread Industry Here," *Dalton Citizen*, March 18, 1954, although a few details are incorrect there, including the name of the McCutchen community, which is written "McCuthey," and the name of Mrs. League, which is given as "Lange." The school talk was printed again in "Mrs. Whitener Began Tufting Industry in 1895 When She Hand-Tufted a Spread," *Dalton Citizen*, March 14, 1958; and it appeared yet again in "If I Had Been a Man," in George O. Wilson and Dalton-Whitfield County Bicentennial Commission, eds., *Today and Tomorrow Become Yesterday: The City of Dalton and the County of Whitfield in the State of Georgia Celebrate the National Bicentennial, Official Souvenir Book, May 1976* (Dalton: Dalton-Whitfield County Bicentennial Commission?, 1976), 74–79.

5 Martin reports that Whitener called this first spread a *star* and circle design, though in her autobiographical text Whitener calls it a *spear* and circle design.

6 Martin, "Daltonite Who Began Tufted Industry."

7 Whitener stated that until Jarvis's orders she made the spreads herself. James D. Prather, "Woman Who Started Bedspread Boulevard," *Atlanta Journal Magazine*, April 11, 1937.

8 "Eugenia Bitting Jarvis," in Mrs. George S. Lowman and Mrs. B. M. Boykin, eds., *Leaders in Georgia: In Education, in Business, and in the Arts* (Atlanta: Curtis, 1955), 56; Thomas M. Deaton, *Bedspreads to Broadloom: The Story of the Tufted Carpet Industry* (Acton, Mass.: Tapestry Press, 1993), 5–7; and "The Hand-Tufted Spread Industry," *Dalton Citizen*, September 17, 1925.

9 Advertisement, John Wanamaker's, "Au Quatrieme 'What is It?,'" *New York Evening Telegram*, December 7, 1915; advertisement, John Wanamaker's, "Candlewick Spreads," *New York Herald*, October 11, 1916. The spreads in the second ad sold for $8.50–$10 ($186–$218 in 2014), down from initial prices of $15 ($328 in 2014) and up.

10 Advertisement, John Wanamaker's, "Summer Bed-Coverings," *New York Evening Post*, April 21, 1917.

11 Murray E. Wyche, "The Tufted Textile Industry in the South," 1948, 3, copied in 1996 by Polly Boggess from a print article found in the Cabin Crafts scrapbooks, Bedspread Industry box, Articles on History, Companies, and Machinery folder, Crown Gardens & Archives.

12 "The Hand-Tufted Spread Industry," *Dalton Citizen*, September 17, 1925.

13 "Miss Evans Made First Bedspread," *Chattanooga Times*, February 1, 1929. Also see the website documenting the exhibition *Peacock Alley: The Early Years of Gordon County's Chenille Industry*, North Georgia Regional Library, http://ngrl.org/calhounlibrary/peacockalley/.

14 William Secord, "The American Candlewick Spread," *HALI: The International Journal of Oriental Carpets and Textiles* 4, no. 2 (1981): 161–62.

15 Phoebe Laing Mosley, "The Pleasant Land of Counterpane," *McCall Decorative Arts and Needlework*, Summer 1932, 22. Catherine Evans Whitener saved a clipping of this article in her scrapbook.

16 "Bedspreads and Pillow Shams," *Ladies' World*, February 1893, 11, clipping in Wykoff's chenille bedspread oral history notebook, Crown Gardens & Archives.

17 Dorothy Dean, "A Talk with the Band," *Des Moines (Iowa) Homestead*, May 18, 1894.

18 "The Hand-Tufted Spread Industry," *Dalton Citizen*, September 17, 1925.

19 Allanstand Cottage Industries was transferred to the Southern Highland Handicraft Guild in 1931. "Craft Revival: Shaping Western North Carolina Past and Present," Western Carolina University, Hunter Library Digital Collections, http://wcu.edu/library/DigitalCollections/CraftRevival/story/index.html; tufted bedspread entries (http://wcudigitalcollection.contentdm.oclc.org/cdm/search/collection/p4008coll2/searchterm/tufted/order/nosort); Katherine Caldwell, "Making History: Allanstand Cottage Industries," from Anna Fariello, ed., Mountain Hands: The Story of

Allanstand Craft Shop's First 100 Years (Asheville, N.C.: Southern Highland Craft Guild, 2008), Western Carolina University, Hunter Library Digital Collections, http://wcu.edu/libraryDigital Collections/CraftRevival/story/allanstand.html.

20 Frances Louisa Goodrich, *Mountain Homespun* (1931; repr., Knoxville: University of Tennessee Press, 1989), 26.

21 "Deerfield Shows Its Work, Exhibit of Village Industries Draws Many Visitors to Old Massachusetts Town," *Christian Science Monitor*, July 15, 1911.

22 Beverly Gordon, "Spinning Wheels, Samplers, and the Modern Priscilla: The Images and Paradoxes of Colonial Revival Needlework," *Winterthur Portfolio* 33, no. 2/3 (Summer/Autumn 1998), 171–72.

23 Advertisement, John Wanamaker's, *Philadelphia Evening Public Ledger*, January 15, 1920; advertisement, Germantown Novelty Shop, *Philadelphia Evening Public Ledger*, June 2, 1922. In the early 1930s, Appalachian Hand Weavers in Tryon, North Carolina, Owens Manufacturing Company in Tullahoma, Tennessee, and Alabama Bedspread Company in Scottsboro, Alabama, also produced candlewick spreads. Bertha M. Nienburg, "Potential Earning Power of Southern Mountaineer Handicraft," *Bulletin of the Women's Bureau*, no. 128 (Washington, D.C.: United States Department of Labor, Women's Bureau, Government Printing Office, 1935), 39, 41. Fireside Industries at Berea College in Kentucky and students at Martha Berry Schools near Rome, Georgia, also tufted spreads. Philis Alvic, *Weavers of the Southern Highlands* (Lexington: University of Kentucky Press, 2003, 44; and Allen H. Eaton, *Handicrafts of the Southern Highlands* (New York: Russell Sage Foundation, 1937), 226–27, plate located between pages 290 and 291. In 1939 the *Christian Science Monitor* reported on tufters in Anguilla, Mississippi, explaining that due to the slump in cotton prices, a group of tenant farmers worked with their employer, Mrs. Tom Fields, to begin making candlewick spreads like the ones Fields had seen in the mountains of North Carolina; thirty-six women and one man made

healthy incomes from the enterprise. Dorothea Kahn, "Homespun Handicrafts Popular in South," *Christian Science Monitor*, April 10, 1939.

24 See for example, advertisement, Georgia Allen, Inc., "Lovely Old Fashioned Candlewick Bedspreads, Stamped to Embroider," *Philadelphia Evening Public Ledger*, November 7, 1922; "'Candlewick' Is a New Embroidery," *Connellsville (Pa.) Daily Courier*, September 29, 1922.

25 "The Hand-Tufted Spread Industry," *Dalton Citizen*, September 17, 1925, and "Many Important Industries Are Located at Dalton, Ga.," *Atlanta Constitution*, May 1, 1927. Retail prices for candlewick spreads ranged from about $6–$9 in 1922 (approximately $85–$128 in 2014), decreasing to about $4–$5.50 in 1925 (approximately $54–$75 in 2014) and about $3–$4 in 1928 (approximately $41–$56 in 2014), and reaching extreme highs and lows in the early 1930s—prices ranged from about $0.84–$9.95 in 1933 (approximately $15–$182 in 2014).

26 Advertisement, Gimbel Brothers, "2500 of the Famous Candlewick Spreads," *New York Times*, January 1, 1924.

27 "Miss Evans Made First Bedspread," *Chattanooga Times*, February 1, 1929; "Kenner and Rauschenberg Ship Bedspreads to Far Corners of Globe" and caption in the rotogravure section, Anniversary Edition, *Dalton Citizen*, August 25, 1932.

28 "Bedspreads Make $1,000,000 Industry," *Washington Post*, June 5, 1934; "Candlewick Wage Situation Defended and Condemned by Bedspread Producers," *Dalton News*, March 8, 1935.

29 Advertisement, John Wanamaker's, "Candlewick Spreads," *New York Herald*, October 11, 1916.

30 Advertisement, John Wanamaker's, "Quaint Candlewick Spreads Have a New Vogue," *Philadelphia Evening Public Ledger*, March 16, 1920.

31 Advertisement, Bloomingdale's, "Bloomingdale's Gives the World Candlewick Prints," *New York Times*, February 11, 1934.

32 "Central Franklin Yarns Famous," Bedspread and Manufacturers' Edition, *Dalton News*, February 29, 1940.

33 W. A. Tarver, president, Franklin Process Company, Providence, Rhode Island, to Mrs. W. L. Whitener, Dalton, Georgia, April 21, 1947, Catherine Evans Whitener Scrapbook.

34 See, for example, advertisement, Lansburgh & Brother, "Ante-Bellum Candlewick Bedspreads Come Back," *Washington Post*, June 4, 1922; advertisement, John Wanamaker's, "Candlewick Spreads for Four-Post Beds," *Philadelphia Evening Public Ledger*, July 17, 1922. A few earlier ads mention colored tufting, including one from Wanamaker's in 1917 that offers white bedspread sets embroidered in pink and blue. Advertisement, John Wanamaker's, "Hand-tufted Candlewick Spreads," *New York Evening Post*, January 18, 1917.

35 Advertisement, Gimbel Brothers, "Candlewick Bed Spreads," *New York Times*, April 27, 1924.

36 "The Hand-Tufted Spread Industry," *Dalton Citizen*, September 17, 1925.

37 "Candlewick Spread First Seen at Fair," *Utica (N.Y.) Observer Dispatch*, February 28, 1937.

38 "Versions at Variance on Origin of Candlewick Spread Industry," *Atlanta Constitution*, March 28, 1937. Before the Civil War, Heath moved to Georgia from South Carolina with her parents and lived in the historic Chief Vann House in Spring Place (a small town east of Dalton noted for its Moravian and Cherokee history), later moving to Dalton and marrying Alexander Heath.

39 Ibid.

40 Cheryl Wykoff, "Stewart's Bedspread Company," based on Wykoff's interviews of Eathel B. Stewart from 1988, Wykoff's chenille bedspread oral history notebook, Crown Gardens & Archives.

41 "Bates Owner Home Made Spread over 150 Years Old," *Dalton News*, May 19, 1942.

42 Mrs. Fred Caldwell and her son Calvin Caldwell, interview by Thomas Deaton, December 10, 1979, transcript, Fred Caldwell folder 012, box 2 of 4, Carpet History 2010.1, MSS 1, Dr. Thomas Deaton Collection, Bandy Heritage Center for Northwest Georgia, Dalton State College, Dalton, Georgia.

43 M. Anna Fariello, *Movers and Makers: Doris Ulmann's Portrait of the Craft Revival in Appalachia* (Asheville, N.C.: Curatorial InSight, 2005), 12.

44 Ibid., 24.

45 Ibid.

46 Alvic, *Weavers of the Southern Highlands*, 123.

47 Advertisement, Strawbridge & Clothier, "Candlewick Bed Spreads from the Georgia Mountains," *Philadelphia Evening Public Ledger*, September 21, 1922.

48 Advertisement, Davison-Paxon-Stokes, "By the Way," *Atlanta Constitution*, July 11, 1926.

49 Alvic, *Weavers of the Southern Highlands*, 6.

50 Ibid., 174.

51 Ibid., 40.

52 Ibid., 134.

53 Ulmann visited the Stiles family twice. On her first visit she shot the images, then she returned to deliver photographs to the family, also bringing new dresses for Frances and her sister and a sack of oranges. Frances Stiles Whitener, interview by author, March 12, 2013, Dalton, Georgia.

54 Frances Whitener recalled that Ulmann tried to visit B. J. Bandy's business, but that it was closed the day they went so they just peeked through a crack. For more on Frances Whitener's recollections of Doris Ulmann's visits, see Rachel Brown, "Dalton Resident Shares Memories of Depression-Era Photography Shoot," *Dalton Daily Citizen*, October 29, 2010.

55 Allen H. Eaton, *Handicrafts of the Southern Highlands* (New York: Russell Sage Foundation, 1937).

56 Ibid., 225, 227.

57 Frances Stiles Whitener, interview by author, March 12, 2013, Dalton, Georgia.

58 Mrs. R. C. Beard family survey, June 6, 1934, Home Workers Candlewick Spreads Schedules, box 232, Records of the Women's Bureau, Department of Labor, National Archives.

59 Kenner and Rauschenberg handwritten notes, Candlewick folder, box 232, Records of the Women's Bureau, Department of Labor, National Archives.

60 These surveys also are discussed in Alvic, *Weavers of the Southern Highlands*, as well as in Jane S. Becker, *Selling Tradition: Appalachia and the Construction of an American Folk, 1930–1940* (Chapel Hill: University of North Carolina Press, 1998).

61 Alvic, *Weavers of the Southern Highlands*, 31, 140. The survey included about one hundred candlewick

workers. There were approximately seventy-five hundred to ten thousand home workers making candlewick bedspreads in Northwest Georgia at about that time. Henry Nevin, "Bedspread Sales Reach High Mark in North Georgia," *Atlanta Constitution*, September 29, 1935.

62 Mrs. Pack survey, June 18, 1934, Home Workers Candlewick Spreads Schedules, box 232, Records of the Women's Bureau, Department of Labor, National Archives.

63 Sally Jo Green survey, June 6, 1934, ibid.

64 Mrs. Mabel Watts survey, June 14, 1934, ibid.

65 Mrs. W. V. Sissin survey, June 5, 1934, ibid.

66 Mrs. Godfrey survey and separate page of notes, June 18, 1934, ibid.

67 Mrs. Webb Coffey survey, June 5, 1934, ibid.

68 Mrs. Stella Bishop survey, June 5, 1934, ibid.

69 Miss Bonnie K. Dunn survey, June 6, 1934, ibid.

70 Mrs. Bradford survey, June 8, 1934, ibid.

71 Mrs. Godfrey survey, June 18, 1934, ibid.

72 Mrs. Bearden survey, June 18, 1934, ibid.

73 Mrs. Gertrude Caldwell survey, June 15, 1934, ibid.

74 Mrs. D. F. Woods survey, June 6, 1934, ibid.

75 Edwards family survey, June 8, 1934, ibid.

76 Mrs. MacDearis survey, June 8, 1934, ibid.

77 Fletcher family survey, June 8, 1934, and Teague family survey, June 8, 1934, ibid.

78 Mrs. John Walker survey, June 6, 1934, ibid.

79 Hill family survey, June 18, 1934, ibid.

80 Mrs. Henderson survey, June 8, 1934, ibid.

81 Mrs. Chadwick survey, June 8, 1934, ibid.

82 Mrs. Scott survey, June 14, 1934, ibid.

83 Mrs. E. Riddenberry survey, June 8, 1934, ibid.

84 Bertha M. Nienburg, "Potential Earning Power of Southern Mountaineer Handicraft," *Bulletin of the Women's Bureau*, no. 128 (Washington, D.C.: United States Department of Labor, Women's Bureau, Government Printing Office, 1935), 4–5.

85 Ibid., 16.

86 Fred Rosen, interview by Thomas Deaton, February 28, 1980, transcript, p. 2, Fred Rosen folder 056, box 2 of 4, Carpet History 2010.1, MSS 1, Dr. Thomas Deaton Collection, Bandy Heritage Center for Northwest Georgia.

87 See Deaton, *Bedspreads to Broadloom*, for more details about the evolution of tufting machines in the Dalton area.

88 "Mid-South Industrial Outlook Grows Encouraging," *Wall Street Journal*, September 2, 1922.

89 Advertisement, W. B. Moses and Sons, "Candlewick Spreads," *Washington Post*, November 26, 1922.

90 Zack Norville, interview by author, July 26, 2013, Dalton, Georgia.

91 "The Tufted Story," in *Textile Manufacturers Association 1950 Directory and Yearbook* (Dalton, Ga.: Tufted Textile Manufacturers Association, 1950), 30; Wyche, "Tufted Textile Industry," 11.

92 For more information on the factory conditions in Dalton, see Douglas Flamming, *Creating the Modern South: Millhands and Managers in Dalton, Georgia, 1884–1984* (Chapel Hill: University of North Carolina Press, 1992).

93 "Chenille Business Is One of Georgia's Newest and Best Sources of Revenue," *Georgia Progress* 3, no. 4 (October 1, 1946): n.p.

94 Deaton, *Bedspreads to Broadloom*, 181; "Business World," *New York Times*, July 28, 1938; Henry C. Ball, "The T.T.M.A.," in *Tufted Textile Manufacturers Association Directory, 1953* (Dalton, Ga.: Tufted Textile Manufacturers Association, 1953), 14. Ball presents a slightly different account, stating that the Bedspread Association was absorbed by the TTMA in 1945 and that the other group, which he does not name, was established in 1939 and short lived. The TTMA published an annual directory from 1950 to 1968 and became the Carpet and Rug Institute around 1969.

95 "TTMA, Serving Tufted Industry, Founded in 1945," Progress Edition, *Dalton Daily Citizen-News*, March 30, 1963.

96 "The Tufted Story," *Textile Manufacturers Association 1950 Directory and Yearbook* (Dalton, Ga.: Tufted Textile Manufacturers Association, 1950), 26.

97 Frank Talley, "How Does Promotion Affect Your Sales?," *Tufted Textile Manufacturers Association Directory, 1953* (Dalton, Ga.: Tufted Textile Manufacturers Association, 1953), 43.

1 Frank J. Reynolds, "Dalton and Whitfield County Set Prosperity Pace; Food Crops, Money in Bank, Highway Completed," *Atlanta Constitution*, January 17, 1915.

2 Edward Caudill and Paul Ashdown, *Sherman's March in Myth and Memory* (Lanham, Md.: Rowman & Littlefield, 2009), 164.

3 "Great Highway Planned, Chattanooga to Atlanta; Association Is Formed," *Atlanta Constitution*, June 13, 1909; "History, Sentiment and Scenic Beauty Combined in Johnston-Sherman Highway," *Atlanta Constitution*, July 2, 1911; "Tourists Follow Historic Route," *Atlanta Constitution*, October 30, 1912.

4 Jeffrey L. Durbin, "Heading South without Getting Sidetracked: The Dixie Highway in Georgia," in Claudette Stager and Martha Carver, eds., *Looking Beyond the Highway: Dixie Roads and Culture* (Knoxville: University of Tennessee Press, 2006), 36–38.

5 "Whitfield and the Highway," *Atlanta Constitution*, January 17, 1915.

6 Durbin, "Heading South without Getting Sidetracked," 43.

7 Howard Laurence Preston, *Dirt Roads to Dixie: Accessibility and Modernization in the South, 1885–1935* (Knoxville: University of Tennessee Press, 1991), 132.

8 Most of Interstate 75 opened in 1965, with its final segment opening between Marietta and Cartersville at the end of 1977.

9 Preston, *Dirt Roads to Dixie*, 39.

10 Frank J. Reynolds, "Dalton and Whitfield County Set Prosperity Pace: Food Crops, Money in Bank, Highway Completed," *Atlanta Constitution*, January 17, 1915.

11 Ibid.

12 Durbin, "Heading South without Getting Sidetracked," 35–36.

13 Ibid., 44–45.

14 Preston, *Dirt Roads to Dixie*, 115.

15 Ibid., 116.

16 Ibid., 124–25.

17 Ibid., 128.

18 Ibid.

19 Some of the earliest published articles giving dates for the beginning of the roadside sales are from the 1940s and suggest that the spreadlines started in the early or late 1920s. Murray E. Wyche, "The Tufted Textile Industry in the South," 3, Bedspread Industry box, Articles on History, Companies, and Machinery folder, Crown Gardens & Archives; "Parlor Pastime Becomes Big Business," *Massillon (Ohio) Evening Independent*, March 4, 1941; R. H. West, "Dalton 'Spreads' Itself," *NC&StL Railway Bulletin* (Nashville, Chattanooga, and St. Louis Railway), September 1949, 8.

20 Lucy O'Brien, "Chenille and Candlewick Spreads Line Both Sides of North Georgia Highways," Women's World column, *Tampa Morning Tribune*, August 11, 1947.

21 "Cannon Company Ships Bedspreads Throughout World," *Dalton News*, March 21, 1929.

22 "Bedspreads Aid Georgia County to Increase Living Standards," *Albany (N.Y.) Evening News*, May 24, 1934 (variations of this United Press article ran in numerous newspapers); "Oklahoma Editor Amazed at 'Washing on the Line' in Bedspread Belt," *Dalton Citizen*, October 10, 1935; "On Georgia's Bedspread Boulevard," *Atlanta Journal*, October 18, 1936; William Boring, "Bedspread Boulevard," *Morning Herald* (Gloversville and Johnstown, N.Y.), October 9, 1938; "Catherine Evans' Bedspreads," *Time*, September 2, 1940, 57–59; Ray G. Jones Jr. and Claude A. Campbell, "The Development of Georgia's Tufted Textile Industry," Research Paper no. 12, Bureau of Business and Economic Research, School of Business Administration, Georgia State College of Business Administration, March 1959, 40; "Millionaires Abound in Georgia Carpet Town," *Nashua (N.H.) Telegraph*, May 16, 1978.

23 "Ancient Industry Revived," *Gastonia (N.C.) Daily Gazette*, May 20, 1938; Henry Nevin, "City of Dalton 'Spreads' Itself to World Fame," *Atlanta Constitution*, September 1, 1942.

24 Wyche, "Tufted Textile Industry."

25 Julian F. Haas, "Candlewick Spreads Helped Georgia Folk," *Hammond (Ind.) Times*, October 23, 1935.

26 Phoebe Laing Mosley, "The Pleasant Land of Counterpane," *McCall Decorative Arts and Needlework*, Summer 1932, 22.

27 "Oklahoma Editor Amazed at 'Washing on the Line' in Bedspread Belt," *Dalton Citizen*, October 10, 1935.

28 William Boring, "Bedspread Boulevard," *Morning Herald* (Gloversville and Johnstown, N.Y.), October 9, 1938.

29 Mrs. Sexton survey, June 8, 1934, Home Workers Candlewick Spreads Schedules, box 232, Records of the Women's Bureau, Department of Labor, National Archives.

30 H. R. Kaye family survey, June 8, 1934, ibid.

31 Fletcher family survey, June 8, 1934, ibid.

32 Jacques H. Upshaw, "Camera Fans Are Still Talking about That Cruise of 400 Miles," *Atlanta Constitution*, August 30, 1938.

33 "Dalton Tufted-Chenille Is Featured on WSB Broadcast," *Dalton News*, July 1, 1947.

34 A bedspread-size tufted sign appears in a photograph in William Boring, "Bedspread Boulevard," *Morning Herald* (Gloversville and Johnstown, N.Y.), October 9, 1938. The sign reads "BEDSPREADS / FOR SALE / HERE" and has landscape elements around the edge—mountains, trees, etc. Wynette Jackson and Sarah Jarrette are in the foreground.

35 "Dalton Neon Sign to Be Erected," *Dalton News*, April 24, 1941; "Lawtex Completing Plant Addition," *Dalton News*, May 22, 1941; "Big Neon Signs to Be Erected Here," *Dalton News*, May 29, 1941.

36 "Candlewick Bedspreads," *Oil-Power: A Magazine of Industrial Romances* 17, no. 5 (May 1942), n.p.

37 "Big Neon Signs to Be Erected Here," *Dalton News*, May 29, 1941. According to the Consumer Price Index Inflation Calculator (http://www.bls.gov/data /inflation_calculator.htm), $2,000 in 1941 equaled about $32,200 in 2014.

38 "Appropriate Signs Would Herald City as 'Chenille Center of the World,'" *Dalton News*, September 10, 1946.

39 Minnie Hite Moody, "Bedspreads Bloom Again," *Saturday Evening Post* 218, no. 27 (January 5, 1946), 74. Moody also described a popular driving game: "Georgia drivers, who accept the spreadlines as a matter of course, often indulge in a neat betting project in which each passenger chooses a side of the road and counts the bedspreads of a certain pattern—say the ever-popular peacock—over a specified mileage. The one whose side yields the greater number of peacocks between, for instance, Acworth and Calhoun, is the winner." The *Christian Science Monitor* also reported a resurgence in the presence of roadside spreadlines after the war. "Bedspread Industry Booms in Georgia," *Christian Science Monitor*, September 8, 1947.

40 Advertisement, Briggs Chenille Shop, *Stroudsburg (Pa.) Daily Record*, December 8, 1964; "Handicraft Shops Popular with Visitors to Poconos," *Pocono Record* (Stroudsburg, Pa.), June 21, 1969.

41 Wyche, "Tufted Textile Industry," 2, Bedspread Industry box, Articles on History, Companies, and Machinery folder, Crown Gardens & Archives.

42 R. E. Hamilton, "Bedspreads Are Big Business," *Christian Science Monitor*, March 15, 1941.

43 Cheryl Wykoff, compiler, *Peacock Alley*, ed. Lydia Stevens (Dalton, Ga.: Prater's Mill Foundation and Whitfield-Murray Historical Society, 1992), 2.

44 R. E. Hamilton, interview by Thomas Deaton, August 5, 1972, transcript titled "R. E. Hamilton—on the History of the Tufting Industry in the Dalton Area," p. 23, R. E. Hamilton folder 031, box 2 of 4, Carpet History 2010.1, MSS 1, Dr. Thomas Deaton Collection, Bandy Heritage Center for Northwest Georgia.

45 Wykoff, *Peacock Alley*, 7.

46 Henry Nevin, "Bedspread Sales Reach High Mark in North Georgia," *Atlanta Constitution*, September 29, 1935.

47 Wykoff, *Peacock Alley*, 7.

48 Ibid., 23.

49 Lucy O'Brien, "Chenille and Candlewick Spreads Line Both Sides of North Georgia Highways," Women's World column, *Tampa Morning Tribune*, August 11, 1947.

50 Allen H. Eaton, *Handicrafts of the Southern Highlands* (New York: Russell Sage Foundation, 1937), 226.

51 Cara Greenberg, "The New Shaggy Chic," *Metropolitan Home* 24, no. 9 (September 1992), 56.

52 Henry Nevin, "Bedspread Sales Reach High Mark in North Georgia," *Atlanta Constitution*, September 29, 1935.

53 "Dalton's Chenille Industry," *Southern Israelite*, December 8, 1950.

54 Jane Garvey, "The Pride of Peacock Alley, North Georgia Chenille," *Georgia Journal* (November /December 1996), 25.

55 John Willis, "Dang Yankees: They Really Went for Those Bedspreads with the Birds on 'em"; John Willis, "'Our Children Would Bag up Red Georgia Dirt and Sell It for 10 or 15 Cents a Bag.' —Emma Stocks," *Rome (Ga.) News-Tribune*, August 26, 2007.

CHAPTER 3. *Handmade Beginnings*

1 William B. Rhoads, "Colonial Revival in American Craft: Opposition to Multicultural and Regional Traditions," in Janet Kardon, ed., *Revivals! Diverse Traditions: The History of Twentieth-Century American Craft, 1920–1945* (New York: Harry N. Abrams, in association with the American Craft Museum, 1994), 41–54,

2 "Girls Who Make Spreads Are Intelligent, Attractive Group," Bedspread and Manufacturers' Edition, *Dalton News*, February 29, 1940; Frederic J. Haskin, "The Haskin Letter: A City Spreads Itself," *Helena (Mont.) Independent*, September 8, 1941.

3 Advertisement, John Wanamaker's, "The Little Home," *Christian Science Monitor*, June 23, 1923; advertisement, Macy's, "Sale of Hand-tufted Candlewick Spreads," *New York Sun*, October 7, 1925.

4 "The Hand-Tufted Spread Industry," *Dalton Citizen*, September 17, 1925.

5 Beverly Gordon, "Costumed Representations of Early America: A Gendered Portrayal, 1850–1940," *Dress* 30 (2003): 3–20. Bridget A. May also provides an in-depth discussion of Colonial Revival dress in "Wearing and Inhabiting the Past: Promoting the Colonial Revival in Late-Nineteenth- and Early-Twentieth-Century America," in Fiona Fisher, Trevor Keeble, Patricia Lara-Betancourt, and Brenda Martin, eds., *Performance, Fashion and the Modern Interior, From the Victorians to Today* (London: Bloomsbury Academic, 2011), 45–58.

6 Gordon, "Costumed Representations of Early America," 16.

7 "Hollywood Came to Cabin Crafts in Dalton for Bedspreads in Bedrooms of Tara Hall," clipping inaccurately marked "*Atlanta Constitution*, 1938," Crown Gardens & Archives; Marie Rose, "Under the Cherokee Rose," *Atlanta Constitution*, February 5, 1939; Bobbie Carmical, "Historical Society Adds a Touch of 'Gone with the Wind,'" *Dalton Advertiser*, April 8, 1987.

8 "Movie Stars to Get Atlanta Souvenirs," *Atlanta Constitution*, December 7, 1939; "Movie Premiere Is Described by Bismarck Woman," *Bismarck (N.D.) Tribune*, December 20, 1939.

9 E. Irving Hanson, "The Reason Why of the International Silk Exposition," *Blue Book of Silks de Luxe*, Spring/Summer 1921, 4.

10 Mallinson scholar Madelyn Shaw suggests that the decoration may be more closely related to the eighteenth-century use of chenille yarns in woven silks for textural effects than to the contemporary candlewicking. The visual effect is remarkably similar, though, regardless of the inspiration. Madelyn Shaw, e-mail to author, April 9, 2014.

11 Advertisement, John Wanamaker's, "Candlewick Embroidery Trims the Newest Frocks for Girls," *Philadelphia Evening Public Ledger*, December 26, 1922.

12 Advertisement, Frederick Loeser, "Candlewick Frocks," *Brooklyn (N.Y.) Daily Eagle*, January 22, 1923.

13 Comparable prices in 2014 were $278–$529 and $626. Advertisement, Lord & Taylor, "Crepe Frocks," *New York Times*, May 10, 1923. Original prices were $3.25 and $2.50. The dresses went on sale in August for $2.75 and $1.95. Advertisement, Lord & Taylor, "Clearance of Crepe Frocks," *New York Times*, August 14, 1923.

14 Advertisement, Gimbels, "Candlewick Kimonos," *Sun and Globe* (New York), November 9, 1923; advertisement, Abraham and Strauss, "Candlewick Kimonos," *Brooklyn (N.Y.) Daily Eagle*, November 14, 1923.

15 The price of $5.05 equaled about $70 in 2014. Advertisement, Joseph Horne, "'Candle-wick'

Kimonos Are New," *Pittsburgh Press*, November 12, 1923.

16 The photograph is marked as Calhoun, where Haney lived, though she was born and raised in Dalton. "Mrs. Haney Dies Monday, Rites Held Tuesday," *Gordon County News*, April 24, 1962.

17 Frances Stiles Whitener recalled the specific peacock design that her mother, Ethel Stiles, an early tufter, used—a peacock with a compact tail, standing on three steps opposite a vase of flowers in an arched trellis, with a large flower and vine underneath. This mirrors the design that appears on the Haney kimono. Frances believed that her mother did not originate the design but, like many other local women, copied the design from someone else. Frances Stiles Whitener, interview by author, March 12, 2013, Dalton, Georgia.

18 Gail Miller DeLoach, Georgia Archives, e-mail message to author, September 1, 2010.

19 "The Hand-Tufted Spread Industry," *Dalton Citizen*, September 17, 1925.

20 Henry Nevin, "Bedspread Sales Reach High Mark in North Georgia," *Atlanta Constitution*, September 29, 1935.

21 Cheryl Wykoff, compiler, *Peacock Alley*, ed. Lydia Stevens (Dalton, Ga.: Prater's Mill Foundation and Whitfield-Murray Historical Society, 1992), 7.

22 Ibid., 2.

23 Allen H. Eaton, *Handicrafts of the Southern Highlands* (New York: Russell Sage Foundation, 1937), 226.

24 Catherine Evans Whitener, "The Tufted Bed Spread Industry: A History," unpublished typed manuscript with handwritten edits, ca. 1938, Catherine Evans Whitener Scrapbook, Crown Gardens & Archives.

25 "The Hand-Tufted Spread Industry," *Dalton Citizen*, September 17, 1925; Walter Rendell Storey, "Making Our Curtains Fit a Decorative Scheme," *New York Times*, November 6, 1927.

26 R. E. Hamilton, interview by Thomas Deaton, August 5, 1972, transcript, p. 17, R. E. Hamilton Folder 031, Box 2 of 4, Carpet History 2010.1, MSS 1, Dr. Thomas Deaton Collection, Bandy Heritage Center for Northwest Georgia.

27 Helen Shope, "From Pin Money to a Cottage Industry," unpublished and incomplete manuscript, February 9, 1994, in notebook marked "Bedspread Articles" (citing interviews and other materials from the 1950s and 1960s), Crown Gardens & Archives.

28 "Handicrafts of Mountain Women," brochure, Tennoga Hooked Rugs, n.d. (ca. 1925), Bedspreads and Booklets on History folder, Bedspreads Industry Material/Clippings, History, Personalities box; Crown Gardens & Archives.

29 "About Tennoga Hooked Rugs," brochure, Tennoga Hooked Rugs, n.d. (ca. 1925), Bedspreads and Booklets on History folder, Bedspreads Industry Material/Clippings, History, Personalities box; Crown Gardens & Archives. After Sims died unexpectedly in 1942, Mrs. H. L. Jarvis continued with her workers. Mary Gene Dykes, granddaughter of both women, ran Tennoga for a while beginning in 1959 until she no longer had enough workers to continue. Cheryl Wykoff, "Mary Eugenia Bi[t]ting (Mrs. H. L.) Jarvis," based on Wykoff's interview of Mary Gene Dykes, February 1988, Wykoff's chenille bedspread oral history notebook, n.d., Crown Gardens & Archives.

30 Advertisement, M. Rich and Brothers Company, "Demonstration Sale, $5.95 Handmade Candlewick Bed Spreads," *Atlanta Constitution*, July 19, 1927.

31 Advertisement, Abraham & Straus, "Spreads—Made by Mountaineer Homemakers," *Brooklyn (N.Y.) Daily Eagle*, October 6, 1929. Demonstrators from Georgia returned in 1930. Advertisement, Abraham & Straus, "Candlewick Spreads," *Brooklyn (N.Y.) Daily Eagle*, April 24, 1930.

32 Advertisement, Sibley, Lindsay and Curr Company, "Candlewick Demonstration," *Rochester (N.Y.) Democrat and Chronicle*, October 14, 1929.

33 Phoebe Laing Mosley, "The Pleasant Land of Counterpane," *McCall Decorative Arts and Needlework*, Summer 1932, 32.

34 Advertisement, Jordan Marsh Company, *Daily Boston Globe*, September 18, 1928.

35 Advertisement, Macy's, "See the Girls from Georgia Actually Making CANDLEWICKS," *New York Times*, April 5, 1931. Woodward and Lothrop in Washington, D.C., described their hand-tufting demonstration

by "girls from Georgia" as providing "an interesting insight into one of America's few surviving 'home industries.'" Advertisement, Woodward and Lothrop, "Girls from Georgia Will Make Candlewick Bedspreads Here," *Washington Post*, April 30, 1931. Additional demonstrations occurred at Joseph Horne in Pittsburgh, by two women from the mountains of Georgia in 1930; at McCreery in New York by two girls from Dalton; at the Wallace Company in Pittsburgh by girls from South Carolina in 1935; and at Macy's in New York City in 1934 by women from Georgia. Advertisement, Joseph Horne, "Demonstration! Candlewick Spreads," *Pittsburgh Press*, April 1, 1930; advertisement, McCreery, "Come In and Watch the Girls Do the Hand Work on These Candlewick Spreads," *New York Times*, October 2, 1932; advertisement, Wallace Company, "Candlewick Spreads," *Poughkeepsie (N.Y.) Eagle News*, March 16, 1935; advertisement, Macy's, "Macy's Does Some Fancy Work with Punchwork," *New York Times*, February 10, 1934.

36 Advertisement, Palais Royal, "Candlewick Bedspreads," *Christian Science Monitor*, March 2, 1936. Representatives of the company Polly Prentiss (Sumter, S.C.) incorporated punchwork examples (a type of embroidery executed with a hand-held needle-gun machine on a spread mounted in an oversized embroidery hoop) with some of their demonstrations by 1936. Advertisement, Hills, McLean and Haskins, "Bedspread-Making," *Binghamton (N.Y.) Press*, September 30, 1936.

37 Cheryl Wykoff, "Kenner and Rauschenberg," Wykoff's chenille bedspread oral history notebook, n.d., Crown Gardens & Archives; Catherine Evans Whitener, "'If I Had Been a Man,'" in George O. Wilson and Dalton-Whitfield County Bicentennial Commission, eds., *Today and Tomorrow Become Yesterday: The City of Dalton and the County of Whitfield in the State of Georgia Celebrate the National Bicentennial, Official Souvenir Book* (Dalton, Ga.: Dalton-Whitfield County Bicentennial Commission?, 1976), 75.

38 "Lion's Shows Candlewick Bedspreads," *San Jose (Calif.) Evening News*, March 20, 1934.

39 Jack Bandy, interview by author, March 14, 2013, Dalton, Georgia. Kitty Carter and Betty Lawton of Dalton also conducted demonstrations in 1930 from Mexico to Canada and across the United States. "Mountaineer Girls of Georgia Display Handicraft Skill," *Hartford (Conn.) Courant*, March 28, 1930.

40 For more on Cannon see "Cannon Company Ships Bedspreads throughout World," *Dalton News*, March 21, 1929.

41 Advertisement, Genung's Department Store, "Candlewick Spreads," *Mount Vernon (N.Y.) Daily Argus*, December 4, 1929.

42 Advertisement, Sibley, Lindsay and Curr Company, "Making Candlewick Bedspreads," *Rochester (N.Y.) Democrat and Chronicle*, May 20, 1931; advertisement, Sibley, Lindsay and Curr, "Demonstration of Candlewick Bedspreads," *Rochester (N.Y.) Democrat and Chronicle*, May 18, 1931.

43 Advertisement, Gimbel Brothers, "Candlewick Spreads," *New York Times*, November 13, 1932. Girls from Georgia returned the next year to give demonstrations. Advertisement, Gimbels, *New York Times*, May 14, 1933.

44 Chlotilde R. Martin, "Product from South Carolina Finds Favor in White House," *Charleston (S.C.) News and Courier*, September 16, 1934.

45 "Cabin Girls to Entertain at Sisson's," *Binghamton (N.Y.) Press*, October 6, 1934; advertisement, Sisson Brothers–Welden Company, "Polly Prentiss Singing Cabin Girls," *Binghamton (N.Y.) Press*, October 8, 1934.

46 "Candlewick Bedspread Artists Demonstrate Ancient Industry," *St. Petersburg (Fla.) Independent*, January 8, 1935; "Candlewick Spreads on Show at Joske's," *San Antonio (Tex.) Express*, February 17, 1935; advertisement, Wallace Company, "All This Week Demonstration and Sale of Candlewick Spreads!," *Poughkeepsie (N.Y.) Eagle-News*, March 14, 1935. The notices for Joske's and the Wallace Company do not mention the women by name but describe them as tufting and singing, consistent with the Rutland notice.

47 Advertisement, Whitney's, "Tufted Bedspreads," *Albany (N.Y.) Evening News*, October 28, 1936;

advertisement, Barney's, Candlewick Spreads," *Schenectady (N.Y.) Gazette*, November 5, 1936. Frances Kolb also gave demonstrations at Gimbels in New York. "See How Candlewick Spreads Are Made," *Olean (N.Y.) Times-Herald*, November 9, 1936. In 1937 Lucy Jarmen represented Polly Prentiss in a demonstration at the Wallace Company in Poughkeepsie. Advertisement, Wallace Company, "Demonstration and Sale Polly Prentiss Candlewick Spreads," *Poughkeepsie (N.Y.) Eagle-News*, May 20, 1937. Kolb began working with Polly Prentiss early in its history and by 1936 was in charge of the production of the company's candlewick spreads. She was considered "an expert color blender, tufter, [and] hand fringer" and a "French knot specialist." Later that year her responsibilities included being in "charge of the entire machine distribution department and . . . of the coordination of production and distribution of the monogram spread and bath mat departments." "Wolff & Marx to Show Candlewick Spreads," *San Antonio (Tex.) Express*, May 10, 1936; "See How Candlewick Spreads Are Made," *Olean (N.Y.) Times-Herald*, November 9, 1936. Kolb appears in the 1940 U.S. Census in Sumter as a "saleslady" for a spread factory. She is twenty-six years old, married to D. R. Kolb, and living with her four-year-old daughter, her parents (Irene B. and J. Frank Watson), and other family members.

48 Fletcher family survey, June 8, 1934, Home Workers Candlewick Spreads, Schedules, box 232, Records of the Women's Bureau, Department of Labor, National Archives; "Oklahoma Editor Amazed at 'Washing on the Line' in Bedspread Belt," *Dalton Citizen*, October 10, 1935.

49 Advertisement, Kann's, "Smart Hand-made Candlewick Aprons and Hoovers," *Washington Post*, November 22, 1934. That price range in 2014 would have equaled $8.70–$28.24.

50 Advertisement, Filene's, "Filene's Apron Shop Presents: 'New Recipes for Thanksgiving Dressing,'" *Daily Boston Globe*, November 23, 1936.

1 Norman Reints, interview by Thomas Deaton, n.d., transcript, pp. 3–4, Norman Reints folder 052, box 2 of 4, Carpet History 2010.1, mss 1, Dr. Thomas Deaton Collection, Bandy Heritage Center for Northwest Georgia.

2 Wylly Folk St. John, "Georgia Bedspreads Cover the Country," *Atlanta Journal Magazine*, September 8, 1946.

3 Advertisement, Best and Company, "When It Comes to American Fashions—You Naturally Think of Best's," *New York Times*, August 18, 1940.

4 Advertisement, Best and Company, "Best's Launches Candlewick Muslins," *New York Times*, May 10, 1934.

5 Fifteen dollars in 1934 equaled about $266 in 2014, $29.75 equaled about $528, $12.75 equaled about $226, and $17.50 equaled about $311. Candlewick bedspreads in 1934 sold for between about $2 and $10, with many around $3–$4.

6 Eileen Earle, "Bedclothes and Curtains Give Fashion Ideas," *New York Sun*, May 12, 1934; Phyllis-Marie Arthur, "When Ladies Meet," *Lowville (N.Y.) Journal and Republican*, May 31, 1934.

7 Mollie Merrick, "The Spotsy Gown Rage," *Daily Boston Globe*, July 2, 1934; "The Newest for Sports Wear," *Chicago Daily Tribune*, June 6, 1934; Rhea Seeger, "Candlewick Bedspread Can Go Places Now," *Chicago Daily Tribune*, June 6, 1934.

8 Evelyn Bolton, "Candlewick Muslin Has Been Shoved into the Fashion Spotlight, Goes to Beach or Dance, as You Wish," *Syracuse (N.Y.) Journal*, June 4, 1934.

9 Virginia Pope, "Tub Styles," *New York Times*, May 13, 1934.

10 The price of $13.95 in 1934 equaled about $248 in 2014. Advertisement, Rich's, "Specialty Shop First to Present the 'Candlewick' Frock," *Atlanta Constitution*, June 3, 1934.

11 The store offered the stamped dresses for $1.00, equal to $17.76 in 2014. Advertisement, R. H. White Company, "Make Yourself a Candlewick Frock," *Boston Daily Globe*, June 28, 1934. Designs for tufting your own candlewick coat were available by 1937. "Candlewick Coat Design," *Laredo (Tex.) Times*, June 29, 1937.

12 Ruth Wyeth Spears, "How to Sew: A Candlewick Frock Strikes a Note of Summer Informality," *Troy (N.Y.) Times*, July 30, 1934. The instructions also ran in the *Washington Post* on August 5, 1934. Instead of instructing women to sew running stitches, as was the general practice for candlewick, Spears instructs them to make a Malta stitch that is sewn in an "x" with a loop at the top and two cut threads hanging from the bottom.

13 "Beach-Bicycling-Sports Frock," *Christian Science Monitor*, July 10, 1935.

14 Janet Treat, "In and about Boston Shops," *Christian Science Monitor*, October 6, 1936.

15 Janet Treat, "Here and There in Boston Shops," *Christian Science Monitor*, September 13, 1937.

16 Dorothy Roe, "Baby Rompers and Pinafores Deck Femininity of All Ages, Childish Type Favorite for Beaches," *Syracuse (N.Y.) Journal*, July 2, 1934.

17 The price of $1.98 equaled about $34 in 2014, $1.00 equaled about $17, and $4.98 equaled about $87. Advertisement, Arnold Constable, "Candlewick Beach Togs," *New York Sun*, July 1, 1935.

18 Ibid.

19 Advertisement, Bloomingdale's, "Sale! Candlewick Play Togs," *New York Sun*, June 26, 1936.

20 Advertisement, Stern Brothers, "Dollar Sale! Beach and Play Togs for Tots and Girls," *New York Sun*, June 3, 1936.

21 Diana Merwin, "Modes of the Moment," *Kingston (N.Y.) Daily Freeman*, June 2, 1936.

22 Dorothy Gentry, "Candlewick Makes Novel Playsuits for Youngsters," *Daily Boston Globe*, June 5, 1936.

23 Advertisement, D. Price and Company, "Beauty at the Beach," *Rome (N.Y.) Daily Sentinel*, June 6, 1940; advertisement, Sisson Brothers–Welden Company, "Cotton Chenille Beach Coats," *Binghamton (N.Y.) Press*, June 6, 1940; advertisement, T. D. Whitney Company, "For a Chenille Summer!," *Daily Boston Globe*, June 11, 1940.

24 Advertisement, John G. Myers, "Washable Chenille Beach Coats," *Albany (N.Y.) Knickerbocker News*, June 3, 1940; advertisement, Harry S. Manchester, "Summer Spree," *Madison (Wis.) Capital Times*, May 19, 1940.

25 Janet Treat Hobbs, "Here and There in the Shops of the Boston Retail District," *Christian Science Monitor*, July 14, 1939.

26 Advertisement, Whitney's, "The Season's Favorites," *Daily Boston Globe*, July 18, 1939; "Beach Blocks," *Binghamton (N.Y.) Press*, January 18, 1940; Mary Brook Lucas, "The Stylefinder Family, Mid Summer Regatta," *Rome (N.Y.) Daily Sentinel*, August 1, 1934; advertisement, T. D. Whitney Company, "For a Chenille Summer!," *Daily Boston Globe*, June 11, 1940; advertisement, Lansburgh's, "Summer Sales!," *Washington Post*, June 16, 1940.

27 Advertisement, Gilchrist's, *Daily Boston Globe*, June 27, 1940.

28 Lucille may have assisted Dessie with the coat. One of the two informational labels attached to the jacket credits Dessie with making it, while the other credits both of the women.

29 "Candlewick Muslin Frocks Latest Thing in Fashion," *Connellsville (Pa.) Daily Courier*, July 23, 1934.

30 Jack Bandy, interview by author, March 14, 2013, Dalton, Georgia.

31 Rhea Seeger, "Candlewick Spread Can Go Places Now," *Chicago Daily Tribune*, June 6, 1934. Rhea Seeger describes one sports dress as having a pale yellow background tufted with ginger, brown, beige, and yellow.

32 "Cotton," *Life*, May 8, 1939, 66.

33 Mary Hampton, "Fashion Outlook," *Bakersfield Californian*, June 23, 1939. She did not explain why they were called "sugar coats."

34 Marshall Adams, "Peggy Townsend Lists Outfits for July 4th," *Washington Post*, June 29, 1939.

35 Nancy Hart, "The Woman's Angle," *Lockhart (Tex.) Post-Register*, June 6, 1935.

36 "New Things Seen in the City Shops," *New York Times*, May 15, 1938.

37 Rhea Seeger, "This Is Season to Revel in New Smart Jackets," *Chicago Daily Tribune*, June 29, 1938.

38 Advertisement, T. D. Whitney Company, "Coquettish and Comfy!," *Daily Boston Globe*, October 29, 1940.

39 Sidney Baxter, telephone conversation with author,

October 23, 2013. The company also had a salesman in New York.

40 Melvin D. Brod, Chenille Slacks, U.S. Patent 121,111, filed March 19, 1940, issued June 18, 1940. He also patented a hooded jacket. Melvin D. Brod, Combined Chenille Jacket and Hood, U.S. Patent 121,036, filed March 19, 1940, issued June 11, 1940.

41 Lisbeth, "Smart New Beach Apparel Marches On, Like Time to Keep Pace with 1937," *Schenectady (N.Y.) Gazette*, July 20, 1937.

42 Advertisement, Hopkins Brothers, "Free! Chenille Cape with Latest Style Spread," *Kokomo (Ind.) Tribune*, August 31, 1939.

43 Richard Martin and Harold Koda, *Splash! A History of Swimwear* (New York: Rizzoli, 1990), 29.

44 Eleanor Gunn, "The Modern Lorelei Wears Gingham," *Washington Post*, June 29, 1921.

45 Eleanor Gunn, "Another Sort of Cape," *Washington Post*, May 12, 1922.

46 Martin and Koda, *Splash!*, 29, 73.

47 Advertisement, Newmans, "Snowy White Candlewick Cape," *Oshkosh (Wis.) Northwestern*, July 6, 1938.

48 "Everything for the Seashore at Gilchrist's Swim Shop," *Daily Boston Globe*, June 4, 1939.

49 Murray E. Wyche, "Tufted Textile Industry," 15, Bedspread Industry box, Articles on History, Companies, and Machinery folder, Crown Gardens & Archives.

50 Ibid.

51 Advertisement, Gilchrist's, *Daily Boston Globe*, June 27, 1940; advertisement, Darleen, "Wed. Morning Special," *North Tonawanda (N.Y.) Evening News*, June 29, 1943. Maude Brooker and William Westbrook, who established a chenille business in Dalton in 1932, started out making beach capes that were large rectangles with drawstrings at the top. Cheryl Wykoff, "Brooker Spread Company," based on Wykoff's interview of Joe Billy Denson and Betti Brooker Denson, February 6, 1989, Wykoff's chenille bedspread oral history notebook, Crown Gardens & Archives; Thomas M. Deaton, *Bedspreads to Broadloom: The Story of the Tufted Carpet Industry*

(Acton, Mass.: Tapestry Press, 1993), 153.

52 Caroline Rennolds Milbank, *Resort Wear: Style in Sun-Drenched Climates* (New York: Rizzoli, 2009), 81.

53 Martin and Koda, *Splash!*, 79.

54 Milbank, *Resort Wear*, 137.

55 Advertisement, Jordan Marsh Company, "White Beauty on the Beach," *Daily Boston Globe*, June 28, 1939.

56 Cape documented on Worthpoint, http://www.worthpoint.com, from an eBay auction ending November 3, 2007. Gimbels department store exhibited chenille spreads by Blue Ridge Spread Company in the Communications Building of the 1939 New York World's Fair. "Blue Ridge Spreads Selected by Gimbels New York for New York World's Fair Chenille Bedspread Exhibit," brochure, 1940, Crown Gardens & Archives. The *Pensky's Style* blogger recalls attending the World's Fair and being given a World's Fair–themed chenille cape by her mother that she hated wearing because she felt like a walking ad. "The World's Fair," *Pensky's Style*, June 9, 2011, http://babastales.blogspot.com/2011/06/worlds-fair.html.

57 Mollie Merrick, "The Spotsy Gown Rage," *Daily Boston Globe*, July 2, 1934.

58 "Hollywood Happenings," *Chicago Daily Tribune*, August 12, 1934; "Candlewick," *Daily Boston Globe*, July 19, 1935.

59 Sheilah Graham, "Deanna's Playtime Outfit Includes Chenille Coat," *Atlanta Constitution*, April 18, 1939; advertisement, Efird's Department Store, "Efird's Annual June Sale," *Danville (Va.) Bee*, May 31, 1939.

60 "Blouse and Apron for Sport Toggery," *Atlanta Constitution*, February 19, 1939.

61 "Bob Jones College 'Classic Players' Widely Known," Bedspread and Manufacturers' Edition, *Dalton News*, February 29, 1940. Though the article, which was excerpted from *Players Magazine*, does not include the names of the costume designers, a program for the debut of the school's production of *King Lear* in 1934 lists the costume designers as Fannie Mae Holmes, Elizabeth Adams, and Ernestine Veazey.

Jeffrey Stegall (principal designer, Classic Players & Opera Association, Department of Theatre Arts, Bob Jones University), e-mail to author, October 20, 2013.

62 Photographs of *My Fair Lady* with captions on backs, Bandy Heritage Center for Northwest Georgia, Carpet and Rug Institute Photograph Collection.

63 Martin and Koda, *Splash!*, 82.

64 Wyche, "Tufted Textile Industry," 15.

65 Zack Norville, interview by author, July 26, 2013, Dalton, Georgia.

CHAPTER 5. *The Rise and Decline of Chenille Robes, an American Fashion Staple*

1 Murray E. Wyche, "Tufted Textile Industry," 15, Bedspread Industry box, Articles on History, Companies, and Machinery folder, Crown Gardens & Archives.

2 Martin S. Richman, "New Look Brings Renewed Interest to Tufted Robes," *Tufted Textile Manufacturers Association Directory, 1960* (Dalton, Ga.: Tufted Textile Manufacturers Association, 1960), 66.

3 Wyche, "Tufted Textile Industry," 15.

4 Ibid., 17.

5 Advertisement, Davison's Basement, "A Party with No Mourning After," *Atlanta Constitution*, June 12, 1940; advertisement, Gimbels, "Candlewick Housecoats," *New York Post*, March 19, 1941.

6 "Georgia Chenille Factories Are Putting on Big Spread," *Washington Post*, July 30, 1947.

7 Advertisement, Smartwear Emma Lange, "Lady Pickwick," *Milwaukee Journal*, April 13, 1934.

8 Advertisement, Abraham & Straus, "Is She Lavender or Is She Lipstick?," *New York Sun*, May 10, 1934.

9 Virginia Lee Warren, "Travelers Need Dressing Gowns That Won't Wrinkle, Show Soil, or Attract Attention," *Washington Post*, July 1, 1934.

10 Advertisement, Gilchrist's Cash and Carry Basement, "Candlewick Robes," *Daily Boston Globe*, August 22, 1934.

11 Advertisement, Arnold Constable, "Candlewick Beach Togs," *New York Sun*, July 1, 1935.

12 Beach, Cruise and Sportswear Newest Lines listing, *New York Times*, November 12, 1935; advertisement,

Bloomingdale's, "Sale! Candlewick Play Togs," *New York Sun*, June 26, 1936.

13 Advertisement, Saks, "The New Saks 34th," *New York Times*, January 9, 1936.

14 See, for example, advertisement, Kann's, "Cotton Candlewick ROBES," *Christian Science Monitor*, October 8, 1945.

15 See, for example, advertisement, Martin's, "Our Candlewick Coat," *New York Post*, March 24, 1943.

16 Sylva Weaver, "Summer Robe of Chenille Ideal for Informal Wear," *Los Angeles Times*, July 18, 1940.

17 Ibid.

18 Advertisement, Dey Brothers, "Candlewick Chenille Robe," *Syracuse Herald-Journal*, January 25, 1944.

19 Janet Treat, "Here and There in the Shops of Boston," *Christian Science Monitor*, February 1, 1939.

20 Sylva Weaver, "Candlewick House Coat Ideal for Leisure Hours," *Los Angeles Times*, December 17, 1940.

21 Sheilah Graham, "Katharine Hepburn's Chenille Robe Combines Comfort and Style," *Atlanta Constitution*, June 20, 1938.

22 Advertisement, Lux Toilet Soap, posted online by The Nitrate Diva, @Nitrate Diva, http://twicsy .com/i/qZLKZc, December 19, 2012.

23 See, for example, advertisement, Keith O'Brien, "Chenille Robes," *Salt Lake City Tribune*, December 21, 1940.

24 Sylva Weaver, "Candlewick Fashioned into Chic Boudoir Robe," *Los Angeles Times*, October 23, 1939.

25 Sylva Weaver, "Candlewick House Coat Ideal for Leisure Hours," *Los Angeles Times*, December 17, 1940.

26 Advertisement, Wallace Company, "Sale! Housecoats in Candlewick to Match Your Bed Spread," *Poughkeepsie (N.Y.) Eagle*, March 2, 1940; "Blend Yourself," *Atlanta Constitution*, September 27, 1940.

27 Advertisement, "Swirlaway Chenille-Gingham Robe," Sears, Roebuck, 1944, posted on *Casey's Elegant Musings* blog, September 2010, https://web .archive.org/web/20120130071338/http://blog .caseybrowndesigns.com/2010/09/sleep-tight.

28 "The Hand-Tufted Spread Industry," *Dalton Citizen*, September 17, 1925.

29 "Textile Standards Kept High by Workers of Long

Training," *Christian Science Monitor*, September 20, 1939; Murray M. Taradash, Chenille Negligee, U.S. Patent 121, 429, filed March 19, 1940, issued July 9, 1940.

30 "Phil Phillips Dies of Heart Ailment in New York City," *Dalton News*, October 21, 1947 (this obituary lists a brother named Charles Shapiro as a survivor); George H. McLaughlin, Chenille Robes, U.S. Patents 151,055 and 151,056, filed February 14, 1948, issued September 21, 1948. McLaughlin is listed in the city directories of New York City in 1945, 1946, and 1948 as working in chenilles. Shapiro also patented a jacket design: Charles Shapiro, Chenille Jacket, U.S. Patent 124,983, filed March 13, 1940, issued February 4, 1941.

31 Bell Bayless, "Bartow Textile Plant Is Producing Large Output, Despite Shortages," *Dalton News*, May 30, 1944.

32 Jack Bandy, interview by author, March 14, 2013, Dalton, Georgia; "Boyce Sells Plant Here to Georgia Man, B. J. Bandy," *Gastonia (N.C.) Daily Gazette*, November 19, 1934.

33 "Designer," Bedspread and Manufacturers' Edition, *Dalton News*, February 29, 1940; A. G. Andre, "Spread Designs Improving," Bedspread and Manufacturers' Edition, *Dalton News*, February 29, 1940.

34 Ivan A. Millender, "Recollections on Growing Up in the Jewish Community of Dalton," in *Ties n' Tidbits: A Supplement to the Official History of Whitfield County, Georgia, 1852–1999* (Dalton, Ga.: Whitfield-Murray Historical Society, 2002), 63.

35 Many accounts relate that the Jewish community was welcomed in Dalton, but an article in the *Southern Israelite* in 1948 observed that though the country club had three Jewish families as charter members, new families were not accepted. Adolph Rosenberg, "The Dalton Story," *Southern Israelite*, June 18, 1948.

36 For more on Dalton's Jewish community, see Aaron Welt, "Dalton's Jewish Community," *Jewish Georgian*, January/February 2010, 28–29. See also the Georgia entries in *Encyclopedia of Southern Jewish Communities*, Goldring/Woldenberg Institute of Southern Jewish Life, http://www.isjl .org/encyclopedia-of-southern-jewish-communities

.html.

37 "Henry Nevin Writes of Optemism [*sic*] of Local Bedspread Plant Managers," *Dalton News*, December 30, 1941.

38 "Bedspread Industry Problems Discussed," *Dalton News*, January 29, 1942.

39 "Georgia Chenille Factories Are Putting on Big Spread," *Washington Post*, July 30, 1947.

40 Helen Johnson (daughter of Emily Bennett) and her husband Paul Johnson, interview by author, March 11, 2013, Dalton, Georgia; Calvin Caldwell (son of Daphne Cleo Sloan Caldwell), interview by author, November 23, 2012, Calhoun, Georgia.

41 Mrs. Fred Caldwell and Calvin Caldwell, interview by Thomas Deaton, December 10, 1979, transcript, Fred Caldwell Folder 012, box 2 of 4, Carpet History 2010.1, MSS 1, Dr. Thomas Deaton Collection, Bandy Heritage Center for Northwest Georgia; and Calvin Caldwell interview.

42 Henry Nevin, "Robes Chenille Have Oomph Appeal," *Dalton News*, May 5, 1942.

43 "G. H. Rauschenburg [*sic*] Company Discontinues Bedspread Manufacture for Duration," *Dalton News*, February 9, 1943.

44 "Blue Ridge Co. Awarded War Contract," *Dalton News*, September 21, 1943.

45 Advertisement, Blue Ridge Manufacturing, "Four Queens Chenille Robes," *Glamour*, November 1944, 134.

46 Both ads note that the robe appeared in *Glamour* and *Mademoiselle*. Advertisement, Three Sisters, "New 1943's Heating System: Candlewick Robes," *Atlanta Constitution*, October 10, 1943; advertisement, Regenstein's, *Atlanta Constitution*, September 26, 1945.

47 Advertisement, "Adrian Evans Chenille Robes," *Marion (Ohio) Star*, June 15, 1944.

48 "Chenille Plant Is Given Contract for Defense Goods," *Dalton News*, March 17, 1942.

49 "Blue Ridge Co. Awarded War Contract," *Dalton News*, September 21, 1943; "War Work," *Dalton News*, July 25, 1944; Seymour Seidman, "Chenille Men Working on Defense Production," *Dalton News*, February 13, 1945, reprinted from the *Daily News Record* of New York.

50 "Dalton Industry Manufactured Variety of Essential Products under War Contracts," Centennial Edition, *Dalton Citizen*, October 16, 1947.

51 Bell Bayless, "Bartow Textile Plant Is Producing Large Output, Despite Shortages," *Dalton News*, May 30, 1944.

52 "Death Blow Struck Chenille Industry," *Dalton News*, January 2, 1945.

53 "Attention! Chenille Housecoat Mfrs.," *Dalton News*, January 4, 1944.

54 Press Huddleston, "Pretty Chenille Products Fill Williams' Shop," *Atlanta Constitution*, January 29, 1945.

55 Advertisement, Williams Chenille Company, *Southern Israelite*, April 5, 1946.

56 "Chenille Robe Makers to Meet OPA Experts," *Atlanta Constitution*, December 30, 1945; "Robe Makers, OPA Meet Here," *Dalton News*, January 15, 1946.

57 Harold Fleming, "OPA Pricing Method Seen as Bottleneck," *Christian Science Monitor*, February 18, 1946.

58 "OPA Promises Survey of Tufted Textile Industry, Will Check on Costs for Fabricating Housecoats," *Dalton News*, April 2, 1946.

59 Wyche, "Tufted Textile Industry," 3.

60 "Tufted Textiles, Stricken Industry Makes a Profitless Recovery—Output Up, Prices Low," *Wall Street Journal*, October 4, 1947.

61 Wyche, "Tufted Textile Industry," 15, 16.

62 "Statistics for the Tufted Industry," *Textile Manufacturers Association 1950 Directory and Yearbook* (Dalton, Ga.: Tufted Textile Manufacturers Association, 1950), 47.

63 "Ads That Created a Market for Tufted Robes— with Success in May, as Well as in December," in *Textile Manufacturers Association 1950 Directory and Yearbook* (Dalton, Ga.: Tufted Textile Manufacturers Association, 1950), 44–45.

64 Wyche, "Tufted Textile Industry," 11, 16.

65 Ibid., 16.

66 "Dalton Tufted-Chenille Is Featured on WSB Broadcast," *Dalton News*, July 1, 1947, partial transcript of (or script for) radio broadcast, Catherine Evans Whitener Scrapbook, Crown Gardens & Archives. Leonard Lorberbaum described the method used at Lawtex of transferring the pattern to the long tufted sheeting: they placed a perforated pattern called a lay on top of the stack of sheeting to be cut, then stamped a chalk powder through the perforations to mark the lines. Leonard Lorberbaum, telephone conversation with author and Julian Saul, June 6, 2013. See also Helen Shope, "From Pin Money to a Cottage Industry," unpublished manuscript, February 9, 1994, in notebook marked "Bedspread Articles," Crown Gardens & Archives; "Tufted Textiles," *Textile Industries* 119 (June 1955): 108.

67 Helen Shope, "From Pin Money to a Cottage Industry," Crown Gardens & Archives.

68 Patsy Cooper, interview by Linda Williams, April 10, 1996, Kennesaw State College, Carpet History Project Oral History Series, Bartow History Museum Archives, Cartersville, Georgia.

69 Queen Carpet brochure, Queen folder, box 1 of 8, 2011.1, MSS 6, Carpet and Rug Institute Records, Bandy Heritage Center for Northwest Georgia. Advertisement, Looper's, rotogravure section, Progress Edition, *Dalton Citizen*, October 2, 1941 (thanks to Nolan Kenner for identifying Swann); "Tufted Bathrobes Take on New Look as Color, Design, Texture Add Interest," *Dalton Citizen*, March 14, 1958; Sada Nell Williams, "New Values Increase Sales in Tufted Robes," *Tufted Textile Manufacturers Association Directory, 1958* (Dalton, Ga.: Tufted Textile Manufacturers Association, 1958), 125.

70 Wyche, "Tufted Textile Industry," 15.

71 Advertisement, Genung's, "The Shorty in Chenille," *Yonkers (N.Y.) Herald Statesman*, November 14, 1945; advertisement, Marting's, "Adrian Evans Original Chenille House Coats," *Portsmouth (Ohio) Times*, April 17, 1946.

72 Advertisement, Ann Lewis of East Houston and Navarro, "Saucy and Surfy . . . Lawtex Candlewick Washenille Beach Robe," *San Antonio (Tex.) Light*, June 25, 1948.

73 "Tufted Robes . . . for Every Need, Every Purse, Every Taste," *Tufted Textile Manufacturers Association Directory, 1951* (Dalton, Ga.: Tufted Textile Manufacturers Association, 1951), 55.

74 "The Ever-Growing Market for Tufted Robes," *Tufted Textile Manufacturers Association Directory and Yearbook, 1952* (Dalton, Ga.: Tufted Textile Manufacturers Association, 1952), 43.

75 Helen Shope, "From Pin Money to a Cottage Industry," Crown Gardens & Archives.

76 Norman Reints, interview by Thomas Deaton, n.d., transcript, pp. 4–5, Norman Reints folder 052, box 2 of 4, Carpet History 2010.1, MSS 1, Dr. Thomas Deaton Collection, Bandy Heritage Center for Northwest Georgia; Thomas M. Deaton, *Bedspreads to Broadloom: The Story of the Tufted Carpet Industry* (Acton, Mass.: Tapestry Press, 1993), 157.

77 Victor Ringel, e-mail to author, November 3, 2013.

78 Cheryl Wykoff, "Lawtex Corporation," based on Wykoff's interview of Leonard Lorberbaum, April 18, 1988, Wykoff's chenille bedspread oral history notebook, Crown Gardens & Archives.

79 "Tufted Chenille Unit Has Valuable Worker in Henry C. Ball, Who Begins His 6th Year," *Dalton Citizen*, July 6, 1950.

80 "Tufted Robes . . . for Every Need, Every Purse, Every Taste," *Tufted Textile Manufacturers Association Directory, 1951* (Dalton, Ga.: Tufted Textile Manufacturers Association, 1951), 55.

81 Wyche, "Tufted Textile Industry," 16.

82 Ibid.

83 Ibid., 8; Ray G. Jones Jr. and Claude A. Campbell, "The Development of Georgia's Tufted Textile Industry," Research Paper no. 12, Bureau of Business and Economic Research, School of Business Administration, Georgia State College of Business Administration, March 1959, 20.

84 Norman Reints interview, pp. 4–5, Dr. Thomas Deaton Collection, Bandy Heritage Center for Northwest Georgia; Deaton, *Bedspreads to Broadloom*, 157.

85 Cheryl Wykoff, "George Hanson," based on Wykoff's interview of Hanson, March 9, 1989, Wykoff's chenille bedspread oral history notebook, Crown Gardens & Archives.

86 See, for example, Warren G. Magnuson and Jean Carper, "Colorful 'Spangle' Cloth Is Highly Flammable," *St. Petersburg (Fla.) Evening Independent*, February 2, 1970.

87 Harry Brandt, *Tufted Textiles*, Federal Reserve Bank of Atlanta Economics Studies no. 2 (Atlanta: Federal Reserve Bank of Atlanta, 1955), quoted in Randall L. Patton with David B. Parker, *Carpet Capital: The Rise of a New South Industry* (Athens: University of Georgia Press, 1999), 89.

88 Ruth M. Clow, "Cheerful Chatter," *Fredonia (N.Y.) Censor*, June 18, 1953.

89 Phyllis Diller, "My Favorite Jokes," *Boston Globe*, March 22, 1964.

90 Jean Shepherd, *Wanda Hickey's Night of Golden Memories and Other Disasters* (New York: Broadway Books, 1971), 128. This quote comes from the short story "Ollie Hopnoodle's Haven of Bliss," from 1968, though Shepherd referred to his mother's chenille robe (sometimes in yellow) in earlier writings as well.

91 Margot Herzog, "Reaching New Heights in Robe Popularity," *Tufted Textile Manufacturers Association Directory, 1953* (Dalton, Ga.: Tufted Textile Manufacturers Association, 1953), 56–57.

92 Margot Herzog, "Greater Style and Comfort," *Tufted Textile Manufacturers Association Directory, 1954* (Dalton, Ga.: Tufted Textile Manufacturers Association, 1954), 75–76.

93 Margot Herzog, "Latest Tufted Robes Stress the 'Ultra Feminine,'" *Tufted Textile Manufacturers Association Directory, 1955* (Dalton, Ga.: Tufted Textile Manufacturers Association, 1955), 106.

94 Ibid., 107.

95 Margot Herzog, "Reaching New Heights in Robe Popularity," *Tufted Textile Manufacturers Association Directory, 1953* (Dalton, Ga.: Tufted Textile Manufacturers Association, 1953), 56–57.

96 Margot Herzog, "Greater Style and Comfort," *Tufted Textile Manufacturers Association Directory, 1954* (Dalton, Ga.: Tufted Textile Manufacturers Association, 1954), 75.

97 Margot Herzog, "Latest Tufted Robes Stress the 'Ultra Feminine,'" *Tufted Textile Manufacturers Association Directory, 1955* (Dalton, Ga.: Tufted Textile Manufacturers Association, 1955), 107; Sada Nell Williams, "New Values Increase Sales in Tufted Robes," *Tufted Textile Manufacturers*

Association Directory, 1958 (Dalton, Ga.: Tufted Textile Manufacturers Association, 1958), 124.

98 "Building Sales with Tufted Robes," *Tufted Textile Manufacturers Association Directory, 1959* (Dalton, Ga.: Tufted Textile Manufacturers Association, 1959), 52.

99 Arthur N. Richman, "Better Products Insure Future," *Tufted Textile Manufacturers Association Directory, 1954* (Dalton, Ga.: Tufted Textile Manufacturers Association, 1954), 80.

100 Sada Nell Williams, "New Values Increase Sales in Tufted Robes," *Tufted Textile Manufacturers Association Directory, 1958* (Dalton, Ga.: Tufted Textile Manufacturers Association, 1958), 126.

101 Ibid.

102 "Tufted Bathrobes Take on a New Look as Color, Design, Texture Add Interest," *Dalton Citizen*, March 14, 1958; Sada Nell Williams, "New Values Increase Sales in Tufted Robes," *Tufted Textile Manufacturers Association Directory, 1958* (Dalton, Ga.: Tufted Textile Manufacturers Association, 1958), 126.

103 *Tufted Textile Manufacturers Association Directory, 1958* (Dalton, Ga.: Tufted Textile Manufacturers Association, 1958), 171, 172.

104 Martin S. Richman, "New Look Brings Renewed Interest to Tufted Robes," *Tufted Textile Manufacturers Association Directory, 1960* (Dalton, Ga.: Tufted Textile Manufacturers Association, 1960), 66.

105 "Heir Apparent: Tufted Pile Becomes Apparel's Newest and Smartest Look," *Tufted Textile Manufacturers Association Directory, 1963* (Dalton, Ga.: Tufted Textile Manufacturers Association, 1963), 58.

106 Jones and Campbell, "Development of Georgia's Tufted Textile Industry," 17; "Building Sales with Tufted Robes," *Tufted Textile Manufacturers Association Directory, 1959* (Dalton, Ga.: Tufted Textile Manufacturers Association, 1959), 52.

107 "Bathe in Smart Luxury with Tufted Beachwear," *News for Women* (Tufted Textile Manufacturers Association), April 1962, Carpet and Rug Institute Records, Bandy Heritage Center for Northwest Georgia.

108 "The Robe," *Tufted Textile Manufacturers Association*

Directory, 1961 (Dalton, Ga.: Tufted Textile Manufacturers Association, 1961), 88.

109 "Tufted Textile Industry—1951–1964," *Tufted Textile Manufacturers Association Directory, 1964* (Dalton, Ga.: Tufted Textile Manufacturers Association, 1964), 8.

110 "Tufted Hemlines Go Up and Down," *Tufting Industry Review, 1965* (Dalton, Ga.: Tufted Textile Manufacturers Association, 1965), 117–18.

111 "Tufted Textiles Set New Pace in Apparel," *Tufted Textile Manufacturers Association Directory, 1967* (Dalton, Ga.: Tufted Textile Manufacturers Association, 1967), 72.

112 "Tufters Build New Markets in the Fashion World," *Tufting Industry Review, 1965* (Dalton, Ga.: Tufted Textile Manufacturers Association, 1965), 132–33.

113 "Tufted Forecast: Space Conquest," *Tufted Textile Manufacturers Association Directory, 1960* (Dalton, Ga.: Tufted Textile Manufacturers Association, 1960), 47, 49; "Heir Apparent: Tufted Pile Becomes Apparel's Newest and Smartest Look," *Tufted Textile Manufacturers Association Directory, 1963* (Dalton, Ga.: Tufted Textile Manufacturers Association, 1963), 55; advertisement, Collins & Aikman, "WE Are in the Tufting Business in a Big Way," *Tufted Textile Manufacturers Association Directory, 1964* (Dalton, Ga.: Tufted Textile Manufacturers Association, 1964), 8; "Tufting Puts the Wear in Wearing Apparel," *Tufting Industry Review, 1966* (Dalton, Ga.: Tufted Textile Manufacturers Association, 1966), 70–71.

114 "Heir Apparent: Tufted Pile Becomes Apparel's Newest and Smartest Look," *Tufted Textile Manufacturers Association Directory, 1963* (Dalton, Ga.: Tufted Textile Manufacturers Association, 1963), 55.

115 Ibid., 55–56.

116 "Looking for Gifts Cute and Cuddly or Prim and Practical? Tufted Products Will Please Those You Choose to Cherish!," *News for Women* (Tufted Textile Manufacturers Association), November 1962, Carpet and Rug Institute Records, Bandy Heritage Center for Northwest Georgia.

117 "Tufters Build New Markets in the Fashion World," *Tufting Industry Review, 1965* (Dalton, Ga.: Tufted Textile Manufacturers Association, 1965), 133;

"Tufted Fabrics: Ski Wear Big Lift to the Tufter, " *Tufted Textile Manufacturers Association Directory, 1964* (Dalton, Ga.: Tufted Textile Manufacturers Association, 1964), 45.

118 "Tufted Textiles Set New Pace in Apparel," *Tufted Textile Manufacturers Association Directory, 1967* (Dalton, Ga.: Tufted Textile Manufacturers Association, 1967), 72.

119 Ibid.

120 "Carpet, from Wall to Wall . . . and . . . Head to Toe," *Tufted Textile Manufacturers Association Directory, 1963* (Dalton, Ga.: Tufted Textile Manufacturers Association, 1963), 40.

121 "Tufted Handbag Is Latest 'Novelty' Item Offered by Tufters," *Tufting Industry Review, 1965* (Dalton, Ga.: Tufted Textile Manufacturers Association, 1965), 125.

122 The company first appears in Dalton city directories in 1967, but several online sites that collect and publish basic business records list the formation date as November 6, 1965.

123 Judy Magid, "A Carpetbagger's Comeback," *Salt Lake City Tribune*, February 13, 2006.

124 "Durable, Divine, and Indestructible: Handbags: Made of Tufted Carpet," *Tufted Textile Manufacturers Association Directory, 1966* (Dalton, Ga.: Tufted Textile Manufacturers Association, 1966), 69.

125 "Larger Bags Back on the Scene," *Yonkers (N.Y.) Herald Statesman*, October 18, 1965.

126 Jerry Terrence, e-mail to author, September 28, 2013.

127 Judy Magid, "A Carpetbagger's Comeback," *Salt Lake City Tribune*, February 13, 2006.

128 Willene Morgan with Janet McKinney, interview by author, July 26, 2013, Calhoun, Georgia.

CHAPTER 6. *Revival and Nostalgia*

1 Christina Lynn Whited, a noted chenille recycler, recalls that in the 1990s large quantities of chenille hit the secondary markets as the original owners aged and downsized their homes. Telephone interview by author, December 11, 2012.

2 Julia Szabo, "Chenille Bedspreads," *Martha Stewart Living*, September 1995, 54.

3 The earliest formal use I have found of the term in print is 1987, in Laurel Garrett, "From Bedspreads to

Broadloom: The Story of Dalton's Carpet Industry," *Rural Georgia* 34, no. 4 (April 1987): 6–7. Tammy Ingram notes that many of the new long-distance roads in the early twentieth century were called "peacock alleys," implying that they were simply corridors along which wealthy Americans could parade their riches. Tammy Ingram, *Dixie Highway: Road Building and the Making of the Modern South, 1900–1930* (Chapel Hill: University of North Carolina Press, 2014), 25.

4 Ruff n' Ready added labels to their clothing featuring silver text stitched on a blue background.

5 Unidentified article from 1972, Vintage Fashion Guild website, "Public Vintage Fashion" forum, http://forums.vintagefashionguild.org/threads/how-old-is-this-and-is-it-a-swimsuit-cover-up.39820.

6 Priscilla Tucker, "The Second Go-Round," *New York Magazine* 5, no. 30 (July 24, 1972), 53.

7 Charlotte Graydon, "Designer 'Turns On' in Attire," *Oregonian*, December 10, 1972.

8 Jack Bradin, e-mail to author, September 23, 2013; Jack Bradin, telephone conversation with author, September 24, 2013.

9 Liz Gardner, "Old-Fashioned Comfort Is as Soft as Chenille," *Los Angeles Times*, November 29, 1991; Kathryn Bold, "Once More . . . with Fabric: Scrappy Designers Find Material Wealth by Recycling Vintage Linens into Clothes," *Los Angeles Times*, September 3, 1993.

10 Karen Newell Young, "Children's Clothes—the Way They Were," *Los Angeles Times*, September 9, 1988.

11 Hyla Wults Fox, "Trend Watch: If You Can't Sleep on It, Wear It," *Globe and Mail* (Toronto), April 16, 1992. Another article addressing chenille's collectability is "Make That Bed," *Collectibles: Flea Market Finds*, Fall 1995, 44.

12 Julia Szabo, "Chenille Bedspreads," *Martha Stewart Living*, September 1995, 55; Louise Pinson of Palm Beach Fashion, Facebook message to author, August 21, 2013.

13 Louise Pinson of Palm Beach Fashion, Facebook message to author, August 22, 2013.

14 Matthew Schneier, "John Waters Brushes Up for the CFDA Spotlight," *New York Times*, May 30, 2014. Waters wore the jacket when he performed "A John

Waters Christmas 2013" at Stage 48 in New York City on December 13, 2013.

15 Clare Collins, "Wayne H. Caron, Chenille Designer," *New York Times*, January 12, 1992; Cara Greenberg, "The New Shaggy Chic," *Metropolitan Home* 24, no. 9 (September 1992): 57.

16 Linda Matchan, "The Real Chenille: The Soft, Nubby, Sentimental Fabric Moves beyond Bedspreads and Bathrobes," *Boston Globe*, March 7, 1999.

17 Christina Lynn Whited, telephone interview by author, December 11, 2012.

18 Linda Matchan, "The Real Chenille: The Soft, Nubby, Sentimental Fabric Moves Beyond Bedspreads and Bathrobes," *Boston Globe*, March 7, 1999.

19 Christina Lynn Whited, telephone interview by author, December 11, 2012.

20 Ibid.

21 Christine Gardner, "Chenille May Be Fluff, but Here It's Taken Seriously," *New York Times*, October 26, 1997.

22 Christina Lynn Whited, telephone interview by author, December 11, 2012.

23 Christine Gardner, "Chenille May Be Fluff, but Here It's Taken Seriously," *New York Times*, October 26, 1997. A friend who worked in the recycling industry told Whited about the use of shredded spreads, selected because they were cotton, as insulation for municipal gas pipes. Christina Lynn Whited, telephone interview by author, December 11, 2012.

24 Roni Denholtz, "Whited Is the Captain of Chenille," *Hunterdon Review* (New Jersey), June 19, 1997.

25 Christina Lynn Whited, telephone interview by author, December 11, 2012.

26 Shelly Phillips, "Chichi Chenille, the Textiles That Fell out of Favor in the '60s Are in Demand Again, and Georgia Factories Are Tufting as Fast as They Can, but Most Highly Sought Are Vintage Linens, Often Recycled as Bathrobes, Baby Quilts and Pillows," *Philadelphia Inquirer*, December 10, 1999.

27 Christina Lynn Whited, telephone interview by author, December 11, 2012.

28 Ibid.

29 Marilyn Wolf, telephone interview by author, March 3, 2014.

30 Wolf's children's robes retailed for about $150 to $200.

31 "Kellwood Acquires Crowntuft," *Wall Street Journal*, October 30, 1989.

32 Victoria Jackson, "Cotton Chenille Robes by Kinnaird Ireland USA: The Success of Stan Herman," Kinnaird Ireland blog, July 21, 2009, http://www .kinnairdireland.com/acatalog/Blog.html; Ruth La Ferla, "Front Row," *New York Times*, October 21, 2003; Joyce Wadler, "Designer Looks Back with Pain and Pride," *New York Times*, September 11, 1998.

33 Harry E. Gordon, letter to author, October 15, 2013; Gail Pallotta, "New Fashion with a Nostalgic Twist," typed manuscript, and "Georgia Chenille" fact sheet from Soft Goods, Inc., Bedspreads Industry Box, Soft Goods folder, Crown Gardens & Archives; Jane M. Roberts, "A Hand-Tufted [remainder of title is cut off in my source]," *Dalton Advertiser*, September 16, 1987; Cheryl Wykoff, compiler, *Peacock Alley*, edited by Lydia Stevens (Dalton, Ga.: Prater's Mill Foundation and Whitfield-Murray Historical Society, 1992), 18.

34 Harry E. Gordon, letter to author, October 21, 2013.

35 Though the address for Edgewood Chenille was Tunnel Hill (located in Whitfield County), it was located in Catoosa County, just north of the Whitfield County line. Harry Gordon, interview by author, November 25, 2013, Tunnel Hill, Georgia.

36 Harry E. Gordon, letter to author, October 21, 2013.

37 Scotti O'Neill, "Tufting Still a Way of Life for Some," *Dalton Citizen-News*, March 10, 1991.

38 "Georgia Chenilles," Soft Goods, Inc., flyer, Soft Goods folder, Bedspread Industry box, Crown Gardens & Archives.

39 Don Chapman, e-mail to author, September 23, 2013.

40 "Chenille Cheap to Chenille Chic," *Mountaineer Times* 6, no. 1 (Spring 1991): 12; Harry E. Gordon, letter to author, October 21, 2013.

41 Recollections regarding the details of the sale of Soft Goods to Damze vary slightly, and it may have taken place in two steps, with a partial transfer in 1989

and the transfer completed in 1991. Don Chapman, telephone interview by author, October 31, 2012; Gordon letters; Don Chapman, e-mail to author, August 22, 2014.

42 Debbie Zomparelli, e-mail to author, December 4, 2013; Don Chapman, e-mail to author, August 22, 2014.

43 Don Chapman, e-mail to author, January 24, 2013.

44 Damze Company trademarked "Canyon Group" in 1995. United States Patent and Trademark Office, Trademark Electronic Search System.

45 Don Chapman, telephone interview by author, October 31, 2012.

46 Demi Moore wore a custom, retro-style robe in HBO's *If These Walls Could Talk* (1996). Lisa Lytle, "TV Offers a Billboard for Newport Couple's Fashion Creations," *Orange County Register* (Santa Ana, Calif.), July 11, 1996.

47 Anne D'Innocenzio, "Broadcast Babes—TV Turns It On," *Women's Wear Daily*, March 23, 1995.

48 Lisa Lytle, "Designers Mold 'Twenty-Something' Look," *Orange County Register* (Santa Ana, Calif.), October 21, 1992.

49 Vicki Jo Radovsky, "Captives of Chenille," *Entertainment Weekly* (June 14, 1996), 47.

50 Ibid.

51 "Surterre Welcomes Don Chapman," Surterre Properties blog, March 18, 2011, http://www .surterreproperties.com/blog/sureterre -welcomes-don-chapman.html.

52 Don Chapman, telephone interview by author, October 31, 2012.

Appendix. Tufted Garment Manufacturers

1 Frances Stiles Whitener, interview by author, March 12, 2013, Dalton, Georgia.

2 "Ann-Lee Chenilles Opens New Plant," *Dalton News*, January 9, 1945; advertisement, Ann Lee Chenilles, *Southern Israelite*, June 22, 1945; list of advertisers, *Southern Israelite*, June 28, 1946.

3 Joy Richman, interview by author, March 28, 2012, Bethlehem, Georgia; Victor Ringel, e-mail to author, November 5, 2013.

4 Art-Rich page, Centennial Edition, *Dalton Citizen*, October 16, 1947.

5 "Art Richman Textile Leader Dies in Dalton," *Southern Israelite*, June 4, 1965.

6 Joy Richman, interview by author, March 28, 2012, Bethlehem, Georgia.

7 Vivian Sparks (daughter of R. P. Bailey), interview by author, July 25, 2013, Dalton, Georgia.

8 Liz Gardner, "Old-Fashioned Comfort Is as Soft as Chenille," *Los Angeles Times*, November 29, 1991; Kathryn Bold, "Once More . . . with Fabric: Scrappy Designers Find Material Wealth by Recycling Vintage Linens into Clothes," *Los Angeles Times*, September 3, 1993.

9 "Big Chenille Plant Coming to Georgia," *Atlanta Constitution*, December 15, 1940; "Miss Evans Made First Bedspread," *Chattanooga Times*, February 1, 1929; "B. J. Bandy One of Pioneer Makers of Bedspreads," Bedspread and Manufacturers' Edition, *Dalton News*, February 29, 1940; Thomas M. Deaton, *Bedspreads to Broadloom: The Story of the Tufted Carpet Industry* (Acton, Mass.: Tapestry Press, 1993), 9; "Boyce Sells Plant Here to Georgia Man, B. J. Bandy," *Gastonia (N.C.) Daily Gazette*, November 19, 1934; "B. J. Bandy, Prominent Businessman, Succumbs," *Dalton News*, December 28, 1948; Randy Patton, "B. J. Bandy and Bartow Textiles: Creating an Industry," Center for Regional History and Culture, Kennesaw State University, 1999, http://www.kennesaw.edu/research/crch/articles /bandy.html; Cheryl Wykoff, "Dicksie Bradley Bandy" and "J. Marvin Muse Spread Mfg.," based on Wykoff's interview of Jack Bandy, March 1992, and Wykoff's interviews of Eathel B. Stewart, David Stewart, and Ruth Kelly, 1988, Wykoff's chenille bedspread oral history notebook, Crown Gardens & Archives; Jack Bandy, interview by author, March 14, 2013, Dalton, Georgia.

10 Randy Beckler and his mother, Claudell Beckler, interview by author, March 13, 2013, Dalton, Georgia; Randy Beckler, telephone conversation with author, September 12, 2013; "About Beckler's Carpet," Beckler's Carpet, http://www.becklerscarpet.com /about; Cheryl Wykoff, compiler, *Peacock Alley*,

edited by Lydia Stevens (Dalton, Ga.: Prater's Mill Foundation and Whitfield-Murray Historical Society, 1992), 20–23; Miriam Longino, "Chenille Spreads Were Warp, Woof of a Region," *Atlanta Journal-Constitution*, October 20, 1996; Deaton, *Bedspreads to Broadloom*, 167–70.

11 "Dixie Belle Reunion," *Calhoun (Ga.) Times and Gordon County News*, May 7, 1986.

12 Advertisement, Bell Textiles, *Polk's Dalton City Directory* (Richmond, Va.: R. L. Polk, 1953), 97.

13 "Belcraft Chenilles, Inc., Is One of Dalton's Largest," Progress Edition, *Dalton Citizen-News*, March 30, 1963; advertisement, Bell Textiles, "Winners All!," *Tufted Textile Manufacturers Association Directory, 1953* (Dalton, Ga.: Tufted Textile Manufacturers Association, 1953), back cover; advertisement, Bell Textiles, "A Winning Combination for '54," *Tufted Textile Manufacturers Association Directory, 1954* (Dalton, Ga.: Tufted Textile Manufacturers Association, 1954), back cover.

14 "Dixie Belle Reunion," *Calhoun (Ga.) Times and Gordon County News*, May 7, 1986.

15 Helen Johnson (daughter of Emily Bennett) and her husband, Paul Johnson, interview by author, March 11, 2013, Dalton, Georgia; Bedspread Industry Material, "Clippings, History, Personalities" box, "Mrs. J. H. Bennett" folder, Crown Gardens & Archives.

16 "Blue Ridge Spread Company to Have New Building," *Dalton Citizen*, August 3, 1933; Blue Ridge page, Progress Edition, rotogravure section, *Dalton Citizen*, October 2, 1941.

17 "L. R. Boyd," obituary, *Chattanooga Times Free Press*, May 29, 2012.

18 Advertisement, Boysell, *Tufted Textile Manufacturers Association Directory, 1950* (Dalton, Ga.: Tufted Textile Manufacturers Association, 1950), 14.

19 Information page on J. W. Bray Company, Wykoff's chenille bedspread oral history notebook, Crown Gardens & Archives; Pam Jenkins, "J. W. Bray Co. a Leader in Footwear," *Dalton Daily Citizen-News*, February 28, 1983; Nina Diamond, "People Have a Way of Walking All over Town," *Chattanooga Times*, October 26, 1975; James Wellborn Bray III, interview by author, December 23, 2012, Dalton, Georgia.

20 Cheryl Wykoff, "Brooker Spread Company," based on Wykoff's interview of Joe Billy Denson and Betti Brooker Denson, February 6, 1989, Wykoff's chenille bedspread oral history notebook, Crown Gardens & Archives; Lloyd Gulledge, "Brooker Spread Co. Ends after 46 Years," *Dalton Daily Citizen News*, April 15, 1983.

21 Calvin Caldwell (son of Daphne Cleo Sloan Caldwell), interview by author, November 23, 2012, Calhoun, Georgia; Calvin Caldwell, Calhoun, Georgia, letter to author, July 16, 2013; Mrs. Fred Caldwell and Calvin Caldwell, interview by Thomas Deaton, December 10, 1979, transcript, Fred Caldwell Folder 012, box 2 of 4, Dr. Thomas Deaton Collection, Bandy Heritage Center for Northwest Georgia; Deaton, *Bedspreads to Broadloom*, 25–27.

22 The company first appears in Dalton city directories in 1967, but several online sites that collect and publish basic business records list the formation date as November 6, 1965.

23 Classified advertisement, *Tucson (Okla.) Daily Citizen*, November 15, 1951.

24 *Tufted Textile Manufacturers Association Directory, 1953* (Dalton, Ga.: Tufted Textile Manufacturers Association, 1953); *Polk's Dalton City Directory* (Richmond, Va.: R. L. Polk, 1953).

25 Jamye K. Landis and Sand Springs Cultural and Historical Museum Association, *Images of America: Sand Springs, Oklahoma* (Charleston, S.C.: Arcadia Publishing, 1999), 66.

26 Deaton, *Bedspreads to Broadloom*, 164.

27 T. F. Chitwood, interview by Thomas Deaton, n.d., transcript, T. F. Chitwood folder 017, box 2 of 4, Carpet History 2010.1, MSS 1, Dr. Thomas Deaton Collection, Bandy Heritage Center for Northwest Georgia.

28 Advertisement, T. F. Chitwood, *Southern Israelite*, June 28, 1946.

29 Linda Matchan, "The Real Chenille: The Soft, Nubby, Sentimental Fabric Moves beyond Bedspreads and Bathrobes," *Boston Globe*, March 7, 1999.

30 Christina Lynn Whited, telephone interview by author, December 11, 2012.

31 "News Notes," *The Record, Official Organ of Southwestern Union Conference of Seventh-Day Adventists* 42, no. 45 (November 17, 1943), 8; R. L. Carr, "Chenille Craft," *The Record, Official Organ of Southwestern Union Conference of Seventh-Day Adventists* 44, no. 3 (October 31, 1945), 8; R. L. Carr, "College Chenille Craft," *The Record, Official Organ of Southwestern Union Conference of Seventh-Day Adventists* 46, no. 3 (January 22, 1947), 6.

32 "News Notes," *The Record, Official Organ of Southwestern Union Conference of Seventh-Day Adventists* 40, no. 46 (November 17, 1941), 6.

33 Diana Cowpe website, http://www.diana-cowpe-quarry.co.uk; Diana Cowpe Mill Shop photograph and comments, Flickr, http://www.flickr.com/photos/rossendalewadey/3586691384/?reg=1&src=comment; Peter Magill, "Burnley Homes Plan for Ex-mill Site," *Lancashire Telegraph* (England), August 29, 2012.

34 "New Spread Company Formed in Dalton," *Dalton Citizen*, January 5, 1939.

35 "Bedspread, Rug, and Carpet Manufacturing in Murray County," Murray County (Ga.) Museum, http://www.murraycountymuseum.com/list_bs.html.

36 Victor Ringel (Mannie Ringel's son), e-mail to author, November 3, 2013; Victor Ringel, e-mail to author, November 5, 2013.

37 "Kellwood Acquires Crowntuft," *Wall Street Journal*, October 30, 1989.

38 Harry Gordon, interview by author, November 25, 2013, Tunnel Hill, Georgia; Don Chapman, e-mail to author, January 24, 2013; Don Chapman, e-mail to author, August 22, 2014.

39 Recollections regarding the details of the sale of Soft Goods to Damze vary slightly, and it may have taken place in two steps, with a partial transfer in 1989 and the transfer completed in 1991. Damze Company trademarked "Canyon Group" in 1995. United States Patent and Trademark Office, Trademark Electronic Search System. Labels for Damze products varied over time. Early labels included the name "Damze," with either "San Diego," "handcrafted with pride in California," or "Made in usa." Canyon Group robe labels typically included "Canyon Group by Damze Co." and an indication that the garment was made in the United States or more specifically California.

40 "Surterre Welcomes Don Chapman," Surterre Properties blog, http://www.surterreproperties.com/blog/sureterre-welcomes-don-chapman.html, March 18, 2011; Canyon Group website, http://www.canyongroup.com/.

41 Legal advertisements, *Rome (Ga.) News-Tribune*, October 2, 1952.

42 "W. E. Dellinger Dies in Rome; Funeral Tuesday," *Calhoun (Ga.) Times*, June 18, 1964.

43 "New Yorker Leases Bedspread Plant," *Dalton News*, May 20, 1941.

44 Debbie Zomparelli, e-mail to author, December 4, 2013.

45 The *Dalton News* reported that Harry Nicholas established an unnamed chenille business with John McCarty in September 1945, and Duchess Chenille was in existence by November 1946. It seems reasonable to assume that Duchess was started in September 1945. "Harry Nicholas Returns," *Dalton News*, September 20, 1945; "Duchess Chenille Workers Reject Union in Vote," *Dalton News*, November 19, 1946.

46 "Designer and Production Manager," *Dalton Citizen*, September 2, 1941; Murray E. Wyche, "The Tufted Textile Industry in the South," 15, Bedspread Industry box, Articles on History, Companies, and Machinery folder, Crown Gardens & Archives.

47 Harry Nicholas became a naturalized citizen in Boston in 1901. Rae Smith Nicholas, United States of America Petition for Naturalization, no. 3562, June 30, 1943, District Court of the United States of America, Atlanta, Georgia, Atlanta Naturalization Petitions 10/42–5/43 (Box 5).

48 Harry E. Gordon, letter to author, October 15, 2013; Gail Pallotta, "New Fashion with a Nostalgic Twist," typed manuscript, Crown Gardens & Archives; "Georgia Chenille" fact sheet from Soft Goods, Inc.,

Bedspreads Industry Box, Soft Goods folder, Crown Gardens & Archives; Jane M. Roberts, "Hand-Tufted," *Dalton Advertiser*, September 16, 1987; Cheryl Wykoff, *Peacock Alley*, 18.

49 Beach, Cruise and Sportswear Newest Lines listing, *New York Times*, November 12, 1935.

50 Advertisement, Luckey's Basement, "Candlewick Hoovertees [*sic*]," *Poughkeepsie (N.Y.) Eagle-News*, May 8, 1937.

51 "Everwear an Old and Leading Bedspread Concern," Bedspread and Manufacturers' Edition, *Dalton News*, February 29, 1940.

52 "Bedspread Association to Sponsor Chenille Show in New York," *Dalton News*, March 16, 1939; advertisement, Everwear Candlewick Company, *Southern Israelite*, June 22, 1945.

53 "Everwear Chenille Repair ahead of Present Schedule," *Dalton News*, August 6, 1946; "Phil Phillips Dies of Heart Ailment in New York City," *Dalton News*, October 21, 1947.

54 Advertisement, Everwear Candlewick Company, Centennial Edition, *Dalton Citizen*, October 16, 1947.

55 "Chenille Spreads Get New Patterns," *New York Times*, June 18, 1951; "Tufted Robes," trade name lists, *Tufted Textile Manufacturers Association Directory, 1953* (Dalton, Ga.: Tufted Textile Manufacturers Association, 1953), 90, and *Tufted Textile Manufacturers Association Directory, 1954* (Dalton, Ga.: Tufted Textile Manufacturers Association, 1954), 112.

56 Everwear Candlewick Ltd. business card, Catherine Evans Whitener Scrapbook, Crown Gardens & Archives.

57 Famous Chenille Corp. business card, Catherine Evans Whitener Scrapbook, Crown Gardens & Archives.

58 "Fireside Handcrafts Specialize in Coats, Robes, Novelties," Bedspread and Manufacturers' Edition, *Dalton News*, February 29, 1940; advertisement, Fireside Handcrafts, "Chenille Products," Bedspread and Manufacturers' Edition, *Dalton News*, February 29, 1940.

59 "Mrs. Alvin White Has Been in Spread Business 20 Years," Bedspread and Manufacturers' Edition, *Dalton News*, February 29, 1940.

60 "Chenille Plant Burns at Dalton," *Atlanta Constitution*, April 26, 1941; "Factory Is Destroyed by Fire," *Dalton News*, April 29, 1941.

61 Henry Nevin, "Robes Chenille Have Oomph Appeal," *Dalton News*, May 5, 1942. An advertisement in the 1969 Dalton city directory gives the founding date as 1936. Victor Ringel, whose father worked for the Gordon brothers in New York, recalls that their company may have been called Gordo and may have moved from New York to Dalton. Victor Ringel, e-mail to author, November 3, 2013.

62 "Mrs. Wrench and Campbell Petty Join Cabin Crafts Staff," *Dalton News*, March 18, 1941; "Henry Nevin Writes of Optemism [*sic*] of Local Bedspread Plant Managers," *Dalton News*, December 30, 1941.

63 Janet McKinney (Susie Wilson's granddaughter) with Willene Morgan, interview by author, July 26, 2013, Calhoun, Georgia.

64 See, for example, advertisement, Keith O'Brien, "Chenille Robes," *Salt Lake City Tribune*, December 21, 1940.

65 Wykoff, *Peacock Alley*, 19–20.

66 Joanne Hall Garner, telephone conversation with author, July 25, 2014.

67 Deaton, *Bedspreads to Broadloom*, 27–28, 37–38, 40.

68 Cheryl Wykoff, "George Hanson," based on Wykoff's interview of Hanson, March 9, 1989, Wykoff's chenille bedspread oral history notebook, Crown Gardens & Archives.

69 Burton J. Bell, ed., *1976 Bicentennial History of Gordon County, Georgia* (Calhoun, Ga.: Gordon County Historical Society, 1976), 501.

70 Niki Hollingsworth, "Serving Where His Roots Are," *Calhoun (Ga.) Times*, February 23, 1994.

71 Victoria Jackson, "Cotton Chenille Robes by Kinnaird Ireland usa: The Success of Stan Herman," Kinnaird Ireland blog, July 21, 2009, http://www.kinnairdireland.com/acatalog/Blog.html; Ruth La Ferla, "Front Row," *New York Times*, October 21, 2003; Joyce Wadler, "Designer Looks Back with

Pain and Pride," *New York Times*, September 11, 1998.

72 Henry Franklin Jones page, Faces of Gordon County website, https://web.archive.org/web/20120327054155/http://facesofgordoncounty.com/henryjones.html; "Final Rites for H. F. Jones Wed. at 4 p.m.," *Gordon County News*, May 11, 1954.

73 Advertisement, Hy-Way Arts, Progress Edition, rotogravure section, *Dalton Citizen*, October 2, 1941.

74 Advertisement, Hi-Way [*sic*] Arts, *Southern Israelite*, June 18, 1948.

75 See, for example, advertisement, Jeldi, *West Australian* [Perth], October 8, 1951.

76 Jerry Terrence, e-mail to author, September 28, 2013; Judy Magid, "A Carpetbagger's Comeback," *Salt Lake City Tribune*, February 13, 2006.

77 Judy Magid, "A Carpetbagger's Comeback," *Salt Lake City Tribune*, February 13, 2006.

78 "Durable, Divine and Indestructible, Handbags: Made of Tufted Carpet," *Tufted Textile Manufacturers Association Directory, 1966* (Dalton, Ga.: Tufted Textile Manufacturers Association, 1966), 69.

79 Advertisement, H. T. Jones and Company, *Southern Israelite*, June 22, 1945.

80 Helen Shope, "From Pin Money to a Cottage Industry," unpublished and incomplete manuscript, February 9, 1994, in notebook marked "Bedspread Articles," Crown Gardens & Archives.

81 Deaton, *Bedspreads to Broadloom*, 160.

82 "Lawtex First Operated on W. King Street in Dalton," Progress Edition, *Dalton Daily-Citizen News*, March 30, 1963.

83 Leonard Lorberbaum, interview by Thomas Deaton, April 21, 1981, transcript, p. 1, Leonard Lorberbaum folder 041, box 2 of 4, Carpet History 2010.1, MSS 1, Dr. Thomas Deaton Collection, Bandy Heritage Center for Northwest Georgia.

84 Advertisement, Lawtex Corporation, *Southern Israelite*, June 22, 1945.

85 Leonard Lorberbaum, telephone conversation with author and Julian Saul, June 6, 2013; Cheryl Wykoff, "Lawtex Corporation," Wykoff's chenille bedspread oral history notebook, Crown Gardens & Archives.

86 Lorberbaum, interview by Deaton, 2–3.

87 Ibid., 5; *Heritage of Gordon County, GA, 1850–1999* (Waynesville, N.C.: County Heritage, 1999), 38.

88 "Looper Is Inventor and Manufacturer," Bedspread and Manufacturers' Edition, *Dalton News*, February 29, 1940.

89 Advertisement, Looper's, Inc., Progress Edition, rotogravure section, *Dalton Citizen*, October 2, 1941.

90 Deaton, *Bedspreads to Broadloom*, 15.

91 Marilyn Wolf, telephone interview by author, March 3, 2014.

92 The 1940 census shows Galt living in Cartersville as the owner of a chenille manufacturing business.

93 "Bedspread Industry Booms in Georgia: Quality Improved Big Business," *Christian Science Monitor*, September 8, 1947; Joseph Lawren, "Georgia Dolls Provide Jobs for Women," *Christian Science Monitor*, April 10, 1945.

94 Joseph Lawren, "Georgia Dolls Provide Jobs for Women," *Christian Science Monitor*, April 10, 1945.

95 Information page, Mary-Anne Novelty Company, ca. 1943, Bartow History Museum Archives, Cartersville, Georgia.

96 "Please Order Early," *Billboard* (December 9, 1944), 54.

97 "Bedspread Industry Booms in Georgia: Quality Improved Big Business," *Christian Science Monitor*, September 8, 1947; Joseph Lawren, "Georgia Dolls Provide Jobs for Women," *Christian Science Monitor*, April 10, 1945.

98 Douglas Lurton, *The Complete Home Book of Money-Making Ideas* (Garden City, N.Y.: Hanover House, 1954), 84–85.

99 Norman Reints, interview by Thomas Deaton, n.d., transcript, p. 4, Norman Reints folder 052, box 2 of 4, Carpet History 2010.1, MSS 1, Dr. Thomas Deaton Collection, Bandy Heritage Center for Northwest Georgia; Deaton, *Bedspreads to Broadloom*, 157.

100 Advertisement, Mason Chenille, *Tufted Textile Manufacturers Association Directory, 1952* (Dalton, Ga.: Tufted Textile Manufacturers Association, 1952), 112.

101 The 1950–52 TTMA directories list Mason Chenille as
a manufacturer of chenille robes. Deaton, *Bedspreads
to Broadloom*, 155–57.

102 Calhoun's Mayfair may have been part of a larger
company, as the *New York Times* reported on October
11, 1950, in "Business Notes," that H. T. Lawrence
was "appointed general manager in charge of super-
vision of all factories of Mayfair Chenilles, Inc."

103 Vivian Sparks (daughter-in-law of William Hansel
Sparks), interview by author, July 25, 2013, Dalton,
Georgia; Alice Young (daughter of W. H. Sparks),
telephone conversation with author, September
24, 2013; advertisement, Sparks, Inc., and Mayfair
Chenilles, Inc., *Polk's Dalton City Directory*
(Richmond, Va.: R. L. Polk, 1953), 116; advertise-
ment, Sparks-Mayfair, *Tufted Textile Manufacturers
Association Directory, 1954* (Dalton, Ga.: Tufted Textile
Manufacturers Association, 1954), 81; advertise-
ment, Sparks-Mayfair, *Tufted Textile Manufacturers
Association Directory, 1955* (Dalton, Ga.: Tufted Textile
Manufacturers Association, 1955), 110.

104 "Togetherness Applies to Dalton and C&A, Says
Bill Sparks," Progress Edition, *Dalton Daily Citizen-
News*, March 30, 1963; "Sparks Named Collins-
Aikman Vice President," *Southern Textile News*,
March 21, 1959.

105 An article in 1939 indicates that the company was
founded three years previously, but it is not listed
in the Fall River city directories until 1939. "Textile
Standards Kept High by Workers of Long Training,"
Christian Science Monitor, September 20, 1939.

106 See, for example, *Fall River Directory, Massachusetts,
for the Year Ending December 1939* (Boston, Mass.: R.
L. Polk, 1938).

107 "Textile Standards Kept High by Workers of Long
Training," *Christian Science Monitor*, September 20,
1939.

108 Advertisement, National Chenille Products
Company, *Southern Israelite*, June 18, 1948.

109 Ed Kisonak, "Begin Construction of New Bates Mill
at Waterloo, Que.," *Lewiston (Maine) Evening Journal*,
June 27, 1956.

110 Zack Norville, interview by author, July 26, 2013,
Dalton, Georgia; Deaton, *Bedspreads to Broadloom*,

178–79; Zack Norville, *Zack's Book* (Dalton, Ga.:
Norville Industries, 1992); Jamie Jones, "50 Years
and Counting: Norville Industries Marks Golden
Anniversary," *Dalton Daily Citizen*, April 22, 2006.

111 Carolyn Carter, "Chenille Industry Looks for
Something to Turn Up," *Atlanta Constitution*,
January 4, 1945.

112 Novelty Mills, Inc., page, Progress Edition, rotogravure section, *Dalton Citizen*, October 2, 1941.

113 Henry Nevin, "Robes Chenille Have Oomph
Appeal," *Dalton News*, May 5, 1942.

114 "Mr. David Ostow," *Calhoun (Ga.) Times and Gordon
County News*, December 6, 1989.

115 "O'Jay Mills Plans to Close," *Calhoun (Ga.) Times
and Gordon County News*, July 3, 1991.

116 Los Angeles telephone directory, 1939;
Los Angeles city directory, 1942; advertisement
for workers, *California Eagle* (Los Angeles),
May 6, 1943.

117 "Minister on Housing, Its Importance in Relation
to Decentralisation," *Goulburn (New South Wales,
Australia) Evening Post*, July 20, 1948.

118 "Dalton Attracts Many Interested in Chenille
Plants," Centennial Edition, *Dalton Citizen*,
October 16, 1947. A jacket from about 1940 sur-
vives with a label including the words "Styled
in Hollywood / SuperTex of California / Pacific
Chenille-Craft," linking the name "SuperTex" to
California as well.

119 The names appear in a variety of formats: "Pacific
Chenille-Craft," "Super-tex," "Supertex," "SuperTex,"
"Pacific Super-Tex of Australia," etc.

120 Tricia L. Silva, "Painted Pony Sews Up an Industry
Niche," *San Antonio Business Journal*, September 20,
1998.

121 Information page, Piedmont Spread Company,
ca. 1940s, Bartow History Museum Archives,
Cartersville, Georgia.

122 Chlotilde R. Martin, "Product from South Carolina
Finds Favor in White House," *Charleston (S.C.) News
and Courier*, September 16, 1934.

123 "Passing of Moore Is Deplored," Bedspread and
Manufacturers' Edition, *Dalton News*, February 29,
1940.

124 Saul Pett, "It's Yard Down, Half Yard to Go in Swim Suit World," *Kingsport (Tenn.) Times-News*, June 6, 1948. The 1940 U. S. Census lists Asch as a beach-wear sales manager.

125 Advertisement, William S. Frankel Company, "Beach and Sports Wear Reduced for Clearance," *Sandusky (Ohio) Star-Journal*, July 17, 1939.

126 Advertisement, M. G. Scher and Associates, *Textile Manufacturers Association 1950 Directory and Yearbook* (Dalton, Ga.: Tufted Textile Manufacturers Association, 1950), 18.

127 Van King, "Council Rejects Planning Recommenda-tion," *Sumter (S.C.) Daily Item*, April 12, 1972.

128 Advertisement, Proffitt Textile Company, Centennial Edition, *Dalton Citizen*, October 16, 1947; advertise-ment, Proffitt Textile Company, *Southern Israelite*, May 30, 1947.

129 Bradley Putnam, interview by author, December 21, 2012, Tunnel Hill, Georgia; Put's Chenille Center brochure, collection of Bradley Putnam; Valerie A. Hoffman, "When Everybody Drove Peacock Alley," Progress Section, *Daily Citizen-News* (Dalton), April 25, 1993.

130 Joann Marston (niece of Ben Putnam), message to author via Ancestry.com, October 30, 2013.

131 Bill Putnam, "The Genealogy Stuff," Georgia Census Reports 1930–1940 page, http://www.billputnam.com/TheGenealogyPage.htm; Sen. Warren G. Magnuson and Jean Carper, "Colorful 'Spangle' Cloth Is Highly Flammable," *St. Petersburg (Fla.) Evening Independent*, February 2, 1970.

132 "The Beginning," Queen Carpet, 1946–96, fiftieth anniversary brochure, Queen folder, Carpet and Rug Institute Records, box 1 of 8, 2011.2, mss.006, Bandy Heritage Center for Northwest Georgia.

133 Advertisement, Queen Chenille Company, *Southern Israelite*, September 7, 1956.

134 Julian Saul, interview by author, June 6, 2013, Dalton, Georgia; Karen Diamond, text for Queen Carpet from exhibition *Main, Market and Beyond: Yesterday's Local Jewish Merchants*, Jewish Cultural Center, Chattanooga, Tennessee, 2013.

135 Cheryl Wykoff, "Kenner and Rauschenberg,"

136 Wyche, "Tufted Textile Industry," 10. The founding date for Kenner and Rauschenberg is uncertain. A handwritten page of notes with the Women's Bureau of the Department of Labor surveys records that Kenner and Rauschenberg started fifteen years earlier, which would be 1919, with $150 in capital, while Rauschenberg's obituary states that the com-pany was officially incorporated in 1925, though it had been operating for several years prior. Kenner and Rauschenberg handwritten notes, Candlewick folder, box 232, Records of the Women's Bureau, Department of Labor, National Archives; "G. H. Rauschenberg Is Laid to Rest Friday in West Hill," *Dalton News*, February 17, 1957.

137 Wyche, "Tufted Textile Industry," 15. The G. H. Rauschenberg page in the Centennial Edition of the *Dalton Citizen* in 1941 states that the company was organized in March 1929, but the fire was in 1937, the business split between Kenner and Rauschenberg was reported in the local newspa-per as completed in March 1938, and 1938 is the first year the Dalton city directory lists the new company. G. H. Rauschenberg page, Centennial Edition, *Dalton Citizen*, October 16, 1947; "G. H. Rauschenberg to Open Up Factory," *Dalton News*, March 10, 1938.

138 Henry Nevin, "Robes Chenille Have Oomph Appeal," *Dalton News*, May 5, 1942.

139 See, for example, advertisement, Henderson-Hoyt Company, "The New Chenille Robe Ensemble," *Manitowoc (Wis.) Herald-Times*, December 3, 1942.

140 G. H. Rauschenberg page, Centennial Edition, *Dalton Citizen*, October 16, 1947.

141 Wykoff, "Kenner and Rauschenberg," Wykoff's chenille bedspread oral history notebook, Crown Gardens & Archives; advertisement, G. H. Rauschenberg Company, *Polk's Dalton City Directory* (Richmond, Va.: R. L. Polk, 1953), 111.

142 Gerhardt H. Zachry (Arthur Linton Zachry Jr.'s son), telephone conversation with author, October 29, 2013.

143 Wykoff, "Kenner and Rauschenberg."

144 Jack Bradin, e-mail to author, September 23, 2013; Jack Bradin, telephone interview by author, September 24, 2013.

145 Unidentified article from 1972, quoted on the Vintage Fashion Guild website, http ://forums.vintagefashionguild.org/threads how-old-is-this-and-is-it-a-swimsuit-cover-up.39820/.

146 Priscilla Tucker, "The Second Go-Round," *New York Magazine* 5, no. 30 (July 24, 1972): 53.

147 "San-Rog Spreads, Inc., among Leading Chenille Manufacturers," Bedspread and Manufacturers' Edition, *Dalton News*, February 29, 1940; "New Spread Concern Files Application for Charter Here," *Dalton Citizen*, October 6, 1938; "Spread Plant Enlarged," *Atlanta Constitution*, October 8, 1939.

148 San-Rog page, Progress Edition, rotogravure section, *Dalton Citizen*, October 2, 1941.

149 By 1953, San-Rog is listed in the Dalton city directory in connection with Rogers but not Sansom. By 1955 San-Rog is not listed. In 1950 and 1951, a separate company, Sansom & Rogers Company, Inc., is listed as a manufacturer of chenille products.

150 "Union Contract Is Signed at North Georgia Factory," *Thomasville (Ga.) Times-Enterprise*, July 13, 1939.

151 Uzair Rauf, Facebook message to author, September 27, 2014.

152 Don Chapman, telephone interview by author, October 31, 2012; Harry E. Gordon, letter to author, October 15, 2013.

153 Zack Norville, interview by author, July 26, 2013, Dalton, Georgia; Deaton, *Bedspreads to Broadloom*, 178; Norville, *Zack's Book*; Jamie Jones, "50 Years and Counting: Norville Industries Marks Golden Anniversary," *Dalton Daily Citizen*, April 22, 2006.

154 "Industrialist Sparks Dies," *Dalton Daily Citizen*, May 2, 1979.

155 Advertisement, Sparks, Inc., *Polk's Dalton City Directory* (Richmond, Va.: R. L. Polk, 1951), 101.

156 Advertisement, Sparks, Inc., and Mayfair Chenilles, Inc., *Polk's Dalton City Directory* (Richmond, Va.: R. L. Polk , 1953), 116; advertisement, Sparks-Mayfair, *Tufted Textile Manufacturers Association Directory, 1954* (Dalton, Ga.: Tufted Textile Manufacturers Association, 1954), 81; advertisement,

Sparks-Mayfair, *Tufted Textile Manufacturers Association Directory, 1955* (Dalton, Ga.: Tufted Textile Manufacturers Association, 1955), 110.

157 Advertisement, Sparks, Inc., Progress Edition, *Dalton Citizen-News*, March 30, 1963; Alice Young (daughter of William Hansel Sparks), e-mail to author, September 29, 2013.

158 Alice Young, telephone conversation with author, September 24, 2013.

159 Vivian Sparks (daughter-in-law of William Hansel Sparks), telephone conversation with author, September 24, 2013; "Industrialist Sparks Dies," *Dalton Daily Citizen*, May 2, 1979.

160 Advertisement, Sparks-Pittman Company, *Southern Israelite*, June 22, 1945; advertisement, Sparks, Inc., Progress Edition, *Dalton Citizen-News*, March 30, 1963.

161 "Dalton Attracts Many Interested in Chenille Plants," Centennial Edition, *Dalton Citizen*, October 16, 1947.

162 The names appear in a variety of formats: "Pacific Chenille-Craft," "Super-tex," "Supertex," "SuperTex," "Pacific Super-Tex of Australia," etc.

163 Brochure, Tennoga Hooked Rugs, "About Tennoga Hooked Rugs;" n.d. (ca. 1925), Bedspreads and Booklets on History folder, Bedspreads Industry Material/Clippings, History, Personalities box, Crown Gardens & Archives; Cheryl Wykoff, "Mary Eugenia Bi[t]ting (Mrs. H. L.) Jarvis," based on Wykoff's interview of Mary Gene Dykes, February 1988, Wykoff's chenille bedspread oral history notebook, Crown Gardens & Archives.

164 Classified advertisements: see, for example, *Lima (N.Y.) Recorder*, March 3, 1949, and *Mt. Vernon (Ky.) Signal*, February 24, 1949.

165 "Mrs. C. B. Wood's Candlewicks First Marketed in 1921," Bedspread and Manufacturers' Edition, *Dalton News*, February 29, 1940.

166 Sidney Baxter (Wood's great-nephew), telephone conversation with author, October 23, 2013; Cheryl Wykoff, "Kate Deck Wood," based on Wykoff's interview of Fannie Lou Wood Bare, June 1988, Wykoff's chenille bedspread oral history notebook, Crown Gardens & Archives.

Selected Bibliography

Alvic, Philis. *Weavers of the Southern Highlands.* Lexington: University of Kentucky Press, 2003.

Becker, Jane S. *Selling Tradition: Appalachia and the Construction of an American Folk, 1930–1940.* Chapel Hill: University of North Carolina Press, 1998.

"Bedspread Industry Booms in Georgia." *Christian Science Monitor,* September 8, 1947.

"Bedspreads Aid Georgia County to Increase Living Standards." *Albany (N.Y.) Evening News,* May 24, 1934.

Boring, William. "Bedspread Boulevard." *Morning Herald* (Gloversville and Johnstown, N.Y.), October 9, 1938.

"Catherine Evans' Bedspreads." *Time,* September 2, 1940, 57–59.

"Craft Revival: Shaping Western North Carolina Past and Present," Western North Carolina, Hunter Library Digital Collections, http://wcu.edu/library/DigitalCollections/CraftRevival/story/index.htm.

Dalton Citizen. Anniversary Edition, August 25, 1932.

———. Centennial Edition, October 16, 1947.

———. Progress Edition, October 2, 1941.

Dalton Daily Citizen-News. Progress Edition, March 30, 1963.

Dalton News. Bedspread and Manufacturers' Edition, February 29, 1940.

Deaton, Thomas M. *Bedspreads to Broadloom: The Story of the Tufted Carpet Industry.* Acton, Mass.: Tapestry Press, 1993.

Durbin, Jeffrey L. "Heading South Without Getting Sidetracked: The Dixie Highway in Georgia." In *Looking Beyond the Highway: Dixie Roads and Culture,* edited by Claudette Stager and Martha Carver, 35–52. Knoxville: University of Tennessee Press, 2006.

Eaton, Allen H. *Handicrafts of the Southern Highlands.* New York: Russell Sage Foundation, 1937.

Fariello, M. Anna. *Movers and Makers: Doris Ulmann's Portrait of the Craft Revival in Appalachia.* Asheville, N.C.: Curatorial InSight, 2005.

Flamming, Douglas. *Creating the Modern South: Millhands and Managers in Dalton, Georgia, 1884–1984.* Chapel Hill: University of North Carolina Press, 1992.

Goodrich, Frances Louisa. *Mountain Homespun.* With introduction by Jan Davidson. Knoxville: University of Tennessee Press, 1989. First published 1931 by Yale University Press.

Gordon, Beverly. "Costumed Representations of Early America: A Gendered Portrayal, 1850–1940." *Dress* 30 (2003): 3–20.

———. "Spinning Wheels, Samplers, and the Modern Priscilla: The Images and Paradoxes of Colonial Revival Needlework." *Winterthur Portfolio* 33, no. 2/3 (Summer/Autumn 1998): 163–94.

Hamilton, R. E. "Bedspreads Are Big Business." *Christian Science Monitor,* March 15, 1941.

Martin, Richard, and Harold Koda. *Splash! A History of Swimwear*. New York: Rizzoli, 1990.

Milbank, Caroline Rennolds. *Resort Wear: Style in Sun-Drenched Climates*. New York: Rizzoli, 2009.

Moody, Minnie Hite. "Bedspreads Bloom Again." *Saturday Evening Post*, January 5, 1946, 74.

Mosley, Phoebe Laing. "The Pleasant Land of Counterpane." *McCall Decorative Arts and Needlework*, Summer 1932, 22, 24, 32.

Nevin, Henry. "City of Dalton 'Spreads' Itself to World Fame." *Atlanta Constitution*, September 1, 1942.

Nienburg, Bertha M. "Potential Earning Power of Southern Mountaineer Handicraft." Special issue, *Bulletin of the Women's Bureau*, no. 128. Washington, D.C.: United States Department of Labor, Women's Bureau, Government Printing Office, 1935.

Patton, Randall L., "Catherine Evans Whitener (1881–1964): The Creation of North Georgia's Tufted Textile Industry." In *Georgia Women: Their Lives and Times*, vol. 2, edited by Ann Short Chirhart and Kathleen Ann Clark, 112–39. Athens: University of Georgia Press, 2014.

———. *Shaw Industries: A History*. Athens: University of Georgia Press, 2002.

Patton, Randall L., with David B. Parker. *Carpet Capital: The Rise of a New South Industry*. Athens: University of Georgia Press, 1999.

Peacock Alley: The Early Years of Gordon County's Chenille Industry. Northwest Georgia Regional Library System, http://ngrl.org/calhounlibrary/peacockalley/.

Preston, Howard Laurence. *Dirt Roads to Dixie: Accessibility and Modernization in the South, 1885–1935*. Knoxville: University of Tennessee Press, 1991.

Rhoads, William B. "Colonial Revival in American Craft: Opposition to Multicultural and Regional Traditions." In *Revivals! Diverse Traditions: The History of Twentieth-Century American Craft, 1920–1945*, edited by Janet Kardon, 41–54. New York: Harry N. Abrams, in association with the American Craft Museum, 1994.

Rosenberg, Adolph. "The Dalton Story." *Southern Israelite*, June 18, 1948.

Secord, William. "The American Candlewick Spread." *HALI: The International Journal of Oriental Carpets and Textiles* 4, no. 2 (1981): 161–62.

St. John, Wylly Folk. "Georgia Bedspreads Cover the Country." *Atlanta Journal Magazine*, September 8, 1946.

West, R. H. "Dalton 'Spreads' Itself." *NC&StL Railway Bulletin* (Nashville, Chattanooga, and St. Louis Railway), September 1949, 4–12.

Wykoff, Cheryl, compiler. *Peacock Alley*. Edited by Lydia Stevens. Dalton, Ga.: Prater's Mill Foundation and Whitfield-Murray Historical Society, 1992.

Index